# The American War
## Vietnam 1960-1975

■ *An excellent view of the Vietnam War, unique in its bold, class-conscious approach. It is very well researched, and especially valuable for its vivid quotations from participants on both sides of the conflict.*
**Howard Zinn** author of A People's History of the United States

■ *Something remarkable and rare—a survey of the American War in Vietnam that is lively, accessible, idiosyncratic, opinionated, and rangy. Neale is unabashedly sympathetic to Vietnamese guerrillas and American activists—including a full chapter on anti-war protest among US soldiers—and unsparing in his criticisms of ruling parties on all sides.*
**Christian G Appy** author of Working-Class War: American Combat Soldiers and Vietnam

■ *Comprehensive in historical and sociological scope, this readable book locates both the logic of the war and the resistance to it in the dynamics of class relations internal to the United States and Vietnam—attention to how the war has played out in both countries is particularly welcome given the light treatment that scholars have given the quarter century since the peace.*
**Jerry Lembcke** author of The Spitting Image: Myth, Memory and the Legacy of Vietnam

# The American War
## Vietnam 1960-1975

*Jonathan Neale*

BOOKMARKS

**The American War: Vietnam 1960-1975 – Jonathan Neale**
First published 2001
Reprinted 2005
Bookmarks Publications Ltd, c/o 1 Bloomsbury Street, London WC1B 3QE
Copyright © Jonathan Neale

ISBN 1 898876 67 3

Printed by The Bath Press
Cover by Rodger Huddle

To Nancy Lindisfarne,
with all my love

# Contents

**Chronology**
xiii

**Introduction**
1

*Chapter 1*
**The Vietnamese**
7

*Chapter 2*
**Why America intervened**
35

*Chapter 3*
**Firepower**
61

*Chapter 4*
**Protesters and guerrillas**
85

*Chapter 5*
**The GIs' revolt**
117

*Chapter 6*
**Vietnam and Cambodia after the war**
147

*Chapter 7*
**America after the war**
175

**Further reading**
199

**Notes**
203

**Bibliography**
213

**Index**
221

# Acknowledgments

My first debt is to books by Marilyn Young, Christian Appy and James Gibson, for their wonderful eyes for quotes. I have often gone to their sources and found myself using the same quotes they chose.

Secondly, Sharon Smith and John Rees encouraged me to write this book. Joel Geier gave very useful advice. Fil Hearn gave me the chance to go to Vietnam in 1998. Ian Birchall, Martin Smith, Dharma Thapa, Nigel Davey, Charlie Hore, Bruce Self and Judith Orr read it and told me what to change and cut. Nancy Lindisfarne and Anthony Arnove in particular read with the eagle eyes of really good editors, and insisted on many changes, most of which I have made. I am very grateful.

Rob Hoveman at Bookmarks began work on this project and was always kind and encouraging. Emma Bircham did the copy editing and saw the book through production. She was a joy to work with.

I owe two personal debts. Liz de Boisgelin stood by me through a difficult time in 1970, and I have not forgotten. Nancy Lindisfarne, by her love and the example of her courage, gave me the strength to write this book.

Finally, I would not have written this book had I not been involved in the movement against the Kosovo war with my comrades in the Amherst branch of the ISO. My thanks for their inspiration, and particularly to Doug Murray.

Jonathan Neale's most recent books are *What's Wrong With America?* (2004) and *You Are G8, We Are 6 Billion* (2002). His other non-fiction books include *Memoirs of a Callous Picket*, *The Cutlass and the Lash* and *Tigers of the Snow*, and there are also two novels (*The Laughter of Heroes* and *Mutineers*) and children's books (*Lost at Sea* and *Himalaya*). He is a member of the Socialist Workers Party and Globalise Resistance in Britain. He teaches creative writing at Bath Spa University.

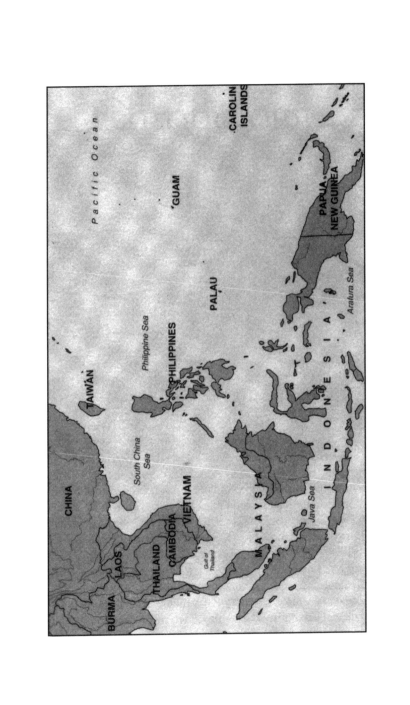

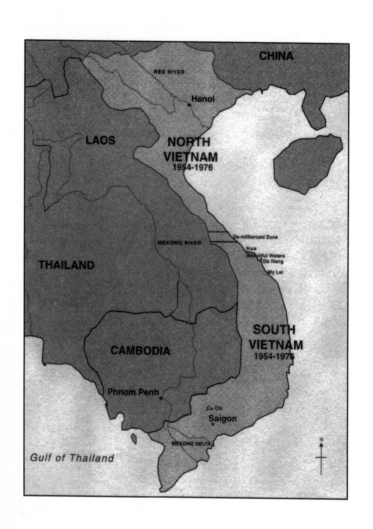

# Chronology

| | |
|---|---|
| 1883 | France completes conquest of Vietnam. |
| 1924 | First Vietnamese Communist organization founded. |
| 1935 | Four friends begin meeting in the village Beautiful Waters |
| 1939 | French round up nationalists and Communists. |
| 1940 | Germany defeats France. French colonialists rule Vietnam under Japanese supervision. |
| 1941 | Ho Chi Minh returns to Vietnam. |
| 1945 | In April, Japan takes over formally from France in Vietnam. In the spring and summer, famine kills 1 million in northern Vietnam. In August, Japan surrenders and crowds led by Viet Minh take power in Saigon and Hanoi, and across the country. In September, Ho Chi Minh declares independence in Hanoi, and in Saigon British-led troops put down a rising and try to restore French power. |
| 1946–54 | War between France and Viet Minh. |
| 1949 | Communists, led by Mao, win power in China. |
| 1954 | French defeated at Battle of Dien Bien Phu. Peace negotiations in Geneva divide Vietnam into two countries, North Vietnam under the Communists and South Vietnam allied to the United States. A great majority of Communist troops and political workers are withdrawn from the South to North Vietnam. |
| 1954–59 | South Vietnamese government of President Diem arrests and executes remaining Communists in the South. Communist leadership in the North urges non-violent response. |
| 1959 | Communists in the South push Northern leadership into backing an insurrection in the South. |
| 1960 | President Kennedy sends the first American troops to Vietnam—3,200 at the end of the year. |

1960–65     Communist-led National Liberation Front (Viet Cong) is winning guerrilla war in the villages in South Vietnam.

1963     Urban unrest and demonstrations led by Buddhists in South Vietnam. US backs coup and assassination of President Diem. President Kennedy assassinated, replaced by President Johnson—18,000 US troops in Vietnam.

1965     US begins sustained bombing of North and South Vietnam. Large numbers of troops committed—180,000 by the end of the year, will rise to over 500,000.

1967     First large demonstrations against war in US. Public opinion shifts against the war.

1968     Tet Offensive by Viet Cong in January shows strength of popular support. President Johnson, shaken, says he will not run for president again that year. My Lai massacre in Vietnam. Peace negotiations in Paris—they will last five years. Bitter demonstrations at Democratic convention in Chicago. Nixon elected president, promising to solve Vietnam problem.

1969     Nixon does nothing. US remains in Vietnam. Very large demonstrations in US in October and November.

1970     US invades Cambodia. In reaction, wave of student demonstrations and strikes in the US, and four students are shot dead. US withdraws from Cambodia and begins serious troop withdrawals from Vietnam. Widespread refusal to fight and killing of officers by US military in Vietnam.

1972     Spring offensive by North Vietnamese army in South Vietnam. Sustained bombing of North by US. Nixon goes to China. US troops still in revolt, being rapidly withdrawn—only 24,200 at the end of the year.

1973     US and North Vietnam sign peace agreement in Paris. US promises to withdraw troops and pay $5 billion compensation. Last troops are withdrawn—money not paid. President Thieu of South Vietnam cannot live with peace settlement. War continues, but Communists do not try to take power.

1974     Nixon resigns in Watergate scandal.

1975     Khmer Rouge take power in Cambodia. South Vietnamese army collapses. Communists take Saigon, set up new South Vietnamese government.

| | |
|---|---|
| 1975–78 | Killing fields of Cambodia under Pol Pot and Khmer Rouge. |
| 1976 | South and North merge into one Vietnam. China cuts aid to Vietnam. |
| 1978 | Refugees, primarily of Chinese ancestry, begin fleeing Vietnam. In December, Vietnam invades Cambodia. |
| 1978–79 | Vietnamese occupation of Cambodia, and war with Khmer Rouge, who are backed by US, Chinese and Thai governments. |
| 1979 | In January, Vietnam takes Phnom Penh and sets up new government there. In February, China invades Vietnam, meets unexpected level of resistance, withdraws. |
| 1985 | Communist leadership in Vietnam formally backs change to partially market economy. |
| 1989 | Fall of Communist governments in Russia and eastern Europe. Vietnam begins to withdraw from Cambodia. |
| 1990 | Last Vietnamese soldiers leave Cambodia. UN arrives. |

# Preface to the second edition

I finished the first edition of this book early in 2000, after the demonstrations at Seattle and before 9/11. Since then we have seen invasion and occupation in Afghanistan and Iraq. And on 15 February 2003 we saw the largest global anti-war demonstration in history. The first edition of this book proved useful to many people in the new peace movement. I will briefly try to explain why.

First, the idea that the United States cannot be defeated is very strong in the peace movement in Europe. This book is the story of the last great defeat of that empire, at the hands of a guerrilla resistance and a global anti-war movement.

Second, this book shows that people change. The American soldiers who were capable of great cruelty were also capable of refusing to fight. Those Americans, like me, who supported the war at the beginning, had mostly turned against it long before the end.

Third, this book is on the side of the American soldiers against their generals and politicians, and in the same way on the side of the Vietnamese peasant communists against their leaders. This is an unusual way of writing history, which usually glorifies the leaders of at least one side. It is helpful, though, to understand the Iraqi resistance, too, as a complex and divided coalition, where the interests of the leaders and the ordinary fighters are very different.

Finally, there is a similar logic to the cruelty of American military policy then and now. In both Vietnam and Iraq the majority of the local people supported the resistance. In such a situation the only way to break the guerrillas is an escalating campaign of terror and bombing against the civilian population. That in turn increases civilian support for the guerillas.

But history does not simply repeat itself. This time round the global movement against the war has grown more quickly. 15 February 2003 was the largest global demonstration ever. It was also the largest peace demonstration in the history of many countries, and the largest demonstration ever in Britain and Spain. The peace movement in the US, also, has grown more quickly than in the Vietnam years.

And the stakes are higher this time round. The 1960s were the end of a long period of economic growth and full employment, when the ideas of the New Deal and the welfare state dominated the world. The Iraq war comes after years of economic uncertainty and unemployment. Now the market dominates the world, while most people hate the market. All this makes for a far angrier, and more unstable, world.

Vietnam exported rice. Iraq has the second largest oil reserves in the world. And the consequences of a defeat in Iraq will be devastating for US power. They would not simply lose control of Iraqi oil. The rulers of other Middle Eastern states, seeing American weakness, would turn to other alliances. In some cases, their people are likely to overthrow them.

But that is not all. American military domination has been closely identified with American economic domination. Bush personifies both. And both dominations have been identified with the idea of the free market—the whole world is for sale. An American defeat in Iraq would threaten both US economic power in the world, and the power of the ideas of the market across the world.

So we now face a situation where the US is losing the war, the peace movement is growing, and the cost of defeat is unthinkable for the rich and powerful in the United States. This will lead to escalation in the war, greater cruelty, more bombing, and more dead Iraqis and Americans. In this situation it matters a great deal what the peace movement does across the world. The scale of the demonstrations has meant that the whole world is watching what happens in Iraq, in a way it was not in Vietnam. That limits the amount of killing and cruelty possible. And we should not let the videos of beheadings obscure the fact that the great majority of killing is done by the American military, and most of that in air strikes. While the global anti-war movement remains strong, that violence will be contained. If not, we should not forget that the American military killed a million people in South Vietnam, a country with the same population as Iraq.

But it does not have to be that way. The monster can be stopped.

To do that, activism is essential. But activism without understanding is helpless. I hope readers will find this book useful in understanding war, empire, and the strengths and weaknesses of the last great peace movement.

**Jonathan Neale**
*January 2005*

# Introduction

The Vietnamese call it the American War. In America it's called the Vietnam War. This is a short history of that war, from the point of view of the peasants and GIs who fought it.

In 1945, when World War Two ended, Vietnam was a French colony. Vietnamese Communists then led a nine-year peasant guerrilla war against the French. In 1954 a peace settlement divided Vietnam in two. North Vietnam became a 'Communist' dictatorship allied to Russia and China, and South Vietnam became a private capitalist dictatorship allied to the United States. Some Communists stayed behind in South Vietnam. The southern government persecuted them, and in 1959 they began a peasant guerrilla insurgency, the Viet Cong or National Liberation Front. By 1965 it looked as if the Communists would soon take power in South Vietnam, and the United States began sending in large numbers of troops to prevent this.

But why another book on the war?

There are a lot of books on different aspects of the war, many of them very good. This is an attempt to synthesize them into a short history that both tells the story and makes sense of what happened. It is particularly written for a new generation of activists who were small children, or not even born, during the war years.

But there are two other audiences that particularly matter to me. One is the Vietnam generation in America—the people who fought in the war, the people who opposed it, and the hundreds of thousands who did both. I have tried to write a book that is true to their experience. The other audience is in Vietnam. Large numbers of young Vietnamese feel a deep sympathy for the guerrilla struggle, but they also feel oppressed by the corrupt government that came to power by winning that war. I hope that this book makes sense to them too.

This is a history from both sides, and from the ground up. It tells what Vietnamese peasants, American soldiers and American protesters did, and how they felt. I also write about what the generals and politicians on both sides did—although I am less concerned with what they felt. And I take seriously the connections between the war and race relations in the United States, and the class struggles within and between America and Vietnam.

Most historians separate class struggle and international relations. One is domestic policy and the other is foreign policy. They exist, in most accounts, in different worlds. This book looks, all the time, at how class struggles affect both international and domestic relations.

So Chapter 1, about why the Vietnamese fought, begins with an account of the class struggle in South Vietnam between a government backed by landlords and businessmen on one side, and a guerrilla army of poor and landless peasants on the other. For both sides it was more of a war over land than over national independence.

But it was not that simple, for the Communist leaders themselves were the children of landlords, business people and government officials. They wanted a strong, independent, socially just Vietnam. But they also wanted to be the new ruling class in that Vietnam, on the model of the people who ruled Russia and China. So at times they led the peasants against the landlords, at times they held the peasants back, at times they exploited the peasants, and at times the peasants forced them to fight. Chapter 1 chronicles the twists and turns of this contradictory struggle.

Chapter 2 is about why the American government intervened. The stated reason was to fight Communism, but after 1945 official American anti-Communism did three jobs at once. First, 'fighting Communism' was the rationale for the Cold War competition with Russia about who would be the dominant power in the world. Second, it was the rationale supporting the rich in poor countries against movements from below. Third, inside America, anti-Communism was in practice a pretext for persecuting radical shop stewards and union representatives.

So when it looked like the Communist-led guerrillas would win in Vietnam, the American government was afraid that it would make Russia more powerful, encourage revolts from below in other countries, and encourage radical tendencies in the American civil rights movements and the unions. It sent troops to Vietnam to stop that happening.

Chapter 3 is about how the war was fought. The American government used bombs and artillery on a scale never seen before in the world. I argue this was because the Viet Cong had won the political war. The majority of Vietnamese supported them, and that meant the American combat troops were outnumbered. To put it in simple terms, there were more guerrillas than GIs, so the Pentagon's strategy was attrition—to kill very large numbers of Vietnamese until they were broken.

This strategy was carried out by American soldiers. But for them it was a working class war.[1] It was not the children of the rich and powerful who were sent to Vietnam. For those who went, being there was part and parcel of their oppression at home, perhaps the worst part of it. And the killing and cruelty they found themselves doing was part of their oppression. What made it worse for them, and sometimes made them more cruel in their actions, was that they could see this. They learned that the people they were fighting in Vietnam were the same sort of people they themselves were in America.

Chapter 4 is partly about the Vietnamese guerrillas, and partly about how racism and the civil rights movement both affected the American soldiers in Vietnam. But the main argument is that, from 1968 on, the rich and powerful in America wanted to withdraw from Vietnam because the protest movement was beginning to threaten their control at home. When push came to shove, power in America was far more important to the American leaders than power in Vietnam. But simply leaving Vietnam would weaken their position with many regimes in the world and weaken their control at home. So they chose a middle road, trying to wind down their involvement without leaving. Protest continued, and many more people on both sides died.

Chapter 5 is about the revolt against the war in the American armed forces. From 1968 on, the American troops killed many of their officers, and by 1971 most of the GIs were refusing or avoiding combat. In early 1973 the US was forced to withdraw completely, and without the support of US troops the southern government fell in 1975. I write about the soldiers' revolt at length because it is a part of the story which rarely gets told, and it is a part of the story that the Vietnam generation needs to have acknowledged. It is also something that people outside the US, particularly in Vietnam, may know little about.

Chapter 6 is about Cambodia and Vietnam after the American War. Again, it concentrates on the class struggle in those countries.

The horror of the killing fields in Cambodia was in part a consequence of the horror of the US bombing that the Cambodians had already been through. But that horror also needs to be understood in terms of the struggle between a new, small, Communist ruling class in Cambodia and the peasants who turned against them.

Vietnam after 1975 was affected by an American-led boycott, Russian exploitation and Chinese enmity. But the chapter concentrates particularly on the attempt of the new Communist ruling class to build a modern economy by taxing the peasants heavily and sweating the workers, and the attempts of peasants and workers to resist that exploitation.

Chapter 7 is about the consequences of the war for the US and the world. The emphasis here is on the 'Vietnam syndrome'—the insistence by the majority of working Americans, passed down from parents to children over the last 30 years, that the government may or may not be right about foreign policy, but the people will not send their children to die for Washington again.

This 'Vietnam syndrome' makes it very difficult for the US government to use ground troops. So the US has become a strange kind of imperial power, effectively a superpower without an army. The chapter traces how the limits imposed on American power by American workers have changed the nature of international relations in the last 25 years. It also traces the backlash in America against the movements of the 1960s. I argue that this backlash has been simultaneously an attack on the memory of Vietnam, on African-Americans, on feminism, on gays and lesbians, on labor unions, and on the incomes and lives of working America. The backlash is part of the class struggle at home, and it is simultaneously an effort to win American workers back to dying abroad. And that class struggle has produced, in turn, the new activists this book was written for.

I have tried to write in a straightforward, accessible style. This has forced me to think carefully. If you make all the steps in an argument explicit, you can notice the gaps, and so can the reader. Tony Cliff, the British socialist, once said that the more complex the argument you want to make, the simpler the language you should use.

Three things make this book complex. First, it was a complicated war, fought in four countries by soldiers from 12 countries, with many twists and turns, and with complex roots and consequences. Second, there is a complex argument about class and war running through the book. Third, the standpoint adopted here is outside the mainstream. Noam Chomsky, the American anarchist, often says how much he hates giving one-minute answers to questions about American foreign policy on radio and television. The reason, he says, is that ideas outside the mainstream are often hard to grasp because people have not heard them before. Many mainstream ideas are complicated too, but because people have heard the arguments many times before they can be explained quickly.

I need to make two small points. First, about 'America.' This is not an anti-American book. It is anti American government, but then I think that the American government is anti most American people. And so I have said 'the American government', or 'the US', or 'Washington' did this or that, because I don't want to assume that the policies of the government and the wishes of the people are the same. I am also aware that everybody in North and South America is American, and most of them say 'North American' where I have used 'American'. I apologize for any offense.

Second, I'm American, and when I was 18 in 1966 I was a supporter of my country's role in Vietnam. If I had been drafted then, I would have gone. I wasn't drafted because my parents were middle class teachers and I could go to college. By 1969 I was marching against the war. In 1970 I was refused conscientious objector status and decided to go to prison rather than the army. I was afraid of prison, but in the long run the people who went to prison had an easier time than the people who went to Vietnam and survived. Then my draft board gave me conscientious objector status on appeal and I did not have to go to jail.

If I had to do it over again, I hope I would go into the army and agitate against the war. I have written this book because I have mixed feelings about the anti-war movement. I am intensely proud of what we did and achieved, but we were ignorant about many things, and particularly about the class system in the US. Our passion helped to end the war, but our mistakes meant that the radical movements of the 1960s were eventually marginalized. I have written this book not out of nostalgia, but in the hope that another generation can learn from our experiences and act more wisely.

# Chapter 1

# The Vietnamese

This chapter is about why the Vietnamese fought. To understand this we have to begin with how French colonialism changed life for rice farmers.

The French conquest of Indochina began in 1859 and was complete by 1888. French Indochina was three neighboring countries—Vietnam, Laos and Cambodia. Vietnam was overwhelmingly the most populous and important of the three. Vietnam had been independent of China for 900 years, but Chinese cultural influence was strong. Before the French, Vietnam, like China, had an emperor served by officials ('mandarins') who were selected by examinations in the Chinese classics.

In 1888 most Vietnamese were rice farmers. There were two great centers of cultivation. In the north the densely populated Red River Valley was irrigated by an ancient system of dykes and canals. In the south the Mekong River Delta was the rice basket of Vietnam, with its thousands of small waterways and low-lying fertile land. North and south were connected by a long thin coastal strip in the center.

The French divided Vietnam into three zones for administrative purposes. The capital of the north was Hanoi, of the center Hue, and of the south Saigon. Eighty five percent of the people spoke Vietnamese as their mother tongue. There were minorities of Chinese and Cambodian speakers, and mountain peoples speaking a variety of languages.

In the irrigated villages where most people lived a small number of landlord families usually owned much of the land. A larger number of families owned enough land to get by, while a majority of the village had to rent land to live. But the emperors and the landlords knew they could only push the peasants so far—Vietnam had a history of peasant revolts. The main protection for the poor peasants was the institution of 'village land'. Part of the land in each village was owned by the village as a whole, and the village council rented fields to the poorer families at reasonable rates. The amount of village land varied from one quarter of the total in some villages to two thirds in others. In most Vietnamese villages in 1888 the rich were rich but the poor could live.

French colonialism didn't make much difference to this at first. But from 1900 on, the colonial government began to transform the village economy into part of the world capitalist system. It did this in four ways.

First, the government took much of the land and gave it to French businessmen to run plantations and mines. Second, the government raised agricultural taxes to about a fifth of the crop so it could fund a strong, modern state.

Third, it needed workers for the expanded mines, plantations and cities. But as long as the Vietnamese peasants could grow enough rice to live, they did not have to work for the low wages business and industry wanted to pay. This was a common problem for colonial governments in many parts of the world in this period. The solution, particularly in French and British Africa, was usually a head tax that had to be paid in cash. Then the country people had to send their sons to the city to earn money even if they grew enough food to survive. Traditional Vietnam already had a head tax, but it was paid in rice and the emperor cancelled it in years of bad harvest. The French doubled the tax, refused to reduce it in bad years, and insisted on cash.

Fourth, and most important, the French government increased the power of the landlords in the villages. This had both political and economic advantages for the colonial authorities. Politically, the French, like all colonial governments, faced a constant problem because there were so few French in Vietnam and so many Vietnamese. The French encouragement of the landlords led the landlords to support the French—it gave colonialism a real social base in the villages.

Economically, the power of the landlords meant that more rice went to the cities. As the landlords became more powerful, they took more and more of the rice produced in the villages and the peasants took less. This meant that more peasants had to become workers in the 'modern' parts of the economy. But it also meant that the landlords could not eat all that rice, so they sold it on to the cities in return for industrial goods produced there and in France.

Inequality in the villages thus strengthened the colonial government, and sent workers and rice to the cities. But at the same time bitterness grew in the villages, and then resistance. *Village at War*, a book by James Trullinger, traces this process in detail in the village of My Thuy Phong (Beautiful Waters), just south of Hue in central Vietnam.[1] During the war Trullinger worked for an American aid agency with shoeshine boys in Hue. Late in the war, in 1974-75, after the last American troops had left but before the South Vietnamese government fell, Trullinger returned to Vietnam as a graduate student and did six months research in Beautiful Waters. His book is a stunning piece of work because he was brave, and smart, enough to talk to both sides. He had permission from the local South Vietnamese commander to do his research. Unlike all other American researchers, he also applied formally to the National Liberation Front for research permission. Supporters of the South Vietnamese regimes talked to him in the village, and local Communists talked to him at secret meetings near the village or in Hue.

When Trullinger asked the old people about the origins of Communism in the village, they explained it to him by telling him about what the French had done.

Before the French came two thirds of the land in Beautiful Waters was owned by the village as a whole, an unusually high proportion. As in the rest of Vietnam, the richer landlords had always dominated the village council that rented out the land to poor villagers. But the villagers said that the council had 'operated more or less fairly and consistently within the expected bounds of hierarchy... It never demanded in taxes more than what people, perhaps in patient submission, accepted'.[2]

Under French rule after 1900, and particularly after 1920, the village councilors found they could charge more for village land, take more rental contracts for themselves and charge larger bribes for distributing land. Some of the councilors were unhappy with this new corruption, but they tended to resign from the council and leave the less scrupulous landlords in charge.

By 1940 five or six families controlled 30 to 40 percent of the land in Beautiful Waters, and the poorest 90 percent of the villagers controlled roughly a third of the land. The 90 percent now had to rent land from the landlords or find wage work. The usual rate for renting land, as throughout Vietnam, was a sum of money equal to half the crop in a good year. In a bad year the rent could be as much as the whole crop, but the tenant still had to pay.

It is important to understand what that meant in human, physical terms. The relationship between peasants and land is not mystical. Vietnam has a landscape of stunning beauty, infinite shimmering greens, which any Vietnamese peasant can see. And of course people love the look, feel and smell of the place in which they grew up. But the question of land, for peasants in Vietnam and anywhere else, is a matter of work, pain and food. It is not an abstract question.

They know that the landlord takes half the rice and the government takes a share on top of that. Their exploitation is not mystified, nor is it hard to understand. They grow the rice, somebody else comes, takes it away and eats it. They feel their work, and their hunger, in their bodies all day every day. And they can see their children are weak and the landlords' children are fat.

That is the reality behind questions of land tenure in every peasant village. And in Beautiful Waters, behind the landlords who took half or more of the crop stood the colonial police. The old Vietnamese imperial government had mostly left the village landlords to deal with the peasants on their own. Under the French there were police in the village. One man told Trullinger:

> The policemen came round with the landlords to force us to pay the rent. Once we had a very bad flood, and the crop was lost, but the policeman came anyway. He said that if we did not pay he would arrest us, or take the land and rent it to someone else.[3]

Another peasant was arrested when he could not pay:

> I was held for a week in the (village) office. They made me sit in a corner, and my family had to bring me potatoes to eat. Finally, my son borrowed money from friends, and they let me go. But I had to give the policeman some money for himself, even after I had paid the rent.[4]

One incident in 1944 stood for many in the preceding decades. That year a few landlord families realized that their fields surrounded the fields of several poor peasant families. They refused the poor peasants the traditional right to walk across their land. The poor peasants could not farm, and they complained to the village council, which backed the landlords. The police backed the village council and the small farmers had no choice but to sell their land cheaply to the big landlords.

Behind the police stood the colonial courts, which always ruled in favor of the landlords. Poor peasants who could not meet the rent had to borrow from money-lenders in the city at interest rates of 50 percent or more a year. The peasants were caught in a spiral of debt, and more and more of them lost their land.

The same thing was happening throughout the country. In the south, by the late 1930s, 6,200 landlords owned 45 percent of the rice land. In the north of Vietnam, in the Red River Valley, 2 percent of households owned 40 percent of the land.[5]

French colonialism was also transforming the old class of feudal landlords and imperial officials into a new class of capitalist landlords and colonial officials. The children of this class became government officials and junior officers in the army and police. They went to the new government schools—usually for three years or less, but they learned to speak French and honor French culture. Moreover, they knew that they owed their increased wealth to French power.

So, in about 1935 five men in the village of Beautiful Waters began to meet and talk. One, about 50 years old, ran a small shop in the village. Another was a low-level clerk for the colonial government in nearby Hue. In his thirties, he owned a bicycle, a little bit of land and a small wooden house. He was poor but educated, and 'always full of opinions on everything'.

The third man, Truong, was a middle peasant of about 40. He could not read, but 'reveled in the long rambling conversations that he sought out and dominated in the village. Many remembered Truong's inquiring mind and quick sense of humor'.[6] The fourth man was a poor peasant who spent much of his spare time maintaining the village shrines and pagoda.

The fifth man, Minh, was about 30. He was the son of one of the big landlords. Trullinger writes:

> Minh was somewhat estranged from his father, and for some reason rejected his father's wishes that he behave as a subservient son, loyal to the large landholding class. Minh had received some schooling, perhaps at a private school in Hue. He was good-humored and, in the words of a peasant related to him, 'frighteningly intelligent'... One elderly peasant said: 'His father was a typical rich man, and did not care about the people. But the son was completely different. He seemed to be interested in the poor people, and always had ideas about how poor people could live better'.[7]

In his twenties Minh left his father's house and became a tradesman.

ˌThe five friends met regularly for years:

> Usually the conversations among the five men were after dark, when
> work was done, and when gatherings were not as obvious to the un-
> friendly eyes of colonial security agents. The men met over small glasses
> of rice wine, beer, or tea. They all gathered as frequently as possible,
> but often only two or three could come. Those who attended passed
> on opinions and reactions to those who could not come or dared not
> attend. A peasant described the conversations among the five:
>
> 'First they talked about the problems and difficulties of life—like
> taxes, land problems, and corruption among local authorities. They
> talked about their own personal problems, their families' problems.
> But that was not all! After a little while they also talked about the
> village, then after about the problems outside this place. They talked
> so much, and after much talk they clearly understood all about the
> Westerners. They knew what France was doing in our fatherland. They
> understood why Westerners were here.'

In 1939, after years of meeting, those five men began to look outside the village to nearby Hue for ideas about how to fight the
French and the landlords. The people they found with those ideas
were Communists.

# Vietnamese Communism

The Vietnamese Communist Party had been founded by Ho Chi
Minh, the son of a mandarin. The majority of mandarins and landlord
families supported French colonialism, but a minority always opposed
it. This reflected a contradiction in the lives of this class. French colonialism made the landlords stronger in relation to the peasants, but
weaker in relation to the French colonial government. So, many mandarins and landlord families were split between supporters and opponents of colonialism, and many mandarins were torn inside themselves.

Ho Chi Minh's father, for instance, was a highly educated young
man when the French first came. In 1885 there was a rebellion against
French rule, called the Scholars' Revolt because it was led by mandarins. Ho Chi Minh's father was part of that revolt. When it failed
the French ruled north and south Vietnam directly, but left a puppet
emperor in Hue in charge of central Vietnam. Ho's father eventually
took a job in the puppet emperor's court under the French, but he
hated it and used to say, 'Being a mandarin is a form of slavery'.[8] His

opinions finally cost him his job. Then Ho's father left his family and wandered across Vietnam and the neighboring French colonies of Laos and Cambodia, working as a story teller, a setter of bones and a letter writer.

Ho Chi Minh himself left Vietnam at the age of 21, in 1911, as a mess boy on a ship. He worked at various jobs, mostly cooking, in the United States and Europe. In 1919 he was in Paris. Fired by American president Woodrow Wilson's rhetoric about the rights of nations, Ho went to the Versailles peace conference to argue for freedom for Vietnam. They showed him the door. Wilson's freedoms were not meant for the colonies.

Ho Chi Minh was already a member of the French Socialist Party. The next year, 1920, he joined the newly formed French Communist Party.

The party he joined was a revolutionary organization, inspired by the Russian Revolution three years before. In 1917 the Russian soldiers had refused to fight in World War One. The workers had taken over the factories, and the peasants had burned down the landlords' mansions and divided up the land. The Russian Communists, the Bolsheviks, backed all this—their slogan was 'Land, peace, bread.' The Russian workers elected committees, called soviets, in their workplaces, and the soldiers elected similar soviets in their barracks. Because the Bolsheviks were the only party backing all the struggles, the workers and peasants elected them to these soviets, and in October 1917 a national congress of all the soviets elected a Communist-led government.

That government took Russia out of the world war, gave full rights to women, legalized homosexuality and appointed women ministers, which was an unusual thing to do at the time. In a country where anti-Semitism was the main form of racism, many of the Communist leaders were Jews. The new government declared that all parts of the Russian Empire had the right to secede, and announced its support for every anti-colonial movement everywhere in the world.

That revolution lit a fire in the minds of men and women in Europe and the colonies. The Russian Revolution is now usually presented as a coup. At the time everybody, left and right, thought that the working class had taken power in Russia

That was the cause Ho Chi Minh joined. By 1923 he was in Moscow working for the Communist International, trying to spread revolution in Asia.

But by 1923 Russian Communism was changing. There is much debate about what happened in Russia in those years.[9] But to put it simply, by 1923 what had been workers' power was becoming a dictatorship of the bureaucrats. A bitter civil war had devastated the economy, and there were now more bureaucrats than factory workers. The Communists had always said Russia was a poor country and they could only build socialism with help from revolutions in the developed West. Now, after the civil war, surrounded by hostile capitalist powers, they needed revolutions abroad or they were finished. But revolutions were smashed in Hungary, Germany and China.[10] Russia stood alone.

The new bureaucracy saw their task as survival. Their spokesman, Joseph Stalin, argued that sooner or later the great capitalist powers would invade. When they did, Russia would need modern industry, the basis for a modern army. They had to build that industry in a hurry. The Russian government had to push the workers and peasants, make profits, invest those profits, push the workers and peasants harder, make more profits, invest them, and so on. This had happened during the industrial revolution in England over a hundred years. The Russian state had to catch up in a decade, so they pushed their people to the limit.

In effect, Russia became a state capitalist economy. It was capitalist because the driving dynamic of the system was to make profits and invest to compete with other countries, just as the driving dynamic of private capitalism is for companies to make profits to invest to compete with other companies. But it was 'state' capitalism, not privately owned.

Stalin's government broke strikes and made independent unions impossible. By 1926 working in a Russian factory was just like working in a factory in any other police state. And in 1929 the government took back control of the land the peasants had won in the revolution. To do that it had to arrest millions of peasants and kill hundreds of thousands. But the peasants' grain now fed the workers in modern industry.

Stalin's state capitalism worked. When Nazi Germany invaded in 1941 Russia had enough modern industry to resist. But it was built on brutal work and terror.

During the 1920s and early 1930s most of the old Bolsheviks broke from Stalin's state. At some point each of them realized the dream had become a nightmare, and that they could collaborate no longer. Those who spoke out were arrested in the 1920s. They were shot in the 1930s, and so too were almost all those who kept quiet, because Stalin and the new bureaucrats saw in them the memory of the revolution.

During these years Ho Chi Minh worked for the Communist International. It was a contradictory organization. The people who joined Communist parties wanted revolution, and the International openly said it did too. But after 1926 the Stalinist machine would not tolerate a democratic workers' revolution anywhere. The example would be too much of a challenge to the Russian regime.

Stalin sacrificed foreign Communists to deals with their rulers. In China, for instance, a joint army of Communists and the nationalist Guomindang marched north in 1926 to take Beijing and Shanghai. In Shanghai there was a general strike and armed workers took power. But the nationalist Guomindang was one of Stalin's few allies in the world. The Communist International told the Communists and workers to turn their guns over to the Guomindang when the army arrived in Shanghai. They did. The Guomindang then killed tens of thousands of workers and Communists, and the few surviving Communists fled to remote rural areas.[11]

Similar things happened in many countries. But the local Communist parties did organize, and led strikes and peasant movements. After all, people became Communists because they wanted to change the world, and Stalin would have nothing to bargain with in international politics if he did not lead a movement.

Ho Chi Minh was in China working for the Communist International for much of the 1920s. In 1924 he founded the first Communist party in Indochina at a meeting of Vietnamese exiles in China. There are conflicting accounts of what he did in the 1930s. For much of the time he lived in Russia and kept his head down, scraping a living teaching other Vietnamese. He also went back to China for the International at some point; he was still part of Stalin's machine. But then in 1939 he left Russia for China, probably on his own account, to build an anti-colonial revolution in Vietnam. He finally got home in February 1941, after 30 years abroad, and found the Communists hiding in small camps in the jungle. They welcomed him. Almost everyone who ever met Ho agreed that he was a nice man—humble, gentle and kind.

His project was to build a state capitalist regime in Vietnam like Stalin's Russia. Ho wanted a proud and independent state with modern industry. The Communists would rule, and the workers and peasants would work, and be arrested if they talked back. Ho wanted, in short, what the Vietnamese now have.

The Communist Party he returned to in Vietnam was a nationalist party with socialist roots. Its members were mostly, like Ho Chi Minh, the educated sons and daughters of landlords and government bureaucrats, but the decent and honest minority among those people. Only the rich got any education in French Vietnam, and they did not get much. In the 1930s only eight Vietnamese in 1,000 had three years of school. These men and women were the majority of the Communists, and the great majority of the leadership of the party.

So when the five men from the village of Beautiful Waters contacted the Communists in Hue in 1939, the party recruited Minh, the radical landlord's son, first. After it trained him, the other four men were allowed to join the party cell in the village: 'Many years later, one of the five men told two friends that the five had considered themselves equals within the cell, but that Minh had served as chief contact man with district and provincial (party) organizations'.[12]

This was how the Communist Party worked. First it recruited educated men like Minh. Then those people recruited and led the villagers they knew.

This produced a party in the image of people like Minh. They were the decent minority of the landlord class. They hated the corruption and brutality of their class. They wanted to sweep aside the old order and replace it with a modern industrial state. They saw that state not in terms of democracy, but in terms of a better world led by people like them. They were in daily, intimate contact with poor villagers and saw themselves as tribunes of the oppressed. They were honest men and women, worthy of respect. You cannot build an underground revolutionary organization in a village unless the people who have known you all your life trust you. But men like Minh were not themselves the oppressed.

This meant the Communist Party was always deeply ambivalent about land reform. Building a new society would mean breaking the old landlords. The rank and file of the party in the villages, the other four men in the party cell in Beautiful Waters, would have no problem taking the land from the landlords and shooting them if necessary. But men and women like Minh would always be torn. They themselves would come out of such a revolution as rulers in the cities, but their families would be impoverished and many of them killed. So the Communist Party was always torn between the leaders and the led, and the leaders were torn between their families and their vision of the future.

For some this suffering increased their resolve. Vo Nguyen Giap, for instance, was a Communist and the son of a mandarin. In the 1939 crackdown the French government jailed his wife, daughter, father, sisters, brother in law and sister in law. Between 1941 and 1943 all of them were killed in jail.[13] Giap escaped and remained a revolutionary all his life. He went on to become the military leader of the resistance against the French and then the Americans.

# The Viet Minh

Ho returned to Vietnam in 1941 with a plan, and persuaded the other Communist leaders of it. They set out to build a mass organization to fight for independence, the Viet Minh (Vietnamese League). This organization would unite everybody—workers, capitalists, peasants and landlords—who wanted to fight the French. The Communists would be the organizers and political leadership of this alliance. This was not a trick. Everybody knew the Communists led the Viet Minh. But the structure of the Viet Minh allowed people to say to themselves, 'The choice is between working with the Communists and working with the French. I am not a Communist, but I do want to fight colonialism. I will join the Viet Minh.'

The structure of the Viet Minh also allowed the Communists to build a mass movement without recruiting too many people to the party. They could pick and choose people they trusted to follow their discipline.

The Viet Minh faced a complicated political situation in the middle of World War Two. Vietnam was a French colony, but Germany had conquered France in 1940. France was then occupied by German troops who set up a puppet French fascist government, the Vichy regime. The French colonial government in Vietnam declared itself loyal to Vichy. Later in 1940 the Japanese army invaded Vietnam. A French colonial government loyal to Vichy remained in place, backed by Japanese military power.

In 1941 the Vietnamese Communists were in no position to launch a general resistance against the Japanese army. They had been shattered by the French crackdown of 1939. They had no arms and few members (four years later, after considerable growth, they would still have only 5,000 members). For the moment they survived in a few small guerrilla camps in the mountains in the north, near the Chinese border. They were unable to launch a guerrilla war. Where they had members they concentrated on talking to people and trying to build underground organization.

But then the Allies drove the German army out of France. De Gaulle's Free French took power in alliance with the French Communists. De Gaulle wanted to hold on to the colonies. The colonial government in Vietnam could see the Allies were winning. It wanted to come out of the war on the winning side and hold Vietnam for France. It began secret talks with de Gaulle's new government. The Japanese army could no longer trust the French colonial authorities, and on 9 March 1945 the Japanese army took over the government directly and interned all the French.

Now Ho's Viet Minh could present themselves as part of the Allies, with America, Russia, France and Nationalist China against Germany and Japan. The American OSS (the forerunner of the CIA) sent a few agents to Ho's camp in the mountains.

One man in Beautiful Waters remembered:

> We knew the war was coming to an end, and we knew the Japanese were going to be defeated by the Americans. We were also sure that the Americans would not let the French come back to Vietnam. We were all hopeful that Vietnam would be independent soon.[14]

A woman in Beautiful Waters said:

> I was a little girl at the time. But I can still remember how much everyone liked the Viet Minh. In my family, my mother and sisters and I spent our time late at night making little Viet Minh flags. We worked on them together. We sewed all the flags with the yellow star, because we knew that the people would want them to celebrate the Viet Minh victory. And we were pretty sure that the Viet Minh was going to take over the country.[15]

Then in the spring of 1945 there was famine in the north. The Mekong Delta in the south had always been the rice basket of Vietnam. From the fall of 1944 on, it was clear that famine was coming to the north. But the only way to get rice north from the Mekong Delta was one two-lane highway and one slow railway line. The

Japanese army needed what transportation lines it had to move rice and war materials for its own troops. The rice did not get through. Of the 10 million people in the north, 1 million starved to death.

There is always food in a famine. During 1943, for instance, the British colonial authorities in India had presided over a similar famine in Bengal, in which between 2 million and 3 million people died. The priority for the British, as for the Japanese, was supplying the front. And in both Bengal and north Vietnam, as in all famines, the rich, the soldiers and the police had enough to eat. In north Vietnam the French colonial police and Japanese army guarded the rice stockpiles from the hungry. The government continued to send troops into the villages to collect taxes—in rice.

The Communists and the Viet Minh told people to attack the rice warehouses and refuse to pay the taxes. They had almost no arms, so they also encouraged people to petition local officials not to collect taxes. According to historian David Marr, unsympathetic officials:

> …found themselves surrounded by angry compatriots wielding bamboo spears, machetes, or knives, escorted to the village ceremonial house, and compelled to apologize publicly for abusing their powers and denigrating the Viet Minh. If the village possessed a small stock of 'charity grain', officials might be persuaded to release it. Grain already collected and about to be turned over to private syndicated tax collectors…sometimes had to be returned… When the district mandarin arrived at Phu Ninh village to collect taxes escorted by a Japanese squad, the alert drum sounded and hundreds of villagers surrounded the party. After a standoff lasting all day, the Japanese fired a volley that killed two people, then withdrew… The district mandarin or An Thi (in Hung Yen) reported that most village officials were now more afraid of being killed than of disobeying repeated orders from superiors to collect taxes…

Sometimes people broke into grain warehouses owned by the government or big landowners. Most commonly a small group of young men armed only with spears and machetes would overpower two or three guards in the middle of the night, break the locks, then urge a much larger group to grab sticks of paddy and disperse as quickly as possible. In other cases, large crowds were mobilized first to cow guards and provide a screen against outside interruption as the warehouse was emptied. Occasionally, it was possible to take advantage of Allied air attacks, when warehouse guards ran for shelter, to seize a quantity of paddy and rice.[16]

There were hundreds of tax refusals and about 75 to 100 warehouse raids. These definitely saved lives, perhaps 100,000, maybe more. But without arms they could not stop the famine.

The Viet Minh had established themselves as the people who fought the famine. Famines change whole societies. Poor people beg from the rich and are refused. People refuse to share with their neighbors and their kin. They have to sell their land cheap and their daughters. Decisions are made inside families about who will eat. The children or the old people do not get their share and they die. This is a daily event, something unspoken, but clear every time people eat. People are ashamed of what they do, and do not talk about it much afterwards. But they do not forget or forgive. After the famine the Communists and the Viet Minh were always strongest in the north.

The new harvest began to come in that summer of 1945. Then the American government dropped atomic bombs on Hiroshima and Nagasaki, and the Japanese government surrendered. Nobody in Vietnam had expected the war to end so quickly and there was a sudden power vacuum. The Japanese had been defeated and the French were still interned. The Viet Minh units in the north marched towards Hanoi, exulting in walking openly in daylight. They were largely unarmed. The main Viet Minh unit in Hanoi had only 800 fighters with 90 firearms, but they had the support of the people. The Japanese army stayed in their barracks, waiting to surrender to the Allies. If the Viet Minh did not attack them, they would not fight.

On 16 August 20,000 people attended a rally in the square facing Hanoi Opera House. A Viet Minh flag was unfurled, the crowd cheered and the police did not dare open fire. Three days later a Viet Minh led crowd of 200,000 seized the palace, the city hall, the civil guard barracks and power.[17]

On 2 September 1945 Ho Chi Minh declared Vietnamese independence in front of a crowd of half a million in Hanoi:

> [He began] 'All men are created equal. The Creator has given us certain inviolable Rights: the right to Life, the right to be Free, and the right to achieve Happiness.' At this point he looked out over the crowd, and gently asked, 'Do you hear me distinctly, fellow countrymen?' And the crowd answered that they did indeed hear him.[18]

Ho was using the words of the American Declaration of Independence. It was a direct appeal for American support against French colonialism.

He didn't get that support.

# The superpowers

The leaders of the great world powers had already agreed what they were going to do with Vietnam. As World War Two came to an end, the leaders of Russia, the United States and Britain held summit meetings in Yalta and Potsdam. There they agreed how to divide up the post-war world into spheres of influence. Russia got Eastern Europe, the United States and Britain got Western Europe, and they split Germany. The US would dominate the Americas, of course, and Britain and the US together would dominate the Middle East.

The British prime minister, Churchill, insisted that France should keep its three colonies in Indochina: Vietnam, Laos and Cambodia. Churchill was dedicated to retaining the British Empire, and was worried that Indochinese independence from France would strengthen the case for Indian and African independence from Britain.

In 1945 France mattered more to America than Vietnam. In March de Gaulle called in the American ambassador to Paris. General de Gaulle was a right wing nationalist and the leader of a new coalition government with the French Communists. The Communists had been the core of the French resistance to the Nazis, and it was not clear then if they would take power in France, or in all Europe. So de Gaulle threatened the American ambassador:

> What are you driving at? Do you want us to become, for example, one of the federated states under the Russian aegis? The Russians are advancing apace, as you well know. When Germany falls, they will be upon us. If the public here comes to realize you are against us in Indo-China, there will be terrific disappointment and nobody knows to what that will lead. We do not want to become Communist; we do not want to fall into the Russian orbit, but I hope you will not push us into it.[19]

De Gaulle was bluffing, but the American ambassador took the point. The Russian, American and British governments agreed that Vietnam, Laos and Cambodia would remain French colonies.

However, they all knew that in 1945 the French government did not have the soldiers, the guns or the ships to retake Indochina. So Russia, Britain and the US agreed that the British army would receive the surrender of the Japanese troops in southern Vietnam, restore order and then hand the country back to the French. The Nationalist Chinese army would do the same in the north.

# The French war

The Viet Minh took power in Hanoi on 19 August 1945. Two days later there was a mass demonstration in Saigon, in the south, led by the Viet Minh. Ngo Van Xuyet was there.

Ngo was a Trotskyist. Leon Trotsky, one of the leaders of the Russian Revolution, had been the leader of the Communist opposition to Stalin's government in Russia. He was arrested and went into exile, where he spent the 1930s trying to build an international movement of socialists opposed to both Western capitalism and the Stalinist dictatorship. When Trotsky was killed by Stalinist agents in Mexico in 1939 he left behind small groups in many countries.

The Trotskyists in Vietnam had a few hundred members in the south, mainly workers on the plantations and workers and intellectuals in Saigon. In the 1930s they won local elections in Saigon and they were central to a general strike there in 1938. But the crackdown of 1939 smashed them, just as it did the Communists. Ngo Van Xuyet and the other survivors began to get released from prison in 1944.

In August 1945 Ngo was worried about the demonstration because it was led by the Viet Minh, who were telling people to remain calm while they negotiated independence with the French. He was sure the French were about to return, in blood. But the demonstration affected him deeply:

> For the first time in the political life of the country, from the morning onwards, veritable masses of people assembled like ants and filled the Norodom boulevard, then the Botanical Gardens near the governor's palace, and then crossed the major arteries chanting slogans…
>
> The Vietnamese police at the service of the occupation no longer knew from where to take its orders: it remained passive in the presence of the procession crossing the city on strike… The demonstration, which owed its initiation to the Viet Minh, was the classic tactic preparatory to the seizure of power—it represented the seal of general approval. But in fact everybody went down the street with different aspirations. The only common but overwhelming sentiment was 'never to see the French back in power'…
>
> The first awakening of these masses, who had been forever in 'chains and gags', emanated an electric tension amid an unusual calm, the calm that precedes a storm. All constraint was broken, and everybody seemed to live in a moment of total liberty…

[But] Roosevelt, Churchill and Stalin had decided our fate at Yalta and Potsdam. We were not to be cast body and soul into a future without a tomorrow. Faced with the imminent arrival of British troops, and faced with the threat of the return of the old colonial regime (General Cedile, the special envoy of the 'New France', was already in the Governor-General's palace in Saigon), everybody decided to look for and obtain weapons; everyone lived in the same electric atmosphere.[20]

In September British troops, mainly Nepali Gurkhas under the command of British officers, arrived in Saigon. The British government was now Labour and Churchill was no longer prime minister, but this made no difference to imperial policy. The British did not have enough troops to attack the Vietnamese on their own. So they released and armed both the Japanese troops and the imprisoned French colonials. On the night of 22 September Nepali, French and Japanese troops under British command occupied the main buildings in Saigon.

The Viet Minh called for restraint and negotiation with the allies. But Saigon rose—the Trotskyists, the Buddhists, the religious sects, the many Communists who could not stomach the party line, and above all the workers. It was spontaneous. A hundred and fifty French civilians were killed, and the rebels held the working class suburbs for several days. But the Viet Minh withdrew from Saigon and the rising was crushed.[21]

The French army replaced the British and slowly reasserted its power in the south. As they all retreated, the Communists hunted down and killed almost all the Trotskyists. For the moment the French were not strong enough to take all of Vietnam, and the Viet Minh still held power in the center and north.

In Beautiful Waters it was a good time. The local Viet Minh held power for 18 months. They did not punish their enemies, and they did not take the land from the landlords. But they lowered many rents and gave the communal land back to the poor peasants. They abolished the land tax on smallholdings and the head tax. They set a ceiling for interest rates of 30 percent, and made strenuous efforts to hold back corruption in their ranks.[22]

It was what the Communists had promised, and what men like Minh had devoted their lives to. It was an attempt to satisfy the poor peasants without losing the support of the landlords and the businessmen in the cities. At the same time Ho Chi Minh was desperately negotiating with the French. The first and last fair elections in Vietnam were held in the center and north in January 1946. The Viet Minh won overwhelmingly.

But they did not have the arms to fight. To the north, in China, there was civil war between Communists and Nationalists. The Viet Minh could get no arms from there. And the Vietnamese Communists were still part of an international movement run from Moscow. The line from there was to negotiate with the French.

So Ho agreed to the landing of French troops in Hanoi in March 1946. In November the French struck and drove the Viet Minh out of Hanoi. In Beautiful Waters the Communists went underground again, but the Viet Minh kept the support of most of the villagers. The guerrilla war against the French lasted eight more years.

The main highway in the country ran through the fields of Beautiful Waters, and the Viet Minh in the village became snipers, firing at French convoys from their hiding places and then running away. The French army made many sweeps through the village looking for rifles, Marxist pamphlets or entrances to tunnels. In the search they would stick their bayonets into the rice storage jars, searching, and the villagers would stand very still and say nothing. They saw the French as cruel and unpredictable. Every sweep took prisoners, and some of them never came back. As the war went on, the Viet Minh grew stronger in Beautiful Waters, and at night small units began to stand and fight the French in the dark.

But not all the villagers in Beautiful Waters supported the Viet Minh, and not all the French supported colonialism. The French Communist Party had supported colonialism as long as it was in the government, but after it left de Gaulle's coalition in 1947 began to organize against the war. Even before that, the French government had assumed it would be politically impossible to use French conscripts in Indochina. So they used 80,000 French career soldiers, 20,000 French Foreign Legionnaires (half of whom had fought for the Nazis) and 48,000 troops from the French colonies. It was not enough, but they also had 300,000 Indochinese troops.[23]

The sergeants and officers among the Indochinese troops were mostly the children of the landlords, the government officials, the money-lenders and the businessmen in the cities. So were the police. The Communists were trying to build an alliance with that class. But the majority of the landlords figured their future was safer with the French. In Beautiful Waters the same few families who had controlled the land in the 1930s now leaned on French support.

Back in the hills, particularly in the north, the Viet Minh were building larger units in the jungle. The war spread across the whole of Indochina. The Vietnamese Communists had called themselves the Indochinese Communist Party. Now they formed separate parties in Cambodia and Laos, which built mass guerrilla organizations modeled on the Viet Minh—the Pathet Lao in Laos and the Khmer Serai in Cambodia. These movements diverted French attention and resources, but the crucial battle was in Vietnam.

In 1949 the Communists in China won their civil war, and the Viet Minh could finally obtain arms from over the border. The Communist Party expanded massively, still favoring people from rich backgrounds, but also recruiting more widely.

This seemed natural and right to the educated Communists. Le Van Tiem, for instance, became party secretary in the village of Son-Duong in the north in 1948:

> The three members of the modern intelligentsia, [elementary school graduates] like myself, all became party members because, with our prestige, our advice to the other villagers was frequently followed. Similarly, many other teachers were also recruited into the Party because of their education, their speaking skills and the prestige they commanded as members of the teaching profession. I can recall only a few cases of teachers who were not invited to join the Party: one because of his competitive and argumentative style of interaction and two others because of their distance from other villagers.[24]

However, the war was making landless peasants more important to the party. The party secretary in Son-Duong village was a teacher, but the commander of the village guerrillas, Te, was a landless laborer. When Te was a boy and his father lay dying very few of the villagers had come to say goodbye to the old man, because the family was poor and of no account, and there was a rumor his father had tuberculosis. Even in that poor household Te had been at the bottom of the hierarchy, because his mother was not his father's favorite wife. From the age of five he had worked for wages. As a teenager he became a plowman for the mayor of a nearby village:

> On the first day he beat me right and left with a bamboo rod in the field as I tried to plow. The following morning, weeping and holding the plow but determined to master the technique, I succeeded at the

task… I always went to work hungry. Even at their family celebrations,
I ate the leftovers when I returned from the field.

Te worked for the mayor for six years, and 'for all those years, my [widowed] mother remained a hired laborer in Son-Duong'.[25] When the war against the French came, Te joined the guerrillas. By 1952 he was the commander in the village where his father and mother had been treated as nothing. In the war, what a person did mattered as much as who they were.

After 1950 Viet Minh propaganda and speeches in Son-Duong and Beautiful Waters, and across Vietnam, began to emphasize class differences and land reform. The war was hardening the Communists. They could see that the landlords were dragging their feet and looking to the French for support. The Communist Party had been founded by revolutionaries. They understood class, and they knew how to mobilize the energy and passion of the oppressed. So in 1953, after eight years of war, they began a thorough land reform in the areas they controlled in the north (but not in their areas in the center and south). In the north the party organized landless peasants to haul the old landlords in front of village meetings, humiliate them, make them apologize, take their land and sometimes kill them. The accounts we have of the land reform are mostly hostile.[26] They all agree that the reform was led by the lowest of the low, and that those people had a lifetime of bitterness to avenge.

Once the landless began, they attacked both the 'feudal' landlords who had supported the French and the 'progressive' landlords who supported the Viet Minh. As we have seen, many Communist leaders came from landlord families. Now, with land reform, the class tensions in the Communist Party came to the surface in stark form. Communists from landlord families found their fathers were publicly humiliated and their families reduced to ordinary poverty. When they went home their mothers looked at them in sullen judgement over the rice bowl. The landless could simply hate exploitation and want their fair share. The Communist party cadres were torn.

The party dealt with this in two ways. At first people from landlord families who protested too loudly were expelled. But in 1955 Ho Chi Minh himself announced that there had been many mistakes and injustices in the land reforms. There were investigations, village by village, many apologies, and some people got some of their land back.

However, the deed was done. The power of the old order in the countryside was broken in the north. And that released, as Ho and the other leaders had known it would, the ferocious energy of the landless. In 1954 the French army dug themselves into the valley of Dien Bien Phu in the mountains near the Laotian border. They built their base in a valley because they knew the Viet Minh in the hills above them had no heavy artillery. But the Viet Minh had organized a civilian transport force of a quarter of a million people, most of them landless peasants, who had carried Chinese heavy artillery, broken down into many pieces, on their backs along paths through the jungle and over the mountains. The French were cut off at Dien Bien Phu and pulverized by that artillery. They surrendered.

The Viet Minh had won the war. But not quite the peace.

# The Geneva negotiations

After Dien Bien Phu the French and the Viet Minh sat down to negotiate in Geneva. It was clear to all that the Viet Minh could defeat the remaining French units and take over the whole country within a year. So there was no question that Vietnam would become independent. The question was whether it would be Communist.

The talks in Geneva were part of larger negotiations between America, Russia and China over the end of the Korean War. Vietnam was a sideshow for these powers, but a sideshow they wanted settled. The big powers agreed that Laos and Cambodia would become independent kingdoms, formally neutral in the Cold War but in practice leaning towards the Americans. Vietnam would be partitioned like Korea and Germany. The Communists would get north Vietnam, and south Vietnam would become a separate state aligned with the Americans.

The Viet Minh wanted the country divided at the 13th parallel, just north of Saigon. More important, they insisted the partition had to be temporary, with elections within six months. The American president, Eisenhower, later wrote, 'I have never talked with or corresponded with a person knowledgeable in Indo-Chinese affairs who did not agree that if elections had been held as of the time of the fighting, possibly 80 per cent of the population would have voted for Ho Chi Minh'.[27]

The French insisted on the 18th parallel, just south of Hanoi, and no elections. The Russian foreign minister, Molotov, proposed the 17th parallel, north of Hue, and elections in two years. Everybody involved knew that two years would give the new southern regime enough time to consolidate power and prevent free elections. So Ho Chi Minh flew to China and personally appealed to Zhou Enlai, the Chinese foreign minister, to overrule Molotov. Zhou told Ho to accept the Russian settlement.[28]

For the Russian and Chinese governments, Vietnam was not worth upsetting the larger deal between the Americans and Russians over Korea and the world. The Viet Minh were dependent on China for weapons, and the Vietnamese Communist Party was still very much part of a world movement led by the Russians. Moreover, the Vietnamese were aware the American government was considering sending troops to Vietnam.

So the Viet Minh accepted partition at the 17th parallel and elections in two years time. The American government refused to sign the final peace settlement so it would not be bound by the promise of elections. North Vietnam and South Vietnam became separate countries. In the North the Communist Party began to build a state capitalist economy modeled on Stalin's Russia and Mao's China. They wanted a modern, industrialized economy in North Vietnam, ruled by the leadership of the Communist Party. South Vietnam became a corrupt American client state.

# The Republic of South Vietnam

The new Republic of South Vietnam was headed by Ngo Van Diem, a Catholic mandarin. Diem had gone into exile during the French war—he hated the Communists yet could not bring himself to support the French. Now his government was the old colonial government, his officials the Vietnamese who had served the French. His army officers had almost all fought for the French against the Viet Minh. A million Catholic refugees came down from the North. Some Catholics had fought for the Viet Minh, but the Catholics who had become refugees had supported the French. Diem was a Catholic too, and now they were his strongest supporters in the South. The big businessmen in the cities were largely Chinese, and they too supported Diem.

In the villages the landlords supported Diem's government. Hue and the center were south of the 17th parallel, so Beautiful Waters was now part of South Vietnam. The same families who had dominated the village council under the French now dominated it under Diem. The individuals differed—under the French it had been one brother, now it was the other brother or a nephew. But the policies continued. The same few families still controlled 30 to 40 percent of the land in Beautiful Waters. And 'many abuses of council authority common under the French became virtually routine' under Diem.[29]

The Communists had accepted the Geneva peace agreement in 1954. They had 60,000 political activists in the South, and all but 15,000 were withdrawn to the North. Of the 100,000 Viet Minh soldiers in the South, 90,000 left for the North, taking almost all the modern weapons with them. The 10,000 soldiers left behind lived secretly in the jungle because their presence was an open violation of the Geneva peace deal. Vo Van An, a Communist activist, defected to the Americans in 1965 and told his interrogators that after 1954:

> These units lived deep in the jungle, 'fleeing from people as if they were tigers'… They maintained no bases, no camps… Each soldier had a hammock which was his home… They were constantly on the move, avoiding contact with anyone, using every means of camouflage, covering their tracks, leaving absolutely no sign at all.[30]

The Communist Party was now run from the North. The strategy was that the party in the South would try to build support for elections. It is unlikely that the Communist leaders believed the elections would actually happen. It was pretty obvious that Vietnam was being divided as Germany and Korea had been divided. Moreover, the Communists had withdrawn three quarters of their political activists from the South. Had they expected democracy and elections, they would have left those people in place. Vo Van An, the Communist defector, told his interrogators that higher level cadres like him had been:

> …certain that general elections would never take place, although this was not discussed at lower levels to maintain morale and so as not to conflict with the Party's public stance that the Geneva Accords were a great victory for the Party. By the summer of 1955 it became apparent to everyone what the higher echelons in the Party had felt all along: there would be no general elections and no steps toward reunification talks. The leadership was not surprised. 'We just considered Diem as a debtor who refused to pay—we would make him pay'.[31]

When the elections did not happen the Communist Party told its members that a revolution might be necessary later. For the moment the task was to build the party, organize and agitate for elections. This was in line with what Communist parties were saying in Europe and India at the same time—don't try to take power, organize campaigns and unions, try to win elections. This line fitted with Russian foreign policy. The Russian government had effectively decided that if the Americans did not challenge its rule in Eastern Europe, it would not challenge American influence in the rest of the world. But it also fitted with the exhaustion of the party in North Vietnam. It felt it needed time to rebuild a working economy in a ravaged land—and for that it needed Russian aid.

But the party cadres left behind in South Vietnam found themselves in desperate times. Diem's new government was a police state. In a sense, Diem had no choice. In the class struggle one side always feels it is on the advance, while the other feels it is on the retreat. The majority of the peasants and workers had supported the Viet Minh. If Diem did not push them back, hard, with repression, they would only become more confident and his government would fall.

And the issue of land remained. The Communist Party in the South had not redistributed all the land as it had in the North. But what the party did in Beautiful Waters it had also done in most of the Mekong Delta. It had rented more communal land to the poor and less to the landlords, and it had reduced rents and controlled debts. Now the landlords were back, but facing tenants who had felt their own power for years. In South Vietnam in 1954 the landless and the peasants could imagine freedom from economic slavery.

The landlords could only claw back their rents in that situation through great fear, and therefore great cruelty. But if they did not take their land back quickly they might lose it forever.

Diem's American advisors urged him to implement land reform to weaken the Communists. The Americans had recommended this strategy in Japan, Korea and the Philippines, and there it had largely worked. But in those countries there had been a powerful native ruling class in the cities, for whom land reform had made sense. They would sacrifice some of their land in the countryside to consolidate the power of their businesses in the city. They could do this because land was not their most important possession.

South Vietnam was different. There the Vietnamese who backed the government relied on their land ownership. Under French colonialism the big businessmen and plantation owners had been French and Chinese. After 1954 they were mostly Chinese. (This does not mean that most Chinese in Vietnam were rich. Most Chinese were poor workers, but most big businessmen and traders were Chinese.) These Chinese capitalists supported Diem's government, but they were not its core, its officials or its officers.

Moreover, capitalism in South Vietnam was more parasitic than productive. The US government bankrolled Diem's government by supplying large quantities of American consumer goods. Diem's government then sold licenses to import these goods cheaply to local capitalists, often Vietnamese ones. (The local capitalists also had to pay large bribes for the licences.) The government used the money from the sale of the licenses to fund government expenditure, the capitalists got a windfall, and the ministers became hopelessly corrupt.[32]

It is probably true that Diem's government would not have lasted a month without American support. It also would not have lasted a year without a real base in the country, among a real class. That base was the landlords and their children in the army. Diem had to defend them.

So Diem agreed to the American idea of land reform and passed a law, but in fact little changed. And he attacked the Communists. In 1956 anybody who had agitated for elections was arrested—about 50,000 people, of whom roughly 12,000 were executed.[33] This is an extraordinary number given that there were probably only 15,000 Communists left after so many withdrew to the North in 1954. The terror smashed half the Communist cells in Tay Ninh province by late 1955, and 90 percent of the party cells were gone by the end of 1956.

The Communists left alive in the villages knew what to do in this situation. They had to kill a few government informers and landlords in the village—that would drive the rest into the provincial towns. The army might come back in sweeps, but the Communists could hide. That is what the Viet Minh had done in the war against the French. The guerrillas fighting the French in the 19th century had done it too. It was the obvious thing to do. And there were still a few thousand armed guerrillas in the jungles, hunted, living like animals, under orders not to fight, but desperate.

The Southern Communists in the villages begged their provincial party committees to let them fight. The provincial committees said no, and simultaneously begged the leadership in Hanoi for the order to fight.

The leadership in Hanoi was torn.[34] The Southern Communists had great moral force on their side. The Southerners who had gone North wanted to fight, but most of the leadership was from the North. More important, they were trying to build state capitalism in one poor country, North Vietnam. They wanted time.

During that time the Southern party was dying, and North Vietnam was part of a world Communist movement undergoing considerable change. Stalin was dead, and in 1956 Khrushchev attacked the worst of Stalin's crimes and announced that the foreign policy of the Communist states would now be peaceful coexistence with the West.

For the Russian leaders, anxious about nuclear armageddon and concerned for their own dictatorship, peaceful coexistence made sense. But when the leadership in Hanoi said 'peaceful coexistence' to its comrades in the South, it was an impossible joke. The Southern regime was killing them all, not offering coexistence.

Still, in 1957 and 1958 the underground party began to recruit again, as Diem's government restored more and more land to the landlords. But then in 1959 repression intensified. 'Le Van Chan' (a psudonym) was a senior party official then. He was captured in 1962, and later told his American interrogators about the:

> ...period toward the end of 1959, when if you did not have a gun you could not keep your head on your shoulders... There was no place where Party members could find rest and security. Almost all were imprisoned or shot... Some village chapters, which had had four or five hundred members during the Resistance [to the French] and one or two hundred members in 1954, were now reduced to ten members, and even those ten could not remain among the people but had to flee into the jungle to survive.
>
> In the face of such activity by the Diem government, the demand for armed activity by Party members increased daily... Party members felt it was no longer possible to talk of political struggle while looking down the gun barrels of the government. Yet, despite the bitterness within the Party and their anger at the Central Committee, the Regional Committee, the zone committee and the village committee, party members were unable to break away from the organization that was killing them. There never were clear factions or groups within the Party demanding armed activity, which might have broken off from the Party organization in the South, or from the Central Committee in Hanoi—that could

never happen. Nevertheless, there were individuals—say, draft-age youths—who became so angry that they took the weapons the Party had hidden and came out of the jungle to kill the officials who were making trouble for them or their families. They did this, not because the Party had condemned those officials, but to preserve their own lives or to defend their families. Sometimes those individuals were so angry at the Party that they allowed themselves to be captured afterwards—just to spite the party.[35]

The Communists in the South were screaming at the North. Their voices had great moral weight. Diem's regime was winning. As Le Van Chan said to his interrogators, 'The Central Committee kept calling for political struggle. If they had kept that up, where were they going to find the cadres to carry it out?'[36] And the movement in the South was beginning to fight on its own. The Communist leaders in the North faced the alternatives of total defeat in the South, or a peasant movement fighting against their orders and outside their control.

In late 1959 the party in the North decided to back the killings of government agents that were already happening in the South, and to organize and broaden them.

At Vietnamese New Year in January 1960 the Communists launched an assassination offensive against secret policemen and village chiefs. In Long An province they had a list of hundreds of names. By the time they had killed 26, the others had all fled to the towns and cities.[37] In Ben Tre province in the Mekong Delta the party organized an uprising as an experiment. According to the historian Gabriel Kolko:

> Virtually unarmed masses briefly took over much of the province; land was distributed during the uprising itself. The formula worked virtually everywhere and soon gave the Party a vast presence and power despite the ARVN's [Diem's Army of the Republic of Vietnam] ability to quickly retake public buildings. Within months a major power shift had taken place in Vietnam.[38]

As in Ben Tre, everywhere the Communists began to share out the land as they drove out the officials and the secret police. The party in the North had been dominated by the educated and torn over land reform. The party in the South was different now. When the party took most of its activists North in 1954, those left behind would have been, by and large, less important in the party. To put it another way, they were less likely to be educated or from landlord families. The party's recruitment since had been among peasants who were angry at the return of the landlords under Diem. And by 1960 the Communists had an ocean of grief to avenge. They were mostly poor men and women, they did not care if they kept any 'progressive' landlords on their side, and they knew that handing out the land would unleash the whirlwind.

A landless peasant who joined the resistance in Long An in 1961 put it this way:

> I was poor. I had lost my land. I didn't have enough money to take care of my children. In 1961 propaganda cadres of the [Communist-led National Liberation] front contacted me… They came to all the poor farmers and made an analysis of the rich and poor classes. They said the rich people had always served the French and had used the authority of the French to oppress the poor… Without any other means to live, the poor had become the slaves of the landlords. The cadres told us that if the poor people don't stand up to the rich people, we will be dominated by them forever. The only way to ensure freedom and a sufficient life was to overthrow them…
>
> In my village there were about forty-three hundred people. Of these, maybe ten were landlords. The richest owned five hundred hectares, and the others had at least twenty hectares apiece. The rest of the people were tenants or honest poor farmers. I knew that the rich oppressed the poor… So I joined the Liberation Front.[39]

For many it had become a matter of human dignity. Chan, the captured Communist, told his American interrogators:

> Previously, the peasantry felt that it was the most despised class… particularly the landless and the poor peasants… At a celebration, they could just stand in the corner and look, not sit at the table like the village notables. Now the communists have returned and the peasants have power. The land has been taken from the landlords… Now the peasants can open their eyes and look up to the sky; they have prestige and social position. The landlords and other classes must fear them because they have the power: most of the cadres are peasants, most of the Party members are peasants, and most of the military commanders are peasants.[40]

# Chapter 2

# Why America intervened

The US government became involved in Vietnam because it looked like the Communists were going to win. The US government was heavily committed to anti-Communist regimes in other parts of the world, and the rich and powerful in the US had found anti-Communism essential to weakening the unions and socialism at home. So they intervened in Vietnam *for reasons that came from outside Vietnam—and some of the reasons came from the class struggle between business and unions in the United States.*

This is hard to grasp. In universities and the media, phenomena that form an organic whole are always divided into compartments. So economics is separated from politics, society from individual psychology, culture from history, science from religion, policy from morality, mental work from manual work, and the body from the mind. In the same way, we are used to thinking that international relations and class struggle are as different as cabbages and goldfish.

And within the US, foreign policy is almost always explained in terms of what is happening in *the other country*. So, for instance, during the war between the US and Serbia in 1999, even anti-war Americans looked for an explanation of the war in terms of what was happening in Serbia. They asked why the Albanians and Serbs were fighting. On the television they could see American bombers and Serb targets. They saw war between the US and Serbia, and asked for its roots in Serbian history, not American history.

There were some on the left, myself included, who suggested to them that the American government was bombing Yugoslavia because Saddam Hussein had successfully defied American bombs in Iraq a few months before. Now the US had threatened the Serbian government with force, the Serbs had defied it, and the American government wanted to demonstrate it could not be defied. This was important to maintaining American power in Europe and the Middle East.

Yes, people would say, that's probably true, but why are the Albanians and Serbs fighting?[1]

For Americans to understand US policy toward Vietnam requires a similar stretch. For the US government, what happened in Vietnam was not the point. It was the effect Vietnam would have in the world, and in America.

After all, while academics and news programs may treat the struggling world as unconnected bits, the people who run American foreign policy do not. They deal, at the top, with Yugoslavia and social security and the death penalty and Iraq and abortion and Monica Lewinsky and China and Teamsters' strikes, one after another, their minds dancing. In their actual lives, and in the world, these things are integrated. If we are to explain them, we have to understand this integration. So the first half of this chapter is about anti-Communism and the rich and powerful *in America*.

# The ruling class

The journalist David Halberstam describes a meeting in 1960 between two ruling class men of this class: president-elect John F Kennedy and Robert Lovett. Lovett was from Texas, the son of a lawyer for the Union Pacific Railroad who became a judge and a member of the Union Pacific board. Lovett went to a private school and Yale, joined the Skull and Bones club there (like George Bush, Sr) and married a banker's daughter. He was one of the Yale pilots who volunteered for World War One and was commander of the Naval Air Squadron. After the war he rose high in his father in law's bank. In World War Two Lovett was a staff man at the Pentagon, and after the war he was under-secretary of state at the Department of Defense. Now he was advising the new president.

Halberstam says that Lovett:

> ...was the very embodiment of the Establishment, a man who had a sense of country, rather than party. He was above petty divisions, so he could say of his friends, as so many of that group could, that he did not even know to which political party they belonged. He was a man of impeccable credentials, deciding who was safe and who was sound, who was ready for advancement and who was not...
>
> Robert Lovett understood power, where it resided, how to exercise it. He had exercised it all his life, yet he was curiously little known... [He was the] financier who is so secure in his job, the value of it, his right to do it, that he does not need to seek publicity, to see his face

on the cover of a magazine or on television, to feel reassured. Discretion is better, anonymity is safer: his peers know him, know his role, know that he can get things done. Publicity sometimes frightens your superiors…

He did not need to impress people with false images. He knew the rules of the game, to whom you talked, what you said, to whom you did not talk, which journalists were your kind, would, without being told, know what to print for the greater good, which questions to ask, and which questions not to ask. He lived in a world where young men made their way up the ladder by virtue not just of their own brilliance and ability but also of who their parents were, which phone calls from which old friends had preceded their appearance in his office. In a world like this he knew that those whose names were always in print…were there precisely because they did not have power, that those who did hold or had access to power tried to keep out of sight…

They were men linked more to one another, their schools, their own social class and their own concerns than they were linked to the country.[2]

John F Kennedy was of this class too. His grandfather had not been. But JFK's father, Joe Kennedy, had been a Wall Street trader, a Hollywood executive, Franklin Roosevelt's head of the Securities and Exchange Commission, and then ambassador to London. The other rich men did not trust Joe Kennedy—it was said he had been a bootlegger, too friendly to Hitler, too dishonest and personally cruel. But his son John was rich, Harvard, personable—he belonged.

Now JFK was looking for men like Lovett to run the country for him. He offered Lovett Secretary of State. Lovett thanked him, but said he was too old. The office went to Dean Rusk, the head of the Rockefeller Foundation.

Kennedy filled his cabinet with such men. Most were Republicans, which was only natural for bankers, lawyers and Wall Street men. Kennedy, a Democrat, was surprised that Robert McNamara, the president of Ford, had voted Democrat, but Kennedy would have made him Secretary of Defense anyway—everybody spoke well of him. McNamara had voted Republican only once, against Governor "Soapy" Williams of Michigan, because Williams was too friendly to the United Auto Workers.

These men were the class who took America into Vietnam. We

need to be specific about this ruling class. They include the owners of corporate wealth—not pension funds or houses, but enough shares to make a difference to how companies are run. They also include the senior management of the corporations, the armed forces, the federal, state and city governments, and the major institutions. To put it differently, the ruling class includes both those who own the system and those who run it. The latter, of course, can hope to become rich in return for running the system.

This class is not a closed group. Some people fall out of it in every generation. Some join it—at different times, for instance, John D Rockefeller, Andrew Carnegie, Lyndon Johnson, Harry Truman, Colin Powell and Bill Gates. And the edges of the class are fuzzy. An under-secretary of state is certainly part of this class, the mayor of New York probably is, and so is the Los Angeles chief of police.

I am not here defining the ruling class by culture or background. I am defining them by their relationship to the rest of society. They are the rich and powerful, who own and run the system.

They have a sense of their collective interests. In public, and often in private, they identify these interests with 'America'. 'We', they say, identifying the interests of the corporations, the government and the people as one. (Most Americans call the corporations and the government 'they'.)

The rich and powerful have social networks built around schools, colleges, charities, balls and vacation homes. But, more important, the boards of the largest 500 corporations are interconnected, because most members of any one board will sit on several others. This means that many small conversations in many cities can form collective opinion and corporate action over the course of a month. Money gives businessmen access to politicians, and increasingly allows the rich collectively to choose political candidates. There are lawyers who exist to put people in touch with other people, to knit the system together. And there are the people, like Robert McNamara—first president of Ford, then Secretary of Defense, then head of the World Bank—who knit the system together in their careers.

It was this class who took the decisions to intervene in Vietnam, and eventually to withdraw from Vietnam. To understand why, we need to begin with how they saw the world in 1945.

# Foreign policy

As World War Two began, the Great Powers in the world were the United States, Britain, France, Germany, Russia, Japan and China. When it ended, Germany and Japan had been decisively defeated, France was no longer a world power, China was locked in civil war, and the Russian and British economies were exhausted. But in America industrial production doubled during the war. In 1945 the US produced half the coal in the world, over half the electricity and two thirds of the oil. And in 1949 the US had military bases in 56 countries. It was the greatest power in the world, with Russia the only serious challenger.[3]

The American ruling class accepted their new mission. The economic and political victors of the war, they would make the world safe for American influence and American business. They were not embarrassed about this. They genuinely thought their way of life was better. They also talked of freedom. Sometimes they sponsored democracy and sometimes they sponsored dictators, as the occasion demanded. The bottom line was business freedom.

That meant supporting the rich in every country against the people who worked for them. In Vietnam, for instance, from 1954 on they supported the government and therefore sided with the landlords against the peasants. This was not an accident or a mistake. The US government abroad always supported the owners. That was the only way they could make the country safe for business.

But this did not always mean supporting the landlords. Where the businessmen in the cities were the real power, the American government could support them and help them give the peasants land reform. And it did not always mean supporting dictators. In Britain both the Conservative Party and the Labour Party did a reasonable job of running the country for business, and the same was true in many other countries. But particularly in the Third World, where people were desperate and the ruling class was often weak, the US regularly supported dictators because they were the only people who could keep inequality safe.

In 1945 the US appeared to be the dominant superpower. By 1948 the Russian state seemed to be gaining ground. In 1945 only the US had the atomic bomb, and the destruction of Hiroshima and Nagasaki had been a very public warning to the rest of the world of what

American power could do. Three years later Russia had the bomb too. In China the Red Army defeated the Nationalists and took power in 1949. In Eastern Europe Communist parties with far less popular support than the Chinese also seized power and began to turn Czechoslovakia, Hungary, Romania, Bulgaria and East Germany into state capitalist copies of the Soviet Union.

These state capitalist countries were a threat not so much because they called themselves 'socialist', but because they were competing capitalist powers and their markets were largely closed to American business. While Russian domination of Eastern Europe had been agreed as the quid pro quo for American domination of Western Europe, China and the bomb had not been agreed. Moreover, the ruling classes in America and Western Europe had not forgotten that a wave of revolution had followed the First World War.

In short, anti-Communism seemed to fit for the American ruling class abroad. We can now begin to look at how it suited them at home.

# McCarthyism

A wave of anti-Communism swept through America between 1947 and 1960. In what follows I will take issue, in some detail, with the received wisdom about this period.[4] Because what happened then was shameful, liberals have since popularized a series of myths about anti-Communism. The wisdom says that the anti-Communism was invented and led by Senator Joe McCarthy, when in fact it was organized by President Truman and FBI director Hoover. It says 'McCarthyism' was Republican, when it was in fact started by Democrats. The myth depicts a witch-hunt, the persecution of people who were innocent of any involvement with socialist ideas or activities. In fact an overwhelming majority of those punished were people who had been socialists or Communists, or had worked with them or spoken out in their support. The myth also says that the anti-Communist 'hysteria' came from the American people. In fact it came from the top—the federal government was the prime mover, and people were mostly punished by their employers.

The force driving this anti-Communism was the opposition of business leaders to labor militancy. In the 1920s business dominated the US. But then the Depression came, and hit America harder than

Europe. In 1933, the year Hitler came to power, unemployment was higher in America than in Germany. People were becoming increasingly desperate. A new president, Franklin Roosevelt, was elected in 1933. He promised people a New Deal, which mainly meant government pensions (Social Security) and workfare for the unemployed. The government also made kindly reference to unions, particularly in the National Recovery Act. It is unclear how serious this was, but working people took it as a green light.

The union leaders were more cautious at first, but by 1936 some unions were recruiting aggressively in the large factories and steel plants where there had been no unions before. The turning point came in Flint, Michigan, early in 1937. The auto workers at the General Motors plant went on strike for union recognition, and sat down inside the plant to stop scabs coming in and taking their jobs. The police came to remove them, and the strikers' wives and other workers in Flint fought the police in the street and defeated them. The new union, the United Auto Workers, won recognition at the plant and the sit-down movement spread across the country. By the end of the year the number of workers in unions had doubled. By 1941 the unions had won recognition in auto, rubber, steel, electrical manufacture, airplane manufacture, the docks, the ships and most mines.[5]

During World War Two the federal government obliged business by regulating wages and outlawing strikes, but obliged labor by insisting the corporations recognized unions. When the war ended in 1945 union members were confident. They felt the war had been fought against fascism and for people like them. Their wages had been held down during the war, but there was full employment now. In late 1945 and early 1946 there were long national strikes in rubber, steel and the mines, and at General Motors. These were seen as trials of strength both by the unions and by the corporations, and on balance the unions won.[6]

Measured in person days on strike, this was the largest strike wave the world had ever seen. This is important. In 1938 American industry had gone from mostly non-union to mostly union. In 1945-46 there was no revolutionary political movement in America, but American business faced the largest challenge from labor in its history. This was not the most numerous movement against American influence in the world: the Chinese Communist movement was bigger. But it was the largest union movement, the largest movement of workers, facing the American ruling class. And the momentum of the last ten years had run against the ruling class.

American business leaders knew they had to turn the momentum around. They did this by using the law and anti-Communist propaganda.

The crucial law was the Taft-Hartley Act in 1947, which effectively made solidarity illegal. It forbade strikes in support of workers in other companies, and made it illegal to honor their picket lines or refuse to work on goods made by scabs. Workers could only take action against their own employers. Most important, the unions were fined for wildcat strikes. Philip Murray, the new head of the Congress of Industrial Unions (the CIO, the militant breakaway from the old AFL, the American Federation of Labor) testified to Congress in 1947:

> If the financial responsibility of the union is to be expanded to include liability for actions of all these 'agents' even when the acts are not authorized or ratified, then this bill is precisely encouraging and insisting that, in self-protection, the unions impose greater centralization so as to confine authority and agency only to the highest and most restricted levels of leadership.[7]

Precisely—that was the point of the bill. As Senator Taft said, 'I think the men are more radical than their leaders in most cases'.[8] His bill also required unions to make all full time officials swear that they were not members of the Communist Party. This was part of the anti-Communist crusade, which was at base an attack on militants in the unions.

The American Communist Party had a few thousand members when the New Deal started. By 1945 it had somewhere in the region of 100,000 members. Even then, it was much more important than its numbers might suggest. It had built the party by building the unions, particularly the CIO. In many cases small party cells had organized for unions in a plant for months or years before the union finally won recognition. Communist Party members were often rank and file leaders of strikes. The CIO had also employed hundreds of party members as full time organizers in the 1930s. By 1945 the Communists led lively left wing oppositions in many unions. In the United Auto Workers and the Steelworkers they seemed to stand a real chance of election to run the union. In the Electrical Workers and several smaller unions they had won the leadership.

Besides unions, the Communist Party had built on two other issues. Its members had been staunch anti-racists, campaigning for integration and running an integrated party. And it had been the organizing core of the American movements protesting against European fascism in Germany and Spain.

The Communist Party was not led by revolutionaries. When Stalin signed a pact with Hitler in 1939, the Communist Party supported it. When Hitler went to war with Stalin, Communist Party was suddenly against all strikes in America because they would disrupt the war effort. It said, 'Communism is 100 percent Americanism', and meant it. But from the point of view of the business leaders in 1946, the Communists were the core of the militant network in the unions, and the clearest socialist voice.

So the ruling class—the federal government and the employers—launched an attack on Communists in America. The organizing force behind this was the Federal Bureau of Investigation, the FBI.[9] Every country has a secret police force that watches the political opposition—the Special Branch in Britain, the Sûreté in France, and so on. The FBI is the American secret police, but it is a secret police that does other things as well, and is never publicly referred to as the secret police. The FBI was founded at the end of World War One, just after the Russian Revolution and during a large strike wave in America in 1919. At this point it was a purely political police, a 'red squad' whose job was to spy on, harass, prosecute and deport socialists, anarchists and Communists in America. But by 1924 the socialist and Communist movement was in disarray, and the Attorney General forbade domestic spying by the FBI. J Edgar Hoover, the director of the Bureau, continued spying secretly, but he also added a public face of ordinary law enforcement, with FBI agents chasing car thieves and a few bank robbers. This public face legitimated the FBI, and gave a cover for its continuing existence. In 1939 the federal government allowed the Bureau to spy legally on Nazis and Communists. That year the FBI had 851 agents. Four years later it had 3,500. In 1945 Hoover and the FBI were ready and waiting, with the lists of Communists they had been keeping for years.

From 1947 on, the usual procedure was for the Un-American Activities Committee of the House of Representatives, or some other arm of the government, to name somebody as a Communist, or former Communist, mostly using FBI lists. The accused person's employer then fired them, their landlord often evicted them, and they usually had a lot of trouble finding another job. Most of the accused were workers and union activists—partly because that is who the

Communists were. Under Democratic President Truman there was a clean-out of Communists in government. The department of the federal government with the smallest percentage of employees fired was the State Department, because few of the elite Ivy League types who worked there were Communists. The department with the highest percentage of employees fired was the Post Office, because so many of the people who worked there were ordinary letter carriers, many of them black, and the union was strong.[10]

When people were accused of having been Communists they could go and testify before the House Committee, say they were sorry and name the names of other Communists in public. They thus became informers and got other people fired, but were allowed to keep their own jobs. The great majority of accused Communists refused to do this. But the few who did had their testimony widely publicized to make Communists look like people without integrity.[11] (Part of the anger in Hollywood about the 1998 Oscar for Elia Kazan was because he was one of the few in Hollywood who informed, while the many who did not inform lost their careers and got no honors.)

The support of union leaders was critical for the attack on Communists. Like the Taft-Hartley Act, anti-Communism divided the union leaders from the militants at the base. The United Auto Workers (UAW), for instance, had been the most important union in the upsurge of 1938 and the strikes of 1945-46. In 1947 politics inside the union were split between a left wing, led by the Communists, and right wing, led by Walter Reuther. (Reuther was right wing in the UAW, but any leader in the UAW was still left wing in terms of national politics.) Reuther used anti-Communism to break the left wing in the car plants. Some Communists and ex-Communists managed to keep their heads down and hold their jobs in the plants, but no Communists could be officials in the UAW.

A similar alliance between employers, union leaders and the federal government operated in Hollywood.[12] There the leaders of the anti-Communist crusade were Walt Disney and Ronald Reagan. Communist activists had played a central part in the unionization of Hollywood in the 1930s. A strike by the animators at Disney had been an important early victory for the unions, and Walt Disney never forgave the Communists. Ronald Reagan, on the other hand, was the leader of the right wing inside the Screen Actors Guild, probably the most important single union. He was also a secret informer for the FBI.

The persecution began when ten men were hauled before the House Un-American Activities Committee in Washington and accused of being Communists. They denied it, and the committee produced copies of their party cards. They lost their jobs, were blacklisted by the Hollywood employers and eventually went to prison. After that many more Hollywood Communists and ex-Communists were blacklisted. The federal government was using show trials. The message was, if they can do this to people in Hollywood, think what they can do to you.

But in Hollywood, as in Detroit, the persecuted Communists were also union activists. Eight of the original Hollywood Ten were writers, and all eight had been activists in their union, the Screenwriters Guild.

In short, the targets of anti-Communism were militant workers, not intellectuals. Of the roughly 20,000 people who lost their jobs in the anti-Communist crusade, the largest single group was 3,000 maritime workers. Again the crusade on the docks was organized by an alliance of the federal government, the employers and some of the union leaders.[13]

Not all the militant workers under attack were Communists. Trotskyists and other revolutionaries were persecuted, and people who supported the Communist Party found themselves in trouble too. Many Communists, understandably, had kept their party membership secret for fear of losing their jobs. So the government investigators used what they called the duck test: 'If someone walks like a duck and swims like a duck and quacks like a duck, he is a duck'.[14] Consistent support for Communist-led campaigns became proof of Communism. These campaigns included the Soviet-American Friendship League during World War Two, support for the anti-fascists in Spain, and writing letters to the American Red Cross to protest its policy of segregating the blood of white and black donors. Many people who had not actually joined the party lost their jobs because of the duck test. Communists or not, all of them had been guilty of supporting social justice, and social justice was what was under attack.

However, that was not what the government said. It focused on the fact that Communism in Russia was a brutal dictatorship and the American Communist Party was a tool of the Russian government. It claimed that some members of the party were spies, all of them followed Moscow's line, and all of them wanted to replace American freedom with a dictatorship like Russia.

This paralyzed the Communist Party. Very few of them were spies, but they did follow Moscow's line. More important, they thought the system in Russia was socialist, while everybody outside the party knew it was a brutal dictatorship. And, although unable to admit it, many people in the party knew it too. So they could not defend themselves properly. They could not hold public rallies and shout, 'Yes, I am a Communist, from the hair on my head to the soles of my feet, and I want for us what they have in Russia, and I'm proud of it.' Instead they defended themselves on the technicalities: 'I didn't break that law,' 'The Fifth Amendment says I don't have to testify,' 'You have no proof I was ever actually in the party.'

That was what made anti-Communism so ideal for the ruling class. The Communists who lost their jobs were not as important as the people who worked with them, and watched them go and didn't defend them. The fear and the shame of those people were what broke the left in the unions.

This process had been the joint creation of the employers, the FBI and the liberals in government. The persecutions began in 1947 under President Truman, a Democrat. The liberal Democrat Hubert Humphrey, later Lyndon Johnson's vice-president, said the Communist Party was 'a political cancer in our society'. Adlai Stevenson, Democratic candidate for president in 1952 and 1956, said Communism was worse 'than cancer, tuberculosis and heart disease combined'.[15]

Later the liberals were ashamed of what they had done. They renamed their crusade 'McCarthyism', and blamed it on Joe McCarthy, a Republican senator from Wisconsin. McCarthy did not get in on the act until 1950, long after anti-Communism started. But he introduced a new twist—he blamed the Democratic Party for shielding Communists in government. Since the Democrats were in fact persecuting all the Communists, he had to make up phony lists of Communists and accuse wholly innocent people, whom the Democrats had not fired precisely because they had not done anything. This was not the style of FBI, the employers or the Democrats, who were all trying to destroy a real social force. But the Democrats had been so hysterically anti-Communist that they had trouble attacking McCarthy at first. And for a time the Republican Party under Taft and Eisenhower used McCarthy as a weapon to smear the Democrats. But after Eisenhower became president in 1953, McCarthy publicly attacked the army for harboring Communists. The establishment could not allow this, and the Senate censured him.

This was possible because anti-Communism had already achieved its purpose. The campaign had been remarkably successful. In all, two Communists were executed, a few hundred people went to prison and just under 20,000 lost their jobs.[16] As political persecutions go, it was not that bad (particularly when compared with what the Communists faced in South Vietnam in the same period). But because so few people defended the Communists, and because they could not defend themselves, the persecution seemed terrible. There was a great fear of speaking socialist ideas, of even using words like 'working class' and 'ruling class'. Then in 1956 the Russian leader Khrushchev revealed that Stalin's crimes were all true, and the majority of the American Communist Party, of the people who had stayed through the persecution, left the party.

The attack on the Communists had not destroyed the unions. The ruling class strategy had been to accept the unions and work with the union leaders to weaken the extremists on the shop floor. They were able to do this because the American economy expanded massively between 1939 and 1960. So union workers in industry won real wage increases of 75 to 100 percent or more over that period. They won medical coverage, pensions and holidays—none of which they had before. The union leaders were able to deliver to the rank and file at the same time as they broke the Communists. But in the long run the attack on the Communists weakened the whole militant left, local democracy in the unions and the power of union locals against their own management. With that came increasing union corruption.

The unions had not been smashed. But from the point of view of the ruling class they had driven back the increasing workers' power they had faced between 1938 and 1946, and they had silenced the voices for socialism in the working class.

That was an important victory, and they would do a lot to defend it. One reason they intervened in Vietnam was that if they simply accepted a Communist victory there it would have weakened anti-Communism at home.

# Korea and Vietnam

Now we turn to anti-Communism in the world. After 1948 the Russian and US governments basically tried to observe the status quo. Neither had much choice. The US was vastly stronger than Russia in military terms, and they both had the H-bomb. The Russian government was on the defensive, but the US could not go in for the kill.

In practice, the Russians did not support the Communist peasant army in the Greek Civil War. The Americans did not support the Hungarian workers when they rose against Russian tanks in 1956. When the Shah arrested the Communists in Iran, the Russians caught them at the border and sent them back to the Shah. And so on, endlessly. Both sides observed their spheres of influence almost everywhere.

But not quite. The Communists in China took power independently of the Russians. And at the end of World War Two Korea, like Germany, had been divided into Russian and American sectors. In North Korea the Russians backed a Communist dictatorship and in South Korea the Americans backed a right wing dictatorship. In 1950 the two Koreas went to war. Controversy still rages about who attacked first. It matters not—both sides were ready to fight. The North Korean army swept all before it, driving the South Korean army and its American allies into a corner of the peninsula. The Americans persuaded the United Nations to back retaliation. A UN force, with largely American troops, then invaded and drove the North Korean army back, almost to the Chinese border. Douglas MacArthur, the American commander, was a well known leader of the lobby in America for returning the Nationalist Chinese to power by force. The Chinese Communist government, expecting an American invasion, struck back across the border and rapidly drove the American forces halfway down the Korean peninsula, roughly to the previous line of division between North and South. And there the Chinese and American armies stayed, grinding each other up.

The Korean War lasted three years. It started under President Truman, a Democrat. Eisenhower, a Republican, was elected president in 1952, in part because of his promise to end the Korean War. At no point did the American people vote for the war. There was little public criticism—people were either patriotic or afraid—but they wanted the war over. Eisenhower in fact ended it in 1953.

Four things about the Korean War were important for Vietnam. First, 40,000 Americans, half a million Chinese and 3 million Koreans, the majority of them civilians, died in Korea. From this the American ruling class learned that it could conduct a bloodbath in Asia with almost no protest at home.

Second, the Chinese army pushed the American army back and held it back. It could be argued that the Chinese won, or that neither side won, but not that the Americans won. The American ruling class and the generals did not forget this. In America the right now claims that the US fought the Vietnam War 'with one hand tied behind our back'. They do not usually say exactly what that hand should have done, but the implication is that the United States should have invaded North Vietnam. However, from 1965 to 1973 China kept large numbers of troops in North Vietnam—170,000 at the high point in 1967. These troops did not fight in South Vietnam, and China refused to lend pilots to North Vietnam, but they did operate anti-aircraft guns. More important, they were there to signal to the US government that an invasion of North Vietnam would mean war with China. They wore their own uniforms and made no effort to keep their presence secret, and the US government knew they were there.[17] And after Korea the American generals feared the Chinese army would win a war with the US. So whenever one or all of the Joint Chiefs of Staff proposed invading North Vietnam, they always immediately mentioned using the atom bomb if China came South. In doing so, they were sounding warlike but in effect ruling out war with China.

Third, the Korean War ended with Russia, the US and China all wanting a real settlement. They met in Geneva in 1954 and divided Korea again, with dictatorships North and South. This was part of a general settlement. China was a poor country—it had lost half a million people. The Chinese government wanted to turn to economic development, and it was satisfied that the US government would now allow it a safe place in the world. The US could not win in Korea and was under pressure at home to end the war. Russia wanted peace and a general agreement among the great powers not to trespass in each other's spheres of influence. And what the Koreans wanted did not matter.

Fourth, from the beginning of the Korean War the American government went from quiet support for France in Vietnam to massive backing. From Washington it all looked like one war. The Chinese Communists had won power in the civil war. Now they were advancing in support of Korean Communists on their northeastern border and arming Vietnamese Communists on their southeastern border. So by 1953 the US was supplying most of the French arms and ammunition, and paying about two thirds of the cost of the war. And the negotiations to end the war between the Viet Minh and France were tacked on to the Korean peace negotiations in Geneva.

# Intervention

The last chapter dealt with the negotiations at Geneva and the history of South Vietnam up to 1960 from the point of view of the Vietnamese Communists. Here we pick up the story from 1960, from the point of view of the American ruling class.

In 1959 the Communist leaders in Hanoi took the decision to back the armed revolt in the South. The Communist cadres from the South who had been withdrawn North in 1954 were sent back down South to lead the guerrilla movement. The Communist policy now was to build a National Liberation Front of all classes like the Viet Minh. This also solved the problem of what to do with the hundreds of thousands of largely landless peasants flooding into the guerrilla army. They would be part of the Front, but not the party.

The party in Hanoi thus kept control of the Southern movement. But the Viet Cong guerrillas were Southerners. At this point there were almost no North Vietnamese soldiers or arms in the South. The Viet Cong captured guns or bought them privately from soldiers of the South Vietnamese army.

In America, John Kennedy became president in January 1961. By then the Front could move in units of 1,000 in the Mekong Delta, and in September briefly took control of a provincial capital. Washington reacted by sending small but growing numbers of American troops: 3,200 by the end of 1961; 11,300 by the end of 1962; 16,300 by the end of 1963. It also sent planes, pilots, bombs, napalm and chemical defoliants. As presidential adviser Walt Rostow said in April 1961:

> We must somehow bring to bear our unexploited counter-guerilla assets on the Viet-Nam problem; armed helicopters; other Research and Development possibilities; our Special Forces units. It is somehow wrong to be developing these capabilities but not applying them in a crucially active theatre. In Knute Rockne's phrase, we are not saving them for the Junior prom.[18]

Rostow's confidence was typical of the Kennedy people at this point. They sent the first troops to Vietnam because they were needed, and that was what you did. Both the CIA and American allies had a very good record of putting down insurgencies between 1945 and 1960. The Americans had not beaten the Chinese army in Korea, but there had been a Communist peasant movement in South Korea and they had smashed it. An American-backed government had also beaten the Communist Huk guerrillas in the Philippines. In Guatemala an elected reformist, non-Communist government under Arbenz had come to power and challenged the American United Fruit Company. The CIA had organized a rag-tag army of a few hundred and sent out false radio broadcasts saying a massive army was marching on the capital. Arbenz fled and the Americans were back in the saddle. In Iran a non-Communist elected government under Mossadegh had tried to nationalize the British and American oil companies, and the CIA had organized a coup which put Mohammed Shah Pahlavi in power. The Belgian Congo became independent in 1960 under a radical nationalist, Patrice Lumumba. African troops attacked white settlers, the UN invaded, and the CIA organized Lumumba's assassination and replaced him with its client, Mobutu.

That was how things worked. When they had to send the troops in, they did. The Kennedy people knew the French had lost in Indochina and the Dutch in Indonesia, but explained that by saying those were colonial powers. South Vietnam was not an American colony. Intervention should work.

It didn't. Between 1962 and 1965 the number of guerrillas in the Front rose from 80,000 to 250,000. The South Vietnamese army (ARVN) fought less and less, not from cowardice, but because it was a conscript army which wanted peace and saw no point dying for Diem.

Diem was already becoming increasingly isolated when Buddhist monks began organizing demonstrations for religious freedom. Vietnam was not a Buddhist country. A million Vietnamese were Catholics and many more were Marxist atheists. The Montagnard peoples in the hills had their own religions. Perhaps another million belonged to the Cao Dai religion, which borrowed from both Christianity and Buddhism. A majority of the rest worshipped at village shrines, honored their ancestors and did not send their sons to the Buddhist monastery, but were for certain purposes sometimes Buddhists.

Many people from all these groups, though, rallied behind the Buddhist monks. They were demonstrating for religious freedom and against the government. They wanted peace and a neutralist coalition government including some Communists. The government fired on a Buddhist procession in Hue, killing nine. Ten thousand demonstrated in Hue, and monks began burning themselves alive on the streets in protest. Madame Nhu, Diem's sister in law, dismissed them as 'barbecues'. It looked bad on American television.

Diem was clearly losing control. Some of the Washington people, and some in the embassy in Saigon, began to argue that Diem was too crazy, too isolated, too Catholic to save South Vietnam. And Diem was resisting the arrival of more American troops. He said they made him look like a lackey, made it harder to win support. Diem could feel American support slipping away, and his brother Nhu contacted Hanoi to talk about getting rid of the Americans and forming a neutralist coalition government. At that, the American ambassador in Saigon, Henry Cabot Lodge, organized a coup and the assassination of Diem and his brother in November 1963.

Later that month John Kennedy himself was shot and vice-president Lyndon Johnson automatically became president. Many people now believe that Kennedy was trying to get out of Vietnam, and had he lived he would have done so. The evidence for this is what his friends and followers remembered him saying, after he was long dead and it was clear Vietnam had been a mistake. Most of them were remarks along the lines of, 'This is a stupid insoluble mess,' which were things that Lyndon Johnson, Richard Nixon and everybody else involved also said privately. It is true that Kennedy threatened Diem with reducing the level of American troops in order to bring him into line. But once Diem was assassinated, Kennedy kept the troops coming.[19]

The Pentagon had been against the anti-Diem coup, so it had been largely kept in the dark. The new military government in South Vietnam under General Minh, rather to Washington's surprise, turned out to have close ties to the Buddhists. General Minh began making moves to form a neutralist government. This time the Pentagon organized the coup and they were hands-on organizers. There was an American officer in the room with the Vietnamese officers as they directed the coup, and the American called his boss every 15 minutes.

This coup produced a South Vietnamese government led by another general, Khanh. But the Front was still winning support in the villages, and those in the cities who did not support the Front wanted peace. General Khanh came to see that the only hope was a neutralist coalition government. He wrote to Huynh Tan Phat of the central committee of the Front, and in January 1965 Phat replied:

> I heartily approve of your determined declaration against American intervention and I congratulate you for having made it. You stated

quite clearly in fact that 'the USA must let South Vietnam settle the
problems of South Vietnam.' In your recent press-conference your attitude was equally clear… The road you have taken is a difficult one…
As you pursue this goal, you may rest assured that you also have our support, as we stated in our last letter.[20]

The Americans got hold of this letter and, the next month, organized a coup against General Khanh. From this coup, the third one,
General Thieu emerged as president and Air Marshall Ky as vice-
president. Both were corrupt in all the usual bribery and export-
import ways. But both were also heavily involved in the heroin trade.[21]
Finally the American embassy had found somebody at the bottom of
the barrel who would do as they were told. They would not talk to the
Communists, they favored the bombing of North Vietnam and they
were prepared to accept a large number of American troops.

Many later American writers have said that the White House and
Pentagon were foolish to be against a neutralist solution. But the
politicians in Washington were clear that neutralism would not work,
and they were right.

Hanoi may have been willing to live with a coalition. But the
Communists and the Front had support on the ground. They were part
of a land war, and there were a lot more poor peasants than landlords. A coalition government would find it hard to prevent elections, and the Communists would win the elections. In any case, the
Communists were on the offensive. If it looked like American support for anti-Communism was faltering, the fence-sitters would jump
to the Communists and it would be all over on the ground, in the villages. While a compromise may be possible after an election, in a
civil war over land somebody has to win.

During 1964 it became increasingly clear that Thieu's government
in South Vietnam would soon fall. But that year Johnson was running
for president against the Republican Barry Goldwater. Goldwater
talked comfortably about nuclear war and was a warmonger ('hawk')
on Vietnam. So Johnson ran against him as a peace candidate ('dove'),
promising 'no wider war' in Vietnam and implying Goldwater might
start World War Three. But Johnson chose his words carefully in his
campaign speeches. In Manchester, New Hampshire, for instance,
he said of Vietnam (emphasis added):

Some of our people—Mr. Nixon, Mr. Rockefeller, Mr. Scranton, and Mr.
Goldwater—have all, at one time or another, suggested the possible

wisdom of going north in Vietnam… As far as I am concerned, I want to be very cautious and careful, and use it *only as a last resort*, when I start dropping bombs around that are likely to involve American boys in a war with 700 million Chinese.

So *just for the moment* I have not thought we were ready for American boys to do the fighting for Asian boys. What I have been trying to do, with the situation that I found, was to get the boys in Vietnam to do their own fighting with our advice and our equipment… We are not going north to drop bombs *at this stage of the game.*[22]

During the campaign the Pentagon staged a phony incident in the Gulf of Tonkin between American naval ships and North Vietnamese gunboats. On that basis the US Congress passed a resolution saying the president could do more or less what he wanted in Indochina.

On 2 November Johnson won the election, and serious planning began in Washington for bombing North Vietnam. On 2 March 1965 the American bombing of North Vietnam began.

But the Pentagon and the Saigon embassy were clear they could not win without hundreds of thousands of American ground troops. There was real argument in Washington over this. It was secret, of course, and conducted in the National Security Council. It never occurred to anybody to involve the American people. But it was a debate, and the decision was not taken lightly. It was clear to many of the men involved that they had only a limited time to win in Vietnam. The American people had turned against the Korean War, and they might well turn against a Vietnam War if it went on too long.

But at the highest level only two men were against sending troops— George Ball, an under-secretary of state, and Lyndon Johnson, the president.[23] Ball and Johnson both said that the government in South Vietnam did not have enough popular support. Even if they sent troops, they would fail. Johnson was, of course, the only man involved in the discussions who faced re-election. He was also the only one who was not a Kennedy appointee. (Those who believe that Kennedy had said America should not be involved in Vietnam nxeed to explain both why he sent troops there and why all his senior advisors but Ball wanted to send more troops.)

Kennedy and Johnson's senior officials had basically one argument for bombing North Vietnam and sending troops—the domino theory. President Eisenhower had formulated this in 1954, when he said in a speech that if French Indochina went Communist, the rest of southeast Asia would 'go over very quickly [like a] row of dominoes'.[24] John F Kennedy, in a speech in the Senate in 1956, had used an architectural metaphor: 'Vietnam represents the cornerstone of the Free World in Southeast Asia. It is our offspring. We cannot abandon it, we cannot ignore its needs'.[25]

Anti-war protesters during the Vietnam War, and liberals since, have pooh-poohed the domino theory. The anti-war protesters felt hemmed in by anti-Communism, so they did not have the courage to say, 'If other countries become Communist because that's what their people want, so be it.' Instead they said, 'What happens in one country does not determine what happens in another country.'

Sometimes it does. Sometimes it doesn't. There are many examples of how the domino theory has worked in great social movements. The Russian Revolution of 1917 gave rise to revolutions in Hungary, Germany, China, Korea, Vietnam and Yugoslavia. The victory of fascism in Portugal and Italy led to fascist governments in Germany, Austria, Hungary and Spain. Indian independence from British colonialism in 1947 was followed by freedom for Indonesia and Vietnam, then Algeria and all French North Africa, Malaya, and French and British Africa. That gave heart to the independence movements in Portuguese Africa, and when they won the South African ANC knew its day would come.

The Islamist revolution in Iran in 1980 inspired mass Islamist movements in Turkey, Lebanon, Palestine, Jordan, Saudi Arabia, Egypt, Tunisia, Sudan and Morocco. In 1989 Gorbachev's reforms in Russia led to the fall of the dictatorships in Poland, Czechoslovakia, Hungary, Bulgaria, Romania, Yugoslavia and finally Russia itself. That inspired mass movements for democracy, often victorious, in Nepal, Thailand and across much of Africa.

Great social movements happen in a domino way. When people see other people like them win in other countries, particularly neighboring countries, they take heart. Politicians know this. The men who ran America in 1965 had seen it happen several times in their lifetimes.

Some people outside this inner circle argued against the domino theory in the Vietnamese case by saying that Ho Chi Minh was basically a Vietnamese nationalist. This was true, but did not solve the American government's problem. Any victory for the National Liberation Front in Vietnam would be a defeat for American power. The

American government was supporting regimes all over the Third World that looked like the governments in South Vietnam. Johnson's advisors were acutely aware that an American withdrawal from Vietnam would cause those regimes to look for other sources of support and give heart to the people who lived under them. If it had been simply a matter of containing Russian Communism, the Russian leaders could have been persuaded to do a deal. But it wasn't. America's mission had become keeping the world safe for the rich, and that was more difficult than just containing Communism. In March 1965 Assistant Secretary for Defense John MacNaughton wrote a memo for his boss, McNamara:

> US aims:
> 70%—To avoid a humiliating US defeat (to our reputation as a guarantor).
> 20%—To keep SVN (and then adjacent) territory from Chinese hands.
> 10%—To permit the people of SVN to enjoy a better, freer way of life.
> ALSO—To emerge from crisis without unacceptable taint from methods used.
> NOT—To 'help a friend,' although it would be hard to stay if asked out.[26]

# Commitment

So in the spring of 1965 Lyndon Johnson gave in to his advisors. The United States sent in the Marines, beginning a build-up of troops that would soon reach 500,000. Four areas of the world bore particularly heavily on Washington's decision. First, Johnson's advisors kept saying that if South Vietnam fell Laos and Cambodia would follow. In fact, when South Vietnam eventually fell, they did follow.

The second area was Latin America. In 1958 the American government withdrew its support for Batista's corrupt regime in Cuba and accepted Fidel Castro as the alternative. On New Year's Day of 1959 the nationalist guerrillas, led by Castro, rode into Havana, greeted by a crowd of a million. Castro's new government was nationalist, not socialist, but it did drive the Mafia out of Cuba and nationalize some American businesses. The US retaliated with trade and aid sanctions. Castro tried to negotiate with the American government and was rebuffed. He then declared that his revolution had been socialist all along and he was now a Marxist. He swung Cuba into the Soviet camp. Russia would buy the sugar the US had banned.

The CIA organized an army of several hundred right wing Cuban exiles and sent them to invade Cuba. They landed at the Bay of Pigs in April 1961. The CIA was expecting a walkover, as in Guatemala. But the Cubans were solid behind Castro and the exiles were cut down on the beaches and surrendered. The US had been humiliated. That gave joy to young nationalists and socialists all over Latin America who began to study the Cuban example of rural guerrilla warfare. Che Guevara, the most radical of the Cuban leaders, would later call for 'One, Two, Three, Many Vietnams!'

The Bay of Pigs had given men like Lyndon Johnson pause. They could lose without local support. But it also meant they did not want to lose again, and not to a guerrilla army.

The third area concerning Washington was Indonesia. On one side there was the Indonesian Communist Party (PKI), with 3 million members, the largest Communist party outside the Communist bloc. On the other side was the Indonesian army with the support of the right wing Muslim parties (the left wing Muslims, even more numerous, were Communists). The economy was in crisis. Unemployment was rising in the cities, and the price of rice had risen so far above wages that workers had trouble eating. But driving the crisis, above all, was land. The government had decreed limited land reform. In Java and Bali, in the center of the country, the Communists on the ground were mobilizing the sharecroppers and tenants to drive down the rent on land. This was happening village by village, town by town, each demonstration a trial of strength.[27]

Everybody could see the crisis was heading towards a resolution. One side would win, one lose. Between the army and the Communists stood Sukarno, the leader of the revolutionary war of independence against the Dutch. Sukarno played the Communists and the army against each other. He and Nehru of India were the leaders of the neutralist bloc in the Cold War. The Communist strategy was to support Sukarno as a progressive leader, praise him to the skies and count on him to protect them from the army.

Indonesia was just south of Vietnam. Vietnam had no important natural resources and did not matter economically. This is important. American businesses were not making significant profits out of Vietnam. Indeed, South Vietnam was costing the American government money. Indonesia, however, was a far larger country. It was strategically important—the islands of Indonesia lie across the trade routes from Japan, China and the Pacific to the Indian Ocean. Indonesia was the fifth most populous country in the world. Vietnam mattered to the American government for the example it set. Indonesia mattered for itself. Vietnam had rice. Indonesia had oil.

President Sukarno of Indonesia had nationalized the oil companies, and the American ruling class hoped to get that oil back. Even if they did not, that oil mattered to Japan. There were real profits to be made in Indonesia. So ever since the revolution American policy had been to arm and build the Indonesian army.

In September 1965 the crisis reached a head. A coup failed. The Communists may or may not have been involved, but it didn't really matter. The class struggle on the ground was throwing the army and the PKI against each other anyway. The army moved against the PKI and the Communist leadership looked to Sukarno for protection. The only thing Sukarno could have done was call on the millions of Communists, the landless and the workers to rise. He was not about to do that. Sukarno let the Communists go. Their leaders, surprised and bewildered, did not organize an insurrection.

But because the Communists were a real mass movement on the edge of power, the army had to organize extensive massacres to break them. The army and the right wing Muslim parties came for the Communists, town by town, village by village, in Java and Sumatra. The American ambassador, Marshall Green, reported 'wholesale killings' to Dean Rusk in Washington, and said he had 'made it clear that the Embassy and USG were generally sympathetic with and admiring of what the army is doing'.[28]

The army asked the embassy for weapons and got them. Ambassador Green kept giving the army lists of Communists to kill. He knew, of course, that the army had perfectly good lists of its own. He was just showing support. According to the historian Gabriel Kolko, 'On December 4, as they were both clamoring for yet more killing, Green wrote to Rusk that over 100,000 but not more than 200,000 had been murdered in northern Sumatra and central and eastern Java alone'.[29] Then the soldiers got in boats, went to Java and started there. By the time it was all over, the CIA estimated 250,000 to 500,000 Communists dead. Some later estimates go up to 1 million, but the official Indonesian estimate a decade later was 450,000 to 500,000.[30]

It was one of the terrible massacres of the 20th century. It destroyed the Indonesian left. The landlords and capitalists were safe, and for 20 years memory and fear ruled Indonesia.

Indonesia was, and is, much more important to the American ruling class than Vietnam. But as Dwight Eisenhower said:

> What do you think caused the overthrow of President Sukarno in Indonesia? What do you suppose determined the new federation state of Malaysia to cling to its independence despite all the pressure from outside and from within?... Well, I could tell you one thing: the presence of 450,000 American troops in South Vietnam...had a hell of a lot to do with it.[31]

Or as Ambassador Green said in 1967:

> The United States military presence in Southeast Asia emboldened the army [in Indonesia], but it had no decisive effect on the outcome... It is perhaps better to look at in negative terms. If we hadn't stood firm in Southeast Asia, if we hadn't maintained a military presence, then the outcome might have been different.[32]

In early 1965 the US government faced a choice in Vietnam—get out and lose, or really go to war. If it had gotten out, then the Communists in Indonesia would have been massively encouraged. The Indonesian army would not have looked to American support. It might well have made its compromises, and it might not have had a choice. One of the things the American government was doing in Vietnam was buying time for the army to smash Communism in Indonesia.

The fourth area of the world that really mattered to the American ruling class was the United States. One of the roots of anti-Communism had been an attack on the left in the American working class. That had worked. But, from 1960 on, there was the civil rights movement in the South and then riots, urban uprisings, in the black ghettoes in the North. Martin Luther King had led a mass demonstration in Washington. Anti-Communism was beginning to sound old fashioned. Lyndon Johnson's great worry about Vietnam in 1965 was that it would be so costly economically and politically that it would destroy his 'Great Society' plan, for civil rights and a war on poverty. That plan was a reaction to the black movement, North and South.

It turned out Johnson was right. Vietnam did wreck his program. More than that, America lost the war. This is now often taken to mean that US involvement in Vietnam was a catastrophically stupid mistake. However, one side always loses a war, and in retrospect their politicians and generals always look stupid. But neither side ever goes to war without a reason to fight and some hope of winning. The US government had both those in Vietnam.

The US government also managed to persuade the governments of Australia, New Zealand, South Korea and the Phillipines to send small numbers of troops to fight alongside their own troops in Vietnam. The other Western governments, including the British Labour Party, backed the US in Vietnam. The only exceptions were France, in part, and Sweden and Canada, which provided refuge for American deserters.

# Chapter 3

# Firepower

Let's pause for a moment, and summarize the argument so far. In Vietnam there was a three-cornered struggle. In one corner were the landlords and business people allied first to French colonialism and then to the United States. In another corner were the poor and landless peasants in the South. Many of them were members of the Communist Party or joined the guerrillas.

In the third corner were the leaders of the Communist Party. They had led the peasants against French colonialism. After 1954, partly under pressure from China and Russia, they had, in effect, decided to let the South go, and concentrate on building their own state in the North. But the class struggle in the South would not go away. The new government in the South had its base among the landlords. They felt they had to fight to regain control of the land, and that meant they had to eliminate the Communists who remained in the South. Those Communists were peasants. Faced with the choice between death and fighting back, the Communists eventually forced the leadership of the party in the North to back them in an insurrection.

By 1965 this insurrection had won the support of the majority of the people in the countryside. It was not, for them, fundamentally a conflict with American imperialism. It was a war over land ownership.

But the United States intervened massively in 1965 for several reasons. It had already sent 18,000 troops and was publicly committed. A defeat in Vietnam would weaken anti-Communism in America, and help to open a space for the new left in the unions and the growing, radicalizing, civil rights movement. A defeat in Vietnam would weaken the position of ruling classes and American-backed regimes in many other countries. A defeat would also be a defeat in the Cold War, where the rulers of America and Russia competed for political and economic power in the world.

In other words, both the Pentagon and the Vietnamese Communist Party found their policies shaped by class struggles they could not avoid. This chapter is about what the war was like for the people who fought it, particularly the GIs. It argues that the cruelty of that war was a response to the class struggle in Vietnam. Once committed, the Pentagon had to be cruel, because it was intervening on the side of a ruling minority, and the subject majority was organized and confident.

This chapter also looks at the experience of American troops in terms of class. At a basic level, being sent to Vietnam was an event in the class struggle in America. The children of the rich did not go. But once the GIs arrived their experience was shaped by the cruelty they were ordered to carry out and the fact that they could see they were defending the rich against the poor in Vietnam. These two things made them desperate. That desperation was a result of class struggle in both Vietnam and America. To see how all this worked, we begin with the air war.

## The air war

The United States bombed South Vietnam, North Vietnam, Laos and Cambodia. The planes dropped over 8 million tons of explosives. This was roughly three times the weight of bombs dropped by *all sides* in World War Two, and the explosive force was equal to 640 of the atom bombs used on Hiroshima.[1]

Just over 58,000 Americans died in Vietnam, and 250,000 soldiers in the South Vietnamese army. There are no precise counts of the number of dead Viet Cong and civilians. The best estimate is between 1.5 and 2 million, though the Vietnamese estimates are higher. Hundreds of thousands more people died in both Laos and Cambodia. That puts the total dead at roughly 3 million, most of them from the air war.

This seems extraordinary, but it made sense. The Pentagon understood more or less clearly that the Viet Cong had the support of the villagers. As Defense Secretary Robert McNamara put it in a memo to President Lyndon Johnson in 1966:

> By and large, the people in the rural areas believe that the GVN [Government of South Vietnam] when it comes to it will not stay but the VC [Communists] will; that cooperation with the GVN will be punished by the VC; that the GVN is really indifferent to the people's welfare; that the low-level GVN are tools of the local rich; and that the GVN is ridden with corruption.[2]

The Viet Cong had roughly 250,000 to 300,000 guerillas in the field. At the height of the war there were 500,000 US troops in Vietnam. Only about one in six were combat troops, and the rest were support. On the ground the Viet Cong outnumbered the American combat troops three or four to one,³ and had the support of most of the villagers.

The Pentagon and the White House decided to equalize with artillery and planes. They were not winning in South Vietnam, so they bombed North Vietnam for years. At first they said they were attacking military targets, industrial sites and infrastructure. They dropped enough bombs to destroy all that, over and over, and still the North Vietnamese fought. The North Vietnamese distributed what industry they had all over the country, they dug shelters, and they got more aid from China to replace the trucks, oil and weapons they lost. On that level, the bombing did not work.

But there was another reason for the bombing, a stronger one, less often stated. The bombs would inflict such 'damage', or 'punishment', by which they meant so many dead, that the people of North Vietnam would force their leaders to negotiate peace. And in the South the bombing would reduce the number of Viet Cong and drive the villagers who supported it into the cities as refugees.

It was the logic of attrition. And it was a bombing war because America was a great industrial capitalist power. That was its strength. It was how the men in Washington thought. They had come out of World War Two the greatest power on earth, not because their soldiers were braver or their officers smarter, but because American industry had mobilized more might, more bangs and bucks, than any other country on earth. That was its strength. It was a corporate, industrial power, and it fought a corporate, industrial war.

In 1967 Malcolm Caldwell, a teacher at the School of Oriental and African Studies in London and a Maoist, visited North Vietnam to investigate the effects of the bombing:

> We interviewed Dr. Oai, who witnessed the repeated bombing of the Quynh leprosarium. The first raid occurred at 8pm on 12 June 1965, the planes flying over and then returning to drop twenty-four bombs and five missiles. A night nurse was wounded. The following morning, all patients had been evacuated, but at 1:45 pm on 13 June 1965 when some of the patients had returned, large numbers of U.S. planes came over and bombed and strafed the hospital in turn. The center was demolished completely. In the following few days, the Americans returned again and

again until the sanitarium had been completely destroyed. The raids of 12-21 June 1965 were reported to have killed 140 patients in all. Dr. Oai was moved to another hospital, while the remaining patients were dispersed to a variety of institutions... Three other eye-witnesses...corroborated the testimony of Dr. Oai in important details—ie, the height of the planes, the fact that the bombs were followed up by strafing of the patients and staff as they sought shelter.[4]

It is a strange picture, the planes flying low, strafing the nurses and the lepers as they fled from a burning building. But this was standard operating procedure—first the reconnaissance flight, then the bombs, then the strafing.

Often the planes dropped anti-personnel cluster bombs the second time round instead of strafing. The South Vietnamese called them 'mother bombs, [because] they exploded in midair and released from 350 to 600 baby bombs. When these hit the ground, each one exploded into thousands of metal pellets. (Later, fiberglass—invisible to X-rays and thus harder and more painful to remove—was used.)'[5] By the end of the war one cluster bomb could hold 180,000 'fleshettes'— particles that cut flesh.[6]

In the North the bombing particularly concentrated on hospitals, schools and churches. By 1967, 391 schools had been destroyed in the North, along with 95 health institutions, over 80 churches and 30 Buddhist pagodas. The lepers Dr Oai worked with were bombed 36 times. This seems monstrous. What was probably happening was that in most parts of North Vietnam hospitals, schools and churches were the only brick or cement buildings of two stories or higher. When the pilots flew over, looking for a target, those buildings were the only things they could imagine were barracks.[7]

Moreover, the US planes had quite rapidly bombed all the 'legitimate targets' in Vietnam. With the tonnage they were dropping, they had to bomb somewhere else. Back in Washington, President Lyndon Johnson was personally picking every target. But in the air, facing the flak and not fooled by the maps, the pilots dropped what they had where they could. If they had any bombs left, it was dangerous to land. So they dropped them in the South China Sea or in 'free fire zones' in South Vietnam. After yet another target mixup Captain Richard Sexton of the United States Air Force confided to his diary what many airmen felt: 'It doesn't matter if we lose the war as long as the paperwork is filled out and some boob keeps his empire'.[8]

And the pilots knew the people below them were not simply civilians. They were also a very concrete enemy. Wilfred Burchett, an Australian Communist journalist, reported from North Vietnam that it had 'become a nationwide duty to study plane silhouettes, to memorize characteristics of speed and altitude; to recognize planes by their sounds; to know how many lengths ahead of a certain type one must aim if it is in level flight and at which point of the nose to fire if it is dive bombing'.[9]

That made it dangerous to fly low. Colonel Jack Broughton, an F-105 fighter-bomber pilot, wrote in his book *Thud Ridge*:

> If he went down, he would have been faced with the intense small arms and automatic weapons fire that even extended down to handguns; and don't even think that a handgun can't knock down a big bird if it hits the right spot. When the bugle blows and thousands of people lie on their backs and fire small-caliber personal weapons straight up in the air, woe be unto him who is unfortunate enough to stray through that fire.[10]

Bombing North Vietnam was the most dangerous job an American could do in Vietnam. For every 40 sorties (flights by a single bomber), one was shot down (the US lost a total of 3,719 planes and 4,869 helicopters in Indochina during the Vietnam War).[11] The crew were often able to eject and parachute down. It is a sign of the strong discipline of the North Vietnamese government that so many of them were not killed by the people who captured them but sent to Hanoi. The North Vietnamese government knew how important those prisoners of war could be in negotiations. The suffering of those airmen in the 'Hanoi Hilton' prisoner of war camp, and they suffered a great deal, can partly be explained by the fact that North Vietnam was a dictatorship and its prisons were not nice places. But much of it can be explained by the fact that their jailers had relatives who lived under those bombs.

As the war went on the US government turned more and more to B-52s. They flew so high they could not be seen or heard before the bombs exploded, so they were safer for the pilots, and they did a lot of damage.

Truong Nhu Tang was not a Communist, but he was a high official in the National Liberation Front. For a time he lived in a camp just across the border in Cambodia. He remembered B-52 raids as:

> …an experience of undiluted psychological terror, into which we were plunged, day in, day out, for years on end. From a kilometer

away, the sonic roar of the the B-52 explosions tore eardrums, leaving many of the jungle dwellers permanently deaf. From a kilometer, the shock waves knocked their victims senseless. Any hit within a half kilometer would collapse the walls of an unreinforced bunker, burying alive the people cowering inside. Seen up close, the bomb craters were gigantic—thirty feet across and nearly as deep.

Truong was lucky. He was living in a high Viet Cong command post and Russian intelligence trawlers often radioed warnings of B-52 strikes to his camp:

> Often the warnings would give us time to grab some rice and escape by foot or bike. Hours later we would return to find, as happened on several occasions, that there was nothing left. It was as if an enormous scythe had swept through the jungle, felling the giant teak and go trees like grass in its way, shredding them into billions of scattered splinters. On these occasions…the complex would be utterly destroyed: food, clothes, supplies, documents, everything. It was not just that things were destroyed; in some awesome way they had ceased to exist. You would come back to where your lean-to and bunker had been, your home, and there would simply be nothing there, just an unrecognizable landscape gouged by immense craters.
>
> Equally often, however, we…had time only to take cover as best we could. The first few times I experienced a B-52 attack it seemed, as I strained to press myself into the bunker floor, that I had been caught in the apocalypse. The terror was complete. One lost control of bodily functions as the mind screamed incomprehensible orders to get out. On one occasion a Soviet delegation was visiting our ministry when a particularly short-notice warning came through. When it was over, no one had been hurt, but the entire delegation had sustained considerable damage to its dignity—uncontrollable trembling and wet pants were the all-too-obvious outward signs of inner convulsions. The visitors could have spared themselves their feelings of embarrassment; each of their hosts was a veteran of the same symptoms.[12]

People lived under the B-52s for years on end. Bao Ninh was a junior officer in the Glorious 27th Youth Brigade of the North Vietnamese army. Five hundred soldiers went South with the brigade in 1969. Bao was one of the ten survivors. His novel *The Sorrow of War*[13] describes living under the B-52s in the jungle, month after month and year after year. The soldiers believed that the ghosts of the ancestors would wander the earth unhappily if they were not buried with proper rites. And there were so many dead in that one jungle that the soldiers, in their fear, listened to the tropical forest sounds at night and heard the ghosts of the dead screaming. They called it the Jungle of the Screaming Souls. Whenever they could, they lit incense at little altars in the tents. They did this secretly, or the political officers would find out and punish them for religious backwardness.

The bombings had a logic, a force of their own. After 1968 the targets kept shifting, but the rate of bombing did not. When there were pauses in the bombing of North Vietnam, more bombs were dropped on South Vietnam, Laos and Cambodia.

In Laos the Geneva peace settlement of 1954 had arranged a neutralist government led by Prince Souvanna Phouma of the royal family, and including the leader of the Communist Pathet Lao guerrillas, Souvanna Phouma's cousin Prince Souvannaphong. But the CIA built a secret army among the Hmong minority in the mountains, and eventually succeeded in organizing a right wing military coup in the capital. In November 1968 President Johnson stopped the bombing of North Vietnam as part of an attempt at peace negotiations. In 1969 there were 300 sorties a day over Laos. George Chapelier, a United Nations official, saw what that did to the main Pathet Lao stronghold, the Plain of Jars:

> Prior to 1967, bombing was light and far from population centers. By 1968 the intensity of the bombings was such that no organized life was possible in the villages. The villagers moved to the outskirts and then deeper into the forest as the bombing climax reached its peak in 1969 when jet planes came daily and destroyed all stationary structures. Nothing was left standing. The villagers lived in trenches and holes or in caves. They only farmed at night. All of the interlocutors [I talked to], without any exception, had their villages completely destroyed. In the last phase, bombings were aimed at the systematic destruction of the material basis of the civilian society. Harvests burned down and rice became scarce.[14]

A quarter of the population of Laos became refugees. Fred Branfman talked to the people in the refugee camps through an interpreter. One man from the Plain of Jars said:

> One day a plane came bombing my ricefield as well as my village. I had gone very early to harrow my field. I thought: 'I am only a village rice farmer, the airplane will not shoot me.' But that day truly it did shoot

me and wounded me together with my buffalo, which was the source of a hundred thousand loves and a hundred thousand worries for me.[15]

Branfman asked people to draw pictures of the bombing. One man drew a man and a boy and explained:

These two, father and son, don't have hands and feet on account of a bomb dropped by the airplanes that didn't explode right away. They thought it would never explode and went to pick it up to look at. It exploded... Now they can't do anything. But [they] did not come away with us. The father said he would not go anywhere if he was killed for it, because he regretted the loss of his land, ricefield, cows and buffalo. Even though they couldn't work, they could still look... Better to die in the village. That was the decision of these two.[16]

Napalm, used extensively in Laos, is a jellied gasoline dropped from planes. The gasoline burns and the jelly makes it stick to the person's body. An American pilot explained:

> We sure were pleased with those backroom boys at Dow [Chemical Company]. The original product wasn't so hot—if the gooks were quick they could scrape it off. So the boys started adding polystyrene— now it sticks like shit to a blanket. But then if the gooks jumped under water it stopped burning, so they started adding Willie Peter [white phosphorous] so's to make it burn better. It'll even burn under water now. And one drop is enough; it'll keep on burning right down to the bone so they die anyway from phosphorous poisoning.[17]

He was exaggerating. People often survived napalm. In 1966 the American reporter Martha Gellhorn visited napalmed children in a hospital in South Vietnam, and wrote in the *Ladies Home Journal*:

> Before I went to Saigon, I had heard and read that napalm melts the flesh, and I thought that's nonsense, because I can put a roast in the oven and the fat will melt but the meat stays there. Well, I went and saw those children burned by napalm and it is absolutely true. The chemical reaction of this napalm does melt the flesh, and the flesh melts tight down their faces onto their chests and it sits there and grows there... These children can't turn their heads, they were so thick with flesh... And when gangrene sets in, they cut off their hands or fingers or their feet; the only thing they cannot cut off is their head.[18]

The American flyers sang songs about their work, in bars and clubs and quarters after flying. Major Joe Tuso, who flew 69 combat missions in 1968-69, later collected these songs. Some are triumphant. Many are full of fear. A few, like 'Chocolate Covered Napalm', are anti-war. 'Strafe the Town and Kill the People' (sung to the tune of Jerry Livingston's 1955 'Wake the Town and Tell the People') is full of angry irony:

> Strafe the town and kill the people,
> Drop your napalm in the square;
> Do it early Sunday morning,
> Catch them while they're still at prayer.

> Drop some candy to the orphans,
> Watch them as they gather 'round:
> Use your twenty millimeter,
> Mow those little bastards down.

Strafe the town and kill the people,
Drop your high-drag on the school;
If you happen to see ground fire,
Don't forget the Golden Rule.

Run your CBU down main street,
Watch it rip off arms and hair;
See them scurry for the clinic,
Put a pod of rockets there.

Find a field of running Charlies,
Drop a daisy-cutter there;
Watch the chunks of bodies flying,
Arms and legs and blood and hair.

See the sweet old pregnant lady
Running cross the field in fear;
Run your twenty mike-mike through her,
Hope the film comes out real clear.[19]

The ranch hands sang 'Spray the Town' to the same tune. They were the men of Operation Ranch Hand, which dropped Agent Orange and other herbicides on the South Vietnamese countryside to kill the trees and destroy the guerrillas' cover. Like much of the bombing in South Vietnam, it was also intended to drive peasants off the land and into the cities so the guerrillas would have nobody to support them. The ranch hands' song goes like this:

Spray the town and kill the people,
Spray them with your poison gas;
Watch them throwing up their breakfast
As you make your second pass.

Get the spray pumps working double
Slightly offset for the breeze;
See the children in convulsions—
And besides it kills the trees.

See them line up for the market,
Waiting for a pound of rice,
Hungry, skinny, starving people—
Isn't killing harvests nice.[20]

# The war on the ground

Now we turn to the ground war.

The politicians who ran the American War in Vietnam did not send their children to fight there. They sent the children of the American working class. About 80 percent of the American soldiers who saw combat came from blue collar families. About 20 percent had fathers in white collar jobs, but mostly routine ones.[21] These men were forced to go to Vietnam. The majority were drafted. Many more joined the military because they were about to be drafted. And some joined to get steady work, or because they were in trouble at home.

The government and the draft boards protected the sons of the rich. College students were not drafted until they finished their studies. And as the demand for men increased the army began taking people who had failed their intelligence tests.

People knew the draft was discriminatory. A firefighter who lost his son Ralph in Vietnam told an interviewer in 1970:

> I'm bitter. You bet your goddamn dollar I'm bitter. It's people like me who gave up our sons for the country. The business people, they run the country and they make money from it. The college types, the professors, they go to Washington and tell the government what to do… But their sons, they don't end up in the swamps over there, in Vietnam. No sir. They're deferred, because they're in school. Or they get sent to safe places. Or they get out with all those letters they have from their doctors. Ralph told me. He told me what went on at his physical. He said most of the kids were from average homes; and the few rich kids there were, they all had big-deal letters [from their doctors] saying they weren't eligible. They looked eligible to Ralph. Let's face it: if you have a lot of money, or if you have the right connections, you don't end up on the firing line in the jungle over there, not unless you want to. Ralph had no choice. He didn't want to die. He wanted to live. They just took him… It's *the Ralphs of America* who pay every time.[22]

In 1970 roughly half of young Americans had at least started college. A fifth of American troops in Vietnam had been to college, and only 7.2 percent had graduated. Almost all of them were officers. And even they were not from elite schools—the Harvard class of 1970 sent two men to Vietnam.[23]

Until late in the war these men did not know, could not know, what they were getting into. Basic training did not teach them. The

American government could not explain to its people that a large majority of the villagers in Vietnam opposed their presence, so the sergeants at boot camp could not explain it either. And without that elementary fact you could not understand the war.

In previous wars American soldiers had served unlimited tours of duty. In Vietnam they did one-year tours. This was a political decision to reduce opposition to the war at home. Officers served six month tours of duty, so every career officer could get a chance to 'punch his ticket' in a real war.

But the short tours made for military disaster. Units were not replaced—men were replaced into units. This made it harder for them to rebel. They counted the days till they left, and by the time they understood the war they were gone. But it also made it harder for them to fight, and an awful lot of time had to be spent teaching new recruits what the war was really like.

The recruits flew out to Vietnam in chartered commercial planes, air conditioned, with seat trays and meals and pretty civilian cabin crew. Gerald Kolb, an enlisted man in the 25th Infantry, flew in that way in 1967. As they approached Vietnam:

> A hush came over the cabin of the plane. All of the joking, singing and cajoling stopped. You could have heard a pin drop. The stewardess was crying, and some of the men were, too. When the door of the plane opened, we were hit with a musty, rank, urine-like odor. It was very hot. We passed a bunch of guys whooping and hollering. They were going home.[24]

Richard Deegan got off the plane in Danang in 1966:

> We were walking by and this crowd of marines waiting to get on the plane to go back to 'The World' [the US] started telling us all this shit: 'You guys ain't gonna make it home'; 'They'll kill every fucking one of you'; 'The gooks are better than you guys.' Yeah! They were really fucking with your mind. They even said, 'Hope you die, you bastards'.[25]

It was their first shock, the first understanding of the scale of death they were walking into. As one veteran, John Hendricks, said in 1985:

> That's what I can't get out of my head—the bodies…all those bodies. Back then we didn't give a shit about the dead Vietnamese. It was like: 'Hey, they're just gooks, don't mean nothin'.' You got so cold you didn't even blink. You could even joke about it, mess around with the

bodies like they were rag dolls. And after a while we could even stack up our own KIAs [killed in action] without feeling much of anything. It's not like that now. You can't just put it out of your mind. Now I carry those bodies around every fucking day. It's a heavy load, man, a heavy fucking load.[26]

The logic was the same as with the air war. American soldiers and marines faced a population who mainly supported the guerrillas, and the guerrillas outnumbered the American forces. The American government, the CIA and the senior generals understood all this. But once they had thrown their support behind the South Vietnamese government, they felt compelled not to lose. There was much at stake and they had few strategic alternatives. They decided to use what General Westmoreland, the American commander in Vietnam, called a 'war of attrition'. But every dead Vietnamese, civilian or guerrilla, was counted as a dead enemy. In effect, the American plan was to kill the Vietnamese until they gave up.

The pressure for this was relentless. The Pentagon demanded statistics. In some rear units the officers chalked the cumulative kills on a board. Officers knew their careers would depend on their numbers. And while the officers seldom said, 'Kill all the civilians you can,' they seldom criticized anybody for doing that, and often praised them.

This put the soldiers in a horrific position. They arrived in Vietnam as individuals and were assigned to companies. They had no training for what they faced, because the army and Marine Corps could not admit what kind of war they were fighting. So the slightly more experienced soldiers had to train the new men, and fast. One marine remembered his training at Khe Sanh:

That first patrol we went to where some Marines had ambushed a bunch of Viet Cong. They had me moving dead bodies, VC and NVA [North Vietnamese army]. Push this body over here out of the way. Flip a body over. See people's guts and heads half blown off. I was throwing up all over the place.

'Keep going. Drag this body over there.'

'For what?'

'You're going to get used to death before you get in a firefight and get us all killed. You're a [machine-]gunner and gunners can't panic on us.'

That first time everything was just coming up. Scared to begin with, then all of a sudden I'm looking at this shit. I moved some more bodies and after a while I stopped throwing up. But I wasn't too happy about the whole situation.

They noticed that I wasn't throwing up no more and they gave me about a ten minute rest. They're laughing and joking.

Next, I had to kick one dead body in the side of the head until part of his brain started coming out the other side. I said, 'I just moved a dead body. What are y'all telling me?' The logic, I didn't see it then, I understood it later. At the time I thought, 'These fuckers been up here too long. They are all insane.' I'm going through my changes and the rest of these guys are laughing.

'Kick it,' they said. 'You are starting to feel what it is like to kill. That man is dead, but in your mind you're killing him again. Man, it ain't no big thing. Look-a-here.' And they threw some bodies off the cliff and shit.

'Go ahead. Pick one up and throw it off. But when you can kick his brains out, you'll know what it is when they say to kick out some-body's brains. So…Kick.' They meant it. The chant started, 'Kick… Kick…Kick.'…

I'm kicking now. I'm kicking and I'm kicking and all of a sudden, the brains start coming out the other side.

Later he understood:

They were serious men, dedicated to what they were doing. [They were] teaching me…not to fall apart. I saw it happen. I saw guys get themselves killed and almost get an entire platoon wiped out, because they panicked or because they gave up or because they got wounded and couldn't deal with their own blood. They had this thing about teaching a boot [a new man] exactly what he's got to deal with and how to accept the fact of what he really is.[27]

What he really was at Khe Sanh was bait. The population either sup-ported the guerrillas or were too scared to betray them. So the Amer-ican generals could only fight the guerrillas by sending the American soldiers and marines out on patrol. If and when the guerrillas chose to attack, the Americans on the ground would then call in artillery and bombers to blast them.

This terrified the GIs—they were always waiting to get hit. Their enemy almost always chose the time and place of battle. And be-tween 15 and 20 percent of Americans killed in Vietnam died from 'friendly fire'—the artillery and bombs they called in.

Another 20 to 25 percent died when they stepped on mines. The ones who didn't die thought about those mines every step they took. Michael Call was in the 25th Infantry division:

> We begin to walk with our eyes fixed on the ground, looking for some telltale sign we should avoid. I ask myself: 'Is that little thing ahead the three prongs of a Bouncing Betty [a mine that springs up to waist height and then goes off] or just three blades of grass?' As my right foot moves in front of my left foot, I carry on a debate in my mind on whether I should place it down on *that* rock just ahead or behind it. Or in front of it. Or on that side of it. But now I face another dilemma. If I choose to step to the side of the rock, which side do I choose? These gooks are very clever. They must figure out I still want to place my foot on hard ground. So, maybe they put the mine under a rock. Maybe I should move over to the left a little or to the right. Then again, why not place my foot in the step of the guy ahead of me. But he is already too far ahead. And if you walk too close to him, he will get pissed off because if I trip a mine he'll get blown away too. What do I do with my right foot? I say, 'I can't stand on my left foot forever.' I finally put my right foot down and nothing happens. My next decision is what to do with my left foot, which, in the act of walking, comes up when the right foot goes down.[28]

Every step, hour after hour, counting off 365 days.

Del Plonka was an officer, a platoon leader in the 25th Division:

> There were these things called stick mines. It's nothing more than taking a dead piece of wood attached to a mine with a trigger device—to knock the stick over and it goes. Usually, they use land mines, and land mines are designed to blow up tanks. Needless to say, when this young man tripped the stick mine and it went off, he lost both legs immediately. He was more or less split open from the groin area to his neck. The best I could do was put him in a poncho. It was a very sickening sight, seeing all that blood and seeing that poor young man with that face just looking at you with those bewildered eyes, and, well, it stays in your mind.[29]

When a mine went off, the GIs could not see the man or woman who set it. But every villager they had passed in the last hour knew where the mine was. The guerrillas told them or left warning marks. Sometimes, often, the soldiers snapped and beat or killed the next Vietnamese they saw.

They were fighting an enemy they could not see. They were constantly afraid, and helpless, and they knew they were losing. The officers were pushing them to report dead Vietnamese. Washington wanted a body count.

Robert McNamara, the Secretary of Defense, had been brilliant at systems, numbers and accounting control at Ford. Now he shone the same brilliance on Vietnam. The reporter David Halberstam writes of McNamara at a military briefing:

> Sitting...for eight hours watching hundreds and hundreds of slides flashing across the screen showing what was in the pipe line to Vietnam and what was already there, he finally said, after seven hours, 'Stop the projector. This slide, number 869, contradicts slide 11.' Slide 11 was flashed back and he was right, they did contradict each other. Everyone was impressed, and a little frightened.[30]

McNamara was in charge of the war, first under Kennedy and then under Johnson. He ran the war like the Ford Motor Company. You had the capital, you had the hardware and you had the men—they were just labor. Halberstam again:

> One particular visit seemed to sum it all up: McNamara looking for the war to fit his criteria, his definitions. He went to Danang in 1965 to check out the marine progress there. A marine colonel in 1 Corps had a sand table showing the terrain and patiently gave the briefing: friendly situation, enemy situation, main problem. McNamara watched it, not really taking it in, his hands folded, frowning a little, finally interrupting. 'Now, let me see,' McNamara said, 'if I have it right, this is your situation,' and then he spouted his own version, all in numbers and statistics. The colonel, who was very bright, read him immediately like a man breaking a code, and without changing stride, went on with his briefing, simply switching his terms, quantifying everything, giving everything in numbers and percentages, percentages up, percentages down, so blatant a performance it was like a satire. Jack Raymond of the *New York Times* began to laugh and had to leave the tent. Later that day Raymond went up to McNamara and commented on how tough the situation was up in Danang, but McNamara wasn't interested in the Vietcong, he wanted to talk about the colonel, he liked him, the colonel had caught his eye. 'That colonel is one of the finest officers I've ever met,' he said.[31]

In all those numbers, the bottom line was the body count. Because the Communists had the support of most of the villagers, the only way to defeat them was to kill so many that the few who were left could bear it no longer. And if you could not find the guerrillas, and usually you couldn't, you killed the people until they told the Communists to stop. The body count was not a trick or a bureaucratic obsession—it was the strategy. The pressure from Washington reached all the way down. Every general and colonel who passed the pressure down, who made the men kill, was making his career: 'Infantry officers knew their opportunities for advancement were largely dependent on the size of the body counts they reported'.[32]

Micheal Clodfelter was an infantryman with the 101st Airborne in 1965:

> We arrived in country expecting to encounter uniformed communist hordes, but found instead this strange small people wearing peasant garb and those inscrutable smiles. We…found it hard to believe that these weak, undernourished-looking peasants could really present a threat and a danger to all our battalions of big, husky, heavily armed GIs. It seemed a laughable country and a laughable war—until we started running into explosive evidence of the enemy's existence, until we started becoming a part of the red results of their cunning and courage. And then, slowly, as fear mounted frustration and rode down a crippled confidence, as callousness started taking over from condescension in our attitude to the Vietnamese, our vision blurred, clouded over, and refocused. Where before we had found it difficult to see the enemy anywhere, now we saw him everywhere. It was simple now; the Vietnamese were the Viet Cong, the Viet Cong were the Vietnamese. The killing became so much easier now.
>
> As the value of Vietnamese life went down in your estimation, so too did the realizations start to sink in that your body and your life was really of very little importance to the men and the machines who ran the war… The machine would not care that a man had died, only that another part of its inventory had been lost and would require replacement, like the destroyed tank. And like the totaled tank, the Army would simply put in another order at another factory—a boot camp, where your replacement was being tooled and trained on a different kind of assembly line. It was just exactly as hard and heartless as that and it was a heavy thing to accept—though accept it we inevitably did.[33]

Clodfelter was in McNamara's army, part of what the GIs called the 'Green Machine'. He was in the 'Hard Core' squad of the First Platoon of Charlie Company. One man in the platoon, Atticus Tate:

> ...wasn't like the rest of us, we said, not even like those of us who, under the burdens and blows we had to take, sometimes gave in to the temptation to cruelty. He enjoyed the killing... He was the company crazy, the regulation madman; the one kill-happy psychotic that every unit seemed plagued with, as if required by some demonic T.O.&E. (Table of Organization and Equipment) chart...
>
> We hated him because what he had done we could do... Maybe one more month in Nam, one more buddy blown apart by a booby trap, maybe the Tate would come out in all of us.[34]

In October of 1966 the Hard Core squad were patrolling the mud and paddies of Phu Yen province. They had killed nobody, and the officers were pushing them. The zero body count 'was making life miserable for all the corpse counters all the way up to the battalion C.O.' Then Tate and some of the other men in the First Squad killed an 'unarmed straggler'. Tate 'taunted us so unmercifully on our lack of scalps that several members of the Second Squad, their "Hard Core" honor at stake, resolved to count coup.'

The next day they passed an old man in a village. Frightened, he just kept repeating, 'No VC here,' in English, over and over. A little further on they found three guerrillas lounging in front of a house. There was a stunned moment, and the guerrillas grabbed their guns and were gone.

The squad had lost the body count. They went back for the old man. The sergeant and two men pulled him out of his house. Clodfelter and the rest 'took up defensive positions in a vegetable garden' surrounding the house to protect the execution. Clodfelter tried to look away from the old man and the sergeant behind him, but his eyes were drawn back, wanting to be a part of it. Yet he kept telling himself it wasn't really going to happen:

> One of the paratroopers pointed his M-79 grenade launcher at the doomed peasant... Hesitation locked the trooper in a sweating embrace, filled the garden with a strangling tension, seemed to stop the very rotation of the earth and the passage of time... I arose from my morass of sweat and dread to scream out words of protest...words that I should

have loosened at the first moments of this horror. A shot reared, drowning out my frantic shout...

I would, in effect, still be shouting those unheeded words of protest in dozens of anti-war marches for years after I left Nam. I am still screaming them out today...too late, far too late.[35]

The old man didn't die immediately. He lay there twitching. The soldiers urged each other to kill him, each one reluctant. Finally one rifleman let loose a volley from his automatic. Still the old man did not die. The rifleman put his gun next to the old man's head and finished him.

They had a body count. They turned away, in shame. And then one man reminded the others they had promised to show Tate the ears. A soldier sliced them off with his bayonet. 'Upon reaching the platoon position, the grenadier proudly displayed his trophies, still dripping blood, to a much impressed Tate. We had joined his ranks'.[36]

It is important to remember that the officers were pushing the body count. That body count was being totaled at battalion headquarters, again in Saigon and again in Washington. Marine Lt Philip Caputo landed at Danang in 1965:

General Westmoreland's strategy of attrition also had an effect on our behavior. Our mission was not to win terrain or seize positions, but simply to kill: to kill Communists and to kill as many of them as possible. Stack 'em like cordwood. Victory was a high body-count, defeat a low kill-ration, war a matter of arithmetic. The pressure on unit commanders to produce enemy corpses was intense, and they in turn communicated it to their troops. This led to such practices as counting civilians as Viet Cong. 'If it's dead and it's Vietnamese, it's VC,' was the rule of thumb in the bush. It is not surprising, therefore, that some men acquired a contempt for human life and a predilection for taking it.[37]

Some units held competitions to see which platoon could get the highest 'box score', like in baseball. A few units gave rest and recreation leave in the rear to men who did particularly well.[38] Of course, with time everybody learned to pad the result. They counted civilians and children. If they found somebody blown to bits, they counted each bit. They counted blood traces, each drop, as a separate kill. They counted the water buffaloes they shot, and the monkeys. Pretty soon they learned to invent dead bodies. In reaction, the more gung-ho officers insisted on 'confirmed kills'—ears.

This meant that men like Tate, the exceptions who enjoyed killing, were almost never punished. In the units where the commanding officer insisted on ears for every body count, nobody said anything— nobody was punished or reprimanded. The Tates delivered for the McNamaras.

# The wrong side

The GIs were under pressure to kill, and they knew they were on the wrong side. Again and again returning veterans in the 1960s said the other side were the only people in the country who knew what they were fighting for.

The tunnels of Cu Chi, more than anything else, give some idea of the courage of the Vietnamese resistance.[39] Cu Chi was in Hau Nghia province, just north of Saigon. The tunnels were originally dug in the 1940s, when the Communist-led Viet Minh were fighting French colonialism, as hiding places for the guerrillas and bomb shelters for the villagers. When the war in South Vietnam began in the 1960s, the Viet Cong dug more tunnels and began to link them together, from one village to another. By the time the American 25th Infantry built a base at Cu Chi in 1966 there were hundreds of miles of tunnels. The Viet Cong lived in the tunnels. At night they could come out, pick off Americans, and dive back into the tunnels, the trap doors hidden by leaves. Some snipers even surfaced inside the barbed wire of the American base.

The tunnels were deep and narrow. They tried to make the passages about five feet in diameter, but in places they were much narrower. If the Americans found the entrance, they had to crawl, knowing there was somebody waiting for them in the dark with a knife, trying to breathe without making a sound. Very few American soldiers went down those tunnels.

But they did use poison gas. The Viet Cong filled the passages with trap doors to block the gas, and learned to lie on the floor of the tunnel, face down, breathing through cloth.

Off the passages they built larger rooms for sleeping, cooking, meetings and storage. They dug every day. Captain Nguyen Than Linh remembered, 'Old men made baskets for carrying the earth, old women did the cooking, young men and women used their strength to dig the earth. Even the children did their share by gathering leaves to cover the trap doors'.[40] (Captain Linh commanded a brigade of

300 guerrillas when the Americans came. Four of them, two officers and two non-coms, survived the war.)

They lived down there for years, eating, cooking, even giving birth. Vo Hoang Le was a guerrilla surgeon. They could not take their wounded to hospital. The government forces would take them, probably torture them, maybe kill them. So Dr Vo did what he could for wounds, which was mainly amputate. He operated with netting above the patient to stop the dirt from the ceiling falling into the wound. Usually he had no anesthetics, and about half the amputation cases died from shock and pain.

But some things drove the guerrillas above ground. The ventilation was bad in the tunnels, so cooking rice took a long time and filled the tunnels with smoke. Whenever they could, the guerrillas cooked above ground at night. Moreover, the women had no rags for menstruation. Vietnam, including Communist Vietnam, was a prudish society. The women were ashamed of the way their clothes smelled and would sneak out at night to wash. And some of the guerrillas, particularly the young, would go above ground some nights to sing together.

They dug deep and repaired weapons in there, even grenade launchers. Once they hid an armored personnel carrier underground.

The 25th Infantry could see the courage of the people living in the tunnels beneath them. Jeri Luici, an infantryman, remembered coming back to the camp after a firefight:

> We humped in just before dawn, and fighting was still going on. There were over a hundred bodies. Later that day, we found more surface graves… To give you an idea of how steadfast the people we were fighting were, I found a dead VC medic who had tied himself to a bamboo clump, with a morphine syringe stuck in his arm, as he was bleeding to death. He had an RPG [rocket propelled grenade] at the ready with the safety off. Another guy was clutching one of our claymores [a mine]: he was going to try to detonate himself on our perimeter. Amazing.[41]

Thomas Giltner was platoon leader at Cu Chi:

> We faced mostly local VC, peasants armed with World War II rifles and no heavy weapons. They were taking on the best army in the world. They received their training from the local cadres. We respected them from day one… They did an awful lot with awful little…
>
> They were tremendously inventive. We used to capture homemade rifles created out of metal pipes and bits of fence post. We never put

out antipersonnel mines: we knew they would be dug up and used against us. Claymores were strictly accounted for, but they were still stolen. We always worried about Charlie getting sophisticated weapons. Once our whole battalion was roused out at night and sent looking for a starlight scope which was lost. We found it. We really worried about him getting a field piece… The Vietnamese were just so ingenious. We all knew they were poor, not stupid.[42]

Vo Thi Mo was one of the women in the tunnels. She came from the village of Ben Suc, a Viet Cong stronghold. In 1967 American troops, led by an officer named Alexander Haig, came to Ben Suc. They killed a few people, and rounded up the rest and took them off to a camp surrounded by barbed wire. They bulldozed all the houses and declared the village and its fields a free fire zone—after that American planes and soldiers would fire at anything that moved. The village was no longer a Viet Cong stronghold.[43]

After her village was destroyed Vo Thi Mo went down into the tunnels and became a platoon leader. One day she was on guard at a tunnel entrance when three American soldiers sat down nearby. They could not see her and she had them in her sights. But she paused. She was curious.

The American soldiers shared cookies and candy with each other. They took out what seemed to be letters from home and read them. Vo Thi Mo was fascinated. They do what we do, she thought. The Americans read each other's letters and began to cry. This also the guerrillas did. She could not shoot them.

Her company messenger, crouched next to her, raised his gun to shoot the Americans. Silently, she knocked it away.

The guerrillas held an inquiry on Vo Thi Mo the next day, in effect a field court martial. She had not done her duty, but her platoon messenger testified passionately in her defense. He worshipped Vo Thi Mo. They had been through several battles together, she leading her platoon of 24 women, the boy messenger running back and forth through the bullets for orders from the higher officers. She had been in the army for four years, she was older than him, and he had only fought for a year. The court martial listened to him and let Vo Thi Mo off with a reprimand.

Vo Thi Mo was 17 years old. Her platoon messenger was ten.

That was what the GIs were up against. They could often see that they were workers oppressing other poor people. In the later stages of the war American soldiers simply refused to fight—Chapter 5 of this book is devoted to that revolt. But in the early stages they felt the only choice was to fight or die. So the knowledge of what they were doing only made them angrier and more desperate. One soldier, like many, returned home to America from Vietnam to be met by his parents at the airport:

> They drove home in silence and sat together in the kitchen, and his mother, in passing, apologized for there being 'nothing in the house to eat.' That did it; he broke. Raging, he went from cupboard to cupboard, shelf to shelf, flinging doors open, pulling down cans and boxes and bags, piling them higher and higher on the table until they spilled over onto the floor and everything edible in the house was spread out in front of them.
>
> 'I couldn't believe it,' he said, shaking his head as he told me. 'I'd been over there…killing those poor bastards who were living in their tunnels like rats and had nothing to eat but mud and a few goddamn moldy grains of rice, and who watched their kids starve to death or go up in smoke, and she said *nothing to eat*, and I ended up in the kitchen shouting: *Nothing to eat, nothing to eat*'.[44]

Those children—the American soldiers expected to be greeted by friendly children. Their fathers and uncles had told them about the children overseas in World War Two. You gave them candy and they loved you. The American soldiers all met children begging for food as soon as they came to Vietnam. If they did not feed the children, the kids screamed abuse at them. If they did, the children fell on them, tearing at their clothes, going through their pockets, making clear their need and their hatred.

The old soldiers told the new soldiers the truth: those children hate us. They know where the mines are. They want us to die.

But still the GIs saw themselves in those children. Most had grown up working class, often very poor. Many of them knew what it was to go hungry or be laughed at in high school because they didn't have the right clothes. And now, suddenly, they were unimaginably rich compared to those children. But they would still be poor when they went home.

So they hated it when the children begged. And because they hated the feeling, they sometimes hated the children. Soldiers in different parts of Vietnam remember throwing full cans of combat rations at children from trucks: throwing them as hard as they could. An army combat engineer said:

> We threw full C-ration cans at kids on the side of the road. They'd be yelling out, 'Chop, chop; chop, chop,' and they wanted food. They knew we carried C-rations. Well, just for a joke, these guys would take a full can…and throw it as hard as they could at a kid's head. I saw several kids' heads split wide open, knocked off the road, knocked into the tires of the vehicle behind.[45]

A marine said:

> When they originally get in country [Americans] feel very friendly toward the Vietnamese and they like to toss candy at the kids. But as they become hardened to it and kind of embittered against the war, as you drive through the ville you take the cans of C-rats and the cases and you peg 'em at the kids; you try to belt them over the head. And one of the fun games that always went was you dropped the C-rats cans or the candy off the back of your truck so that the kid will have time to dash out, grab the candy and get run over by the next truck.[46]

And a peasant woman in Beautiful Waters remembered the marines:

> I was walking along the road with my son, who was wearing a hat. There was a string to hold the hat to his chin. One of the American soldiers grabbed the hat, and pulled my son up and under the wheels of the truck. The truck stopped, but it was too late. [The boy was crushed]… He was my only son, and my sadness is so deep that it will never end.[47]

The historian Christian Appy says that these stories are 'not easy to understand, and veterans who are plagued with guilt for incidents like this do not themselves fully understand what led them to behave so cruelly or how they might have found in it a "joke" or a "fun game".'[48] But the soldiers saw the children's hatred and need, and could not bear it.

# Chapter 4

# Protesters and guerrillas

Three weeks before the Marines arrived in Vietnam and the massive build-up of troops began, the American student movement against the war began too.

In March 1965 30 teachers at the University of Michigan met. They had mostly supported Johnson against Goldwater, and felt they were campaigning for peace and against war. Now Johnson was giving them war. They decided to stop normal classes for one day and make the university 'a massive classroom against the war'.[1] They got the support of 50 teachers on a petition, and the university administration became threatening. The teachers got cold feet and met again. One of them, a young anthropology instructor named Marshall Sahlins, suggested a compromise tactic—something called a teach-in. The teachers would meet with interested students in the evening after class.

Three thousand students showed up and debated the war until 8am the next day.

There were teach-ins at over 100 universities that spring. At the University of California in Berkeley, another radical stronghold, the teach-in lasted 36 hours. Thirty thousand students attended in all, with up to 12,000 there at any one time.[2]

The Students for a Democratic Society called a national demonstration in Washington on 17 April 1965. SDS was by far the largest organization of the left, with 100,000 members on college campuses. Many of them were beginning to think of themselves as revolutionaries. But everybody was astonished by the size of the protest in Washington—25,000 people.

That doesn't seem like a lot now. But then it was amazing. Doug Dowd was a professor at Cornell University and had been a radical right through the 1950s:

> I was teaching at Berkeley during the Korean War. Jesus Christ, you couldn't get *anybody* to say *anything* against the Korean War... Everybody was scared shitless to identify themselves with being against that

war because it meant, quite obviously that you must be a ranking member of the Communist Party... [In 1965] it was as though spring had arrived after a very, very long fucking winter.[3]

On the weekend of 15 and 16 October 25,000 people demonstrated in New York, 15,000 in San Francisco, and a total of 100,000 across the country. In November 30,000 demonstrated in New York City, and in March 1969 there were 50,000 in New York.

What had changed America since the Korean War was the civil rights movement. It had legitimated dissent. Many people, white and black, had been through the movement. Most of the whites and some of the blacks had started out as liberal middle class students. They expected America to deliver equality. In the South they expected the federal government to protect them from the sheriffs and the Klan. What they found out was that the FBI followed them, and did not follow the Klan. Blacks were terrorized out of the vote in Mississippi, and civil rights activists organized a Mississippi Freedom Democratic Party delegation to the Democratic Party convention in 1964. The Democrats seated the old white racist Mississippi party instead.

Many former liberals had learned that American society was systematically racist and unfair, that the government and the Democratic Party lied to you, and that the only way to change society was to organize, sit in and demonstrate.

When the Vietnam War came along it was not that hard to see it was a racist war. Stokely Carmichael of SNCC, the main radical civil rights organization, said in 1967 that the draft was 'white people sending black people to make war on yellow people in order to defend the land they stole from red people'.[4]

Muhammad Ali was the world heavyweight champion boxer, a black man and a Muslim. He refused to be drafted, saying he had no quarrel with the Viet Cong (and implying he had a quarrel with somebody else). He was threatened with prison, stripped of his title and banned from working at his trade. He stuck to his principles.[5]

Greg Payton was a marine in Vietnam in 1968:

> The first sergeant was telling me one day about gooks [Vietnamese]...gooks this, gooks that. That was the first time I [realized]... 'A gook's the same as a nigger,' I remember telling him; then he said, 'You're a smart nigger.' He said that to me, just me and him.[6]

Martin Luther King, Jr, was privately opposed to the war. He was a pacifist, after all. But his whole political project was to unite the liberals, the labor leaders and the civil rights leaders in a bloc that could change the Democratic Party. And his funding came from those same liberals and labor leaders. They told him again and again throughout 1966 that if he spoke out on Vietnam publicly it would damage the civil rights cause. The real powers in Washington would never take him seriously. King was quiet. But he was haunted by a picture of napalmed children he had seen in *Ramparts* magazine. The black struggle was moving from the South to the North, and the ghetto uprisings there had not been non-violent. Young black workers respected Dr King—they cried when they listened to his speeches—but they were moving beyond him politically, beyond non-violence and the Democratic Party. Under pressure from them and his conscience, King gave a speech at Riverside Church in New York on 4 April 1967:

> As I have walked among the desperate, rejected and angry young men I have told them that Molotov cocktails and rifles would not solve problems... They asked me if our own nation wasn't using massive doses of violence to solve its problems, to bring about the changes it wanted. Their questions hit home, and I knew that I couldn't ever again raise my voice against the violence of the oppressed in the ghettos without having first spoken clearly to the greatest purveyor of violence in the world today—my own government...
>
> [Blacks are dying] in extraordinarily high proportions relative to the rest of the population...to guarantee liberties in Southeast Asia which they had not found in Southwest Georgia and East Harlem.[7]

The White House liberals said King's speech made no difference. But it had a shattering effect on the generals. They did not say anything in public. But in 1965 almost a quarter of combat deaths were black. In 1966 it was 16 percent. In 1968, after King's speech, it was 13 percent, in 1970 down to 9 percent, and by 1972 only 7.6 percent. Year by year the generals were pulling black men out of combat. Overall blacks accounted for 12.6 percent of combat deaths in Vietnam, roughly equivalent to their share of the population.[8]

White radicals too could see the war was racist. They believed that if the Vietnamese were white they would not have suffered cruelty and killing on the same scale (in this they may have been wrong.)

Moreover, from 1964 the black movement was becoming nationalist and separatist. The black radical students were constantly told by King and the Southern Christian Leadership Conference that they couldn't go too far because the white people wouldn't like it. By this they meant the white people in Washington and leading the UAW. But the black radicals turned away from all white people. The Communist Party had been a serious organization in the working class, with black leaders and black activists on the ground. After the 1950s that was gone. The radical tradition that did survive in the ghettoes was the black nationalism of Marcus Garvey and the Nation of Islam. The major movement people saw in the world in the 1950s and 1960s was the movement for colonial freedom. So when Stokely Carmichael stuck his fist in the air on a march in Mississippi and said 'Black Power' it made sense.

That left a lot of white radical students from the civil rights movement with nothing to do, and a feeling they ought to organize white people like themselves. Enter the war. And it was natural to organize teach-ins after civil rights sit-ins, natural to meet and demonstrate, and to march on Washington.

These radicals found a ready audience. The students they were talking to were patriotic liberals. But there was a contradiction in their heads. Many people now say that the media brainwashes everybody with constant lies. That is partly true—the media does lie, on a grand scale. But the reason it has to lie is that people are not brainwashed. Most of us have fundamentally different values from the values of the ruling class. The people in the White House knew that South Vietnam was a dictatorship and mass murder was happening there—they had organized the coups and were counting the bodies. But the government and the media had to say that America was defending democracy and not committing mass murder, because most Americans were against dictatorship and mass murder. And the radicals could show pretty easily that South Vietnam was a dictatorship and the war was cruel.

In 1965 15 year old Craig McNamara had an argument with other boys at his prep school about the war. He phoned his father, the Secretary for Defense, and asked for more information so he could show those boys they were wrong. His father sent him more and more information, but it didn't make sense to Craig. By the time he got to Stanford University, Craig McNamara was marching against the war.[9]

Anti-war feeling was higher among workers than among the middle class. This is in part because people with more money tend to be more interested in preserving the status quo. They are also likely to have more education which might lead one to presume they would be more anti-war—everyone is taught that the education system makes people more liberal and tolerant. This widely held view is not, however, supported by opinion polls in Europe and North America.

The historian Marilyn Young writes that:

> …from the start, opposition to the war was strongest among poorer and less educated Americans, those who would have to fight and die. In 1966, according to a survey conducted by the University of Michigan, only 27 percent of those with college educations favored withdrawal from Vietnam as opposed to 41 percent of those with an eighth grade education.[10]

In a referendum in 1966, 41 percent of people in Dearborn, a white working class suburb of Detroit, voted for American withdrawal:

> Later research found [the vote] was inversely associated with citizens' socioeconomic level, with blue-collar workers more disapproving of the war than professionals and managers.[11]

Educated left wing people often find this point difficult to grasp. As the historian Mike Marqusee says:

> Until 1970 blacks, low-income families and the over-sixties were the only sections of the population in which greater numbers favored withdrawal rather than escalation. Yet the notion that anti-war sentiment was largely a white middle-class student phenomenon remains widespread, among both critics and some (white, middle-class) veterans of the movement.[12]

The historian James Loewen, in his useful book on teaching American history, *Lies My Teacher Told Me*, reports an experiment he ran with students in courses at the University of Vermont. He asked them to guess the percentages of college graduates, high school graduates and high school dropouts who supported American intervention in Vietnam in a poll late in the war. They quite consistently assumed that the more educated were more against the war.[13] So did students at Dartmouth College when my friend Nancy Lindisfarne ran the same experiment. The reason, in both cases, was that they knew middle class professionals were more liberal than working class rednecks.

The children of the working class were coming back from Vietnam. They told their friends and relatives that the only people worth respecting over there were the enemy. Those people came back to working class neighborhoods and jobs long before the television turned against the war. Many of the middle class people who changed their minds thought it was television that moved people. Those who were close to somebody who went felt differently.

And even if, in the end, middle class young men did not have to go to Vietnam, they thought they would have to. They were afraid, but, more importantly, they didn't want to be cruel. Most of them were headed for lives as teachers or social workers, or in minor office jobs. In America then and now about half of young people start college and about a quarter finish. That quarter have an easier life, but they aren't the ruling class. They mostly still have to make a living.

On 15 April 1967, 300,000 people marched against the war in New York. Fred Halstead, a leader of the anti-war movement, and an old socialist, exulted, 'It was a hugey'.[14]

On 20 October the demonstrators started coming to Washington. They were going to march to the Pentagon. The Yippies, a loose network of young, white, hippie, dope-smoking anarchists, announced they were going to levitate the Pentagon.

The ruling class was scared. That night it filled the Pentagon with troops, 'rifles, tear gas machines, helmets…trucks and jeeps of the First Army'. At the White House first lady Lady Bird Johnson told her diary, there was 'much talk of tomorrow' at dinner: 'There is a ripple of grim excitement in the air, almost a feeling of being under siege'.[15] The next day 150,000 demonstrators marched through Washington, with signs saying both 'Negotiate' and 'Where is Oswald when we need him?' They listened to speeches and marched on the Pentagon. There they met a wall of troops. A demonstrator went down the line of soldiers, putting a flower in each rifle barrel. There was pushing and hitting as the demonstrators tried to break through the nervous soldiers and arrests were made.

On the roof of the Pentagon generals watched and 'army sharpshooters crouched uneasily, weapons in hand.' The ruling class watched from the windows. Richard Helms was the head of the CIA. He later told the historian Tom Wells, I don't think there was any doubt that they took a look at that mob around the Pentagon and nobody liked the look of that at all. And I certainly least of all. I'd had experiences with mobs all over the world and I didn't like the look or sound of this one bit.' Secretary of the Army Stanley Resor told Wells, 'It was a very impressive thing, thirty-five thousand people right there under your nose.' Paul Nitze was the official in charge of organizing the defense of the Pentagon that day. Three of his four children were in the crowd.[16]

Many, if not most, of the warlords had at least one child who turned against the war. It hurt them. Dean Rusk's son Richard, 'caught between love for my father and the growing horror of Vietnam', had a nervous breakdown. In October 1969 staffer William Watts was working in the White House on a speech for President Nixon 'announcing a major escalation of the war'. He took a break from work to walk on the White House lawn and went over to the gate to get a better look at the protesters outside, part of a nationwide Moratorium. He saw his wife and children walk by, 'each holding a candle'. He felt like throwing up: 'It was very painful to be on the other side of the fence'.[17]

Demonstrations worked. It wasn't just the family pain. After all, almost all those men lived with the pain rather than hurt their careers. It was the experience of having a mass of people against you, and sudden vulnerability at home, in America. Richard Helms had certainly seen angrier mobs when he worked for the CIA—the people outside the Pentagon were non-violent. But it was far beyond anything Helms could have imagined happening in America.

In late 1966 Pentagon whiz kids explained to Lyndon Johnson that they could save lives by carpet-bombing Hanoi and the port of Haiphong, and thus ending the war sooner than otherwise. They had fed numbers into their computers and proved that dropping the atom bombs on Hiroshima and Nagasaki in 1945 had saved 750,000 lives. Johnson said to them, 'I have one more problem for your computer— will you feed into it how long it will take five hundred thousand angry Americans to climb the White House wall out there and lynch their President if he does something like that?'[18]

Massive demonstrations legitimated dissent about the war. Every big demonstration sends home people who argue for the cause of the demonstration and inclines people to listen to them. By November 1970 a majority in the opinion polls thought the Vietnam War was a mistake. Only 35 percent approved of the president's 'handling of the war'. And MacGeorge Bundy wrote in a memo to Johnson, 'Public discontent with the war is now wide and deep'.[19]

And then came Tet.

# The Tet Offensive

Tet, 1968, changed everything. It was a shattering defeat for both the Southern guerrillas and the American ruling class.

In late December of 1967 the invitations to the New Year's Eve party at the American embassy in Saigon said, 'Come see the light at the end of the tunnel'.[20] It was a joke. For months the generals had been telling Lyndon Johnson, and he had been telling the American people, there's light at the end of the tunnel. Things are dark now, we can't see clearly, but hang on a bit longer and we'll win.

That was American New Year in Saigon. Vietnamese New Year, the festival of Tet, was on 31 January 1968. US Navy Lieutenant Dick Shea wrote a poem about Tet in 1965:

tet
vietnamese new year
today tomorrow and the day after
the viet cong sent a message saying
they were not fighting during tet
all vietnamese went home
or disappeared somewhere
very few guards still on duty
interesting
how they call the war off
and put their toys away for three days
hard for an american military mind to comprehend[21]

The American embassy was expecting the same thing for Tet in 1968. But the Front had been assembling its forces for weeks. The North Vietnamese Army had created a massive diversion at Khe Sanh, in the 'Demilitarized Zone' (DMZ) along the border with North Vietnam. General Westmoreland had thrown everything he could into Khe Sanh. It was the kind of battle he understood—artillery, air strikes and American machine-guns mowing down human waves of Orientals. A real battle, like Korea, like the movies. But while Westmoreland read body counts from the DMZ, the National

Liberation Front moved into position to take the cities.

All Vietnamese over 35 remembered where they were in August 1945, when Hanoi, Saigon and every town of any size rose against the Japanese and the French. For all of them, those days defined a revolution. Now, in 1968, they were going for urban insurrection, finally. The Front had been fighting for a long time, with great courage. Its generals were not sure they could continue. One big push, they told their people. We march into the cities and the people will rise with us.

On Tet they struck, throwing in everybody they could. The tunnels of Cu Chi were the base for the assault on Saigon. Fighters flooded into the city. That morning sappers from the tunnels assaulted the American embassy in the heart of Saigon and held part of it for hours. The world saw the television pictures and saw one of the sappers was a woman.

There was fighting in the streets of Saigon. In Hue the Front took almost the whole city, and the guerrillas of Beautiful Waters joined the fight.

With great courage, they failed. On the streets of Saigon the chief of police blew out the brains of a captured guerrilla, and a cameraman captured the moment for American TV. In Hue the guerrillas held the old imperial city and its beautiful buildings, fighting house to house with exhausted US marines. The world saw the pictures of a guerrilla on a ruined wall, gun in hand, and the tired and desperate stare of a wounded marine. More than half of Hue had been destroyed by the time the Marines retook it.

In the city of Ben Tre, in the Mekong Delta, the American army flattened every building. The American officer in charge told reporters, 'It was necessary to destroy the city in order to save it,' and newspapers around the world carried that quote.

What the world, and the American people, saw was that the White House had been lying to everybody. Two days into Tet, Lyndon Johnson gave a press conference. He said that the Tet Offensive was a failure, it was all over, and anyway he had known about it beforehand. These were lies and, what was worse, obvious lies. There was no more light at the end of the tunnel. The American people had been told that the Viet Cong were North Vietnamese soldiers who had invaded South Vietnam and terrorized the peasants, and that America was winning the war in the countryside. Now people in

America could see what the GIs had seen—the courage of the Vietnamese resistance.

The American photographers, the TV cameramen, and the reporters in Saigon and in the newsrooms were already opposed to the war. Now they saw their chance. Enraged, exultant and professional, they raced through the streets, filming, screaming down the phone home, making them run those pictures, hoping that the newsroom forced the editor to run the story, that the word got out, that people could see.

What the world saw was that the greatest power on earth, with all those weapons, all those big white men, had been humbled by peasants.

The guerrillas, however, experienced a shattering defeat. They had expected Saigon and Hue to rise. It didn't happen.

The problem was that the Communists could not organize the working class. Six years later Tran Bach Dong, the man in charge of the Communist underground in Saigon, said during a conference underground in the jungle, that the National Liberation Front's organization in Saigon was 'wonderfully successful—the intellectuals, students, Buddhists, all of them'—except for the workers, where organization was 'worse than bad'.[22] He was removed from office and humiliated, not because the organization was worthless, but because he said so, and what he said was both true and embarrassing for the Communist Party.

The party, after all, claimed to be a communist party, a Marxist party. The core idea of Marx's Marxism was that the working class can take over the world and liberate all humanity. But party bureaucrats, not workers, ran North Vietnam. The party spoke of a proletarian line and the leading role of the proletariat, but what they meant was the line they chose and the leading role of the party.

They had particular difficulties building any organization among workers in the South. The obvious way to do that was to organize unions, to support strikes, to sell a regular underground newspaper and try to build underground committees in each workplace opposed to both the employer and the state. This was the classic Communist way of organizing. There were workers in the South, and strikes. By 1973 the bombing in the South had created so many refugees that 70 percent of people now lived in the cities. The peasants had become workers, or were at least scrabbling for a living in the city.

But the Vietnamese Communists were committed to building an alliance of classes in the National Liberation Front. Crucial to that alliance were the 'progressive bourgeoisie'. These people were the employers and managers of the workers. If the Communists tried to organize the workers over daily grievances on a daily basis, as they did try to organize the peasants, they would lose the support of the businessmen and managers. Faced with the choice, the Communists did better at organizing the managers.

This was partly because party leaders felt a natural affinity with businessmen and managers. The same sort of people, with the same sort of education, ran both North and South. And most of them had relatives of the same class on the other side.

But there was a deeper problem. Because the party had pushed through land reform in the North, they were able to advocate it in the South and in that way respond to peasants' economic grievances. But because they did not allow workers in the North to have unions or strikes or independent workers' committees or meetings or newspapers they could not advocate these practices in the South without raising the question of why this wasn't happening in the North. In other words, if the party had made strikes and workers' power central to its work in Saigon, it would have had to change in Hanoi.[23]

And that is why Saigon was weakest at Tet, Hue was stronger and Ben Tre was strongest of all. In Saigon the rising had to have the workers. Hue was smaller, closer to the countryside. Ben Tre was a small city in a sea of peasants. But Saigon was the capital, the key.

There was one more problem. Workers' risings do not happen with a secret command. They take the form of mass strikes, then demonstrations, then more little strikes and protests, and more mass demonstrations, building up to a moment of general strike and insurrection. The strength of such a rising is that in the end it pits a whole city against the police and the army, and the soldiers will not fire on the crowd because included in that crowd are their friends and family. The risings of 1945 had been like that. Such risings are protean, creative, democratic and chaotic. The whole tradition of the Vietnamese Communists to that point had been military. So by 1968 they could only conceive of an urban rising as a military event, happening by command, with the people supporting the army.

Had they concentrated on deepening and extending the sort of movement that was seen in the demonstrations of the Buddhist monks, they might have organized a march of all Saigon. By 1968 it would have been politically impossible for the American army to fire on a crowd of a million—and the GIs would probably have refused to do it. But the Communist leaders could not organize that crowd.

So after Tet the guerrillas had to retreat, carrying their wounded where they could, their cover blown. Bao Nihn, a North Vietnamese veteran, wrote in a novel of the retreat from Saigon:

> For the infantry scouts even the sky was dangerous in those two weeks of withdrawal, carrying the wounded, dragging their feet through the jungles headed west towards the Cambodian border. In less than a fortnight they had been encircled twice, and twice in utter desperation had broken out of the traps, fighting fearlessly.
>
> Kien's unit was in total disarray and badly beaten up. They fought a rearguard struggle as they headed west and together with three men from another company crossed the Poco River and wormed their way toward the Black Hill, which had been ground to powder by B52s. From that relative safety they ran for their lives into the sunset.
>
> As they were crossing some low-lying jungle areas at the foot of the Ngoc Bo Ray mountain, the group came across a team of stretcher bearers heading for Cambodian territory. Against his better judgment, Kien and his men joined the stretcher-bearers from the Sa Thay river area and went along with them. They were all short of food and their units had been torn to shreds… American troops were all around them in this area and their ragged unit saw traces of them having passed earlier at various places, and other signs of their presence. They expected to run into them at any time, especially near water-holes; it was the dry season and there were precious few water sources left, so they were natural ambush sites.
>
> Overhead there were the spotter planes and bombers to contend with. After some unexpected encounters with the enemy they took more wounded, including the stretcher-bearers. They reformed with groups of three carrying two stretchers each.[24]

The guerrillas took a terrible beating in many areas. In Long An province, south of Saigon, one unit of 1,430 had only 640 survivors after Tet. Another of 2,018 had only 775 survivors. And then the B-52s came. By the end of the war the guerrillas had lost 84,000 'combatants' in a province with a total population of 350,000 men, women and children—one person in four.[25]

In Cu Chi district the local guerrillas lost 883 killed and 3,670 wounded in the first six months of 1968. The 7th Battalion, with a normal complement of 320, lost 122 killed and 116 wounded during Tet. A captured guerrilla finance officer told his interrogators:

> We had lost many cadre during the 1968 offensive and its aftermath… My own operations were becoming more and more difficult and dangerous. The taxation situation had deteriorated tremendously, because the people were disenchanted with us. We had promised to topple the puppet government with the [Tet] General Offensive and had collected extremely heavy taxes on the basis of this pledge. In 1969, when I attempted to tax again, the people were angry about this. This attitude combined with the decimation of our cadre and the enemy build-up, resulted in a great drop in taxes collected.[26]

The B-52s created craters deeper than the tunnelers of Cu Chi could dig. Many guerrillas were buried in the tunnels, and for those who remained the passages lay open to the sky. The guerrillas left the tunnels of Cu Chi.

The guerrillas were stronger in some areas of South Vietnam than others, but everywhere they were weaker than before. Now they faced the Phoenix program.[27] Phoenix was organized under William Colby, then the CIA station chief in Saigon, and later the director of the whole CIA. The staff were CIA agents, South Vietnamese soldiers and South Vietnamese police. The aim was to target the 'Viet Cong Infrastructure' (the people in the resistance) and assassinate them. The difficulty was in knowing who they were. So under Phoenix anybody could inform on anybody else anonymously for a cash reward. That way many Communist and Front leaders were eliminated. But so were a lot of other people. It was an extortionist's paradise, and President Thieu also used it to kill many of the supporters of a rival general, 'Big' Minh. Tens of thousands died. The CIA insisted on some proof—not proof of guilt, but proof that a person had died, a body. One agent complained that the local police were bringing in every body they came across. But Phoenix was also an opportunity for the landlords hiding in the cities, who did know who their enemies in the villages were, to get their revenge.

Phoenix agents also worked with American military sweeps. The GIs would go through a village and round everybody up. The Phoenix people took away anybody who looked suspicious and anybody on their lists of minor Viet Cong supporters. Some of these people were

killed, but the majority were sent to local and provincial torture centers and then released after a few days or weeks. If they went home,
or to another village, they were picked up again pretty soon in another
sweep and sent to the torture center again. This happened over and
over. The Phoenix people were not making a mistake—they had
quotas.

After Tet the 101st Airborne came to the village of Beautiful
Waters. Micheal Clodfelter, who screamed in protest as his platoon
cut off the old man's ear, served with the 101 in 1965. Now the
'Screaming Eagles' built a base, Camp Eagle, on the land of Beautiful Waters.

The villagers told Trullinger they found the Americans cruel and
nervous like the French. Sometimes the 101 just went crazy, and fired
for minutes into the night. That was especially hard for the villagers
with fields near the base. The 101 seemed to like shooting water buffaloes too, and children had to stop sitting on their buffaloes. There
were endless searches of the village, beatings and some rapes.

Before Camp Eagle came the guerrillas had been strong in Beautiful Waters. As one peasant said, the villagers had spoken of the
men who oppressed them, and finally had the courage to say their
names aloud. But in 1968 the guerrillas had to leave the village, only
returning sometimes at night. Trullinger estimates that support for the
Viet Minh and then the National Liberation Front had always been
70 to 80 percent of the village. But after 1968 solid support was down
to about 50 percent. Government support, usually 5 to 10 percent, had
climbed to 15. The other 35 percent of villagers were exhausted, and
waiting.

The Front told the villagers not to take jobs at Camp Eagle, and
most of the civilian workers on the base came from other villages.
The villagers found the Americans almost unimaginably rich, these
men who had grown up the hard way in their own country. All of
their food was imported, everything they needed was imported, and
a lot of it was wasted, dumped on the garbage dump outside the base.
Poor villagers, particularly old people and children, picked through
that garbage dump regularly and found things they could use or sell.
The dump trucks kept coming as they searched, and the bulldozers
would level the dump regularly. Occasionally children from Beautiful Waters died when they didn't see the bulldozer coming and it
buried them.

In one sense the strategy of attrition was working. The bombs, the guns and Phoenix were killing an awful lot of civilians, but they were wiping out the guerrillas in the process. After 1968 the Viet Cong had almost no organization left in Saigon. When the Communists finally won in 1975, there were many villages that could no longer produce a Communist committee.

# Prostitution and rape

The American armed forces were winning the war in the villages. But at the same time the war was hollowing out the society of South Vietnam. Remember Vo Thi Mo, the 17 year old woman platoon commander in the Cu Chi tunnels. She was fighting for land. But women like Vo Thi Mo were fighting for other reasons as well. If she had not gone down the tunnels, she could easily have become one of Saigon's prostitutes.

Vietnam had long had prostitution. Prostitution by the poor for the rich had always been an important family value. But there was an explosion with the Americans and the new rich in the cities. Women, men and children did it to live.

Frank Snepp was a CIA analyst and interrogator in Saigon. In 1973 the last American troops had left but the South Vietnamese government still held power in the cities. Snepp went to Mimi's Flamboyant Bar for a beer:

> I heard for the millionth time a bar girl drone on about her long-lost American GI. He's gone. She's a mother. But now, unlike 1969 or '70, she who tells the tale is no more than thirteen or fourteen, only beginning to discover what so many others before her are trying to forget. 'I'm no animal,' she says, 'but the Americans make love to me as if I was.' And she pounds her fist in her hand to demonstrate. But then one of her favorite customers comes in and she is all smiles and sweetness. Soon she is gone for the night.[28]

Snepp had a Vietnamese lover, 'Tu Hua' (a pseudonym). In 1975 the Communists were closing in and a pilot in the South Vietnamese Air Force bombed the presidential palace in Saigon. Snepp, at work in the embassy, got a call from Tu Hua. He asked if she was all right:

> 'Okay,' she said, 'but scared. When the big bang went off I was...'
> 'Yes,' I coaxed, trying to sound calm and unconcerned.

'I was taking a shower.'

'Well, you were lucky,' I said, unable to keep from laughing. 'That bathroom's a safe place. Well away from the windows.'

'No, it was terrible,' she insisted. 'I don't want to die with no clothes on.'

I laughed again and reassured her all was well. But as I hung up the phone I couldn't help wondering at how curious her reaction was. Tu Hua, after all, had spent much of her childhood dodging shrapnel in the streets of her native village in the delta, and a good many of her teenage years working in the bars of Tu Do. And now, as if she were still an innocent in the world, she was worrying about dying in the buff![29]

For Snepp it's a joke. He does not understand why a prostitute would be afraid of dying naked.

When the GIs went to those prostitutes some were angry and hurt, and used the woman to hurt back. Some were looking for love, and trying to give it, or just wanted someone to hold them. Some were looking for sex because they were in a world full of death. Some built relationships of love with Vietnamese women. But the war and the inequality degraded both the prostitutes and the GIs.

And there were hundreds of thousands of rapes. Duong Thu Huong went south as an officer in a North Vietnamese Communist Youth Brigade when she was 21. In 1990, after she was expelled from the Communist Party for dissent, she wrote a novel about the war. She writes of a patrol:

> We moved towards the corner of the forest from which the horrible odor seemed to emanate. We found six naked corpses. Women, their breasts and genitals had been cut off and strewn on the grass round them. They were northern girls: We could tell by their scarves made out of parachute cloth and the lotus-shaped collars of their blouses. They must have belonged to a group of volunteers or a mobile unit that lost its way. Perhaps, like us, they had come here to search for bamboo shoots or vegetables. The soldiers had raped them before killing them. The corpses were bruised violet.[30]

This is a novel, and perhaps Duong saw that and perhaps she did not. But that is what women soldiers like Duong feared all the time. The British photographer Philip Jones Griffiths took this picture:

Photograph by Philip Jones Griffiths (Magnum Photos)

For a picture caption, Griffiths wrote:

> Captured VietCong. The woman was the sole survivor of a Communication squad caught in the open. Wounded in the spine, she was forced to crouch all day with her hands tied behind her back before being taken off by helicopter. When reproached, a US officer replied, 'What's the hurry? When the GVN boys have interrogated her, she'll only be raped and killed anyway.[31]

Just after the Tet Offensive in 1968 Leonard Gonzalez was on almost constant patrol with a 'Charlie Company' under Captain Ernest Medina of the 11th Infantry in Quang Ngai province along the coast. Some of the men raped on every patrol. Gonzalez remembered:

> Take one squad say, it's a small village, one squad would go from the back, one goes from the front, and the other is going through. Now the one that is going through is having their fun...
>
> One squad got one girl—one lady. Then they told me, 'Go in there,' and I said, 'No, I won't.' So what I did is I went inside and she looked real bad. The only thing I can do for the lady is, like, I got the canteen and wiped her. She was awful perspiring. I wiped her forehead. I tried to hold her up. She got scared of me, I was part of them. I tried to tell her I don't have nothing to do with it. I helped her up to her feet. I took her to the well, got some water from the well...
>
> Then another squad heard about the thirteen guys who did their thing with this woman, and were going to try her out and I told them to leave her alone, and then at that time I just walked off. I said: 'Forget it.' I don't want to kill my own men. I tried to tell her: 'Get out of here—go,' She was going to run...but, like after thirteen guys got to her it's hard to walk.[32]

After repeated patrols Captain Medina called Charlie Company together one evening in March 1968 and told them that the next day they would be taking a village that was a Viet Cong stronghold. He ordered them to kill everybody in the village, My Lai.

Varnado Simpson was a rifleman in Charlie Company. He was 19 when he entered the village the next day. He shot a woman. Years later, he remembered:

> I went to turn her over and there was a little baby with her that I had also killed. The baby's face was half gone. My mind just went. The training came to me and I just started killing. Old men, women, children,

water buffaloes, everything. We were told to leave nothing standing. We did what we were told, regardless of whether they were civilians. They was the enemy. Period. Kill. If you don't follow a direct order you can be shot yourself. Now what am I supposed to do? You're damned if you do and you're damned if you don't. You didn't have to look for people to kill, they were just there. I cut their throats, cut off their hands, cut out their tongue, their hair, scalped them. I did it. A lot of people were doing it and I just followed. I just lost all sense of direction.

Simpson personally killed about 25 people. Lieutenant 'Rusty' Calley, the officer in charge on the day, shot over 100. Rape and killing went together, both part of a larger terror. Simpson said later:

Do you realize what it was like killing five hundred people in matter of hours? It's just like the gas chambers—what Hitler did. You line up fifty people, women, old men, children, and just mow 'em down. And that's the way it was—from twenty-five to fifty to one hundred. Just killed. We just rounded them up, me and a couple of guys, just put the M-16 on automatic, and just mowed 'em down.[33]

That day Leonard Gonzalez was with another platoon 500 meters away. He saw the sergeant take a girl of about 16 into a house. When she came out she had no pants. Gonzalez had watched two hours of killing, not knowing what to do. Now he begged the girl's mother, in English, to get her some pants. But other men moved in on the girl. According to the historians of the massacre, Michael Bilton and Kevin Sim:

Several men saw three GIs with the girl. One had penetrated her, one was having oral sex with her…

In a pile outside a hootch [Gonzalez] saw seven naked women aged between 18 and 35—their corpses dotted all over with tiny dark holes. The sight really sickened him… Roschevitz was explaining how they came to be naked to a group of men standing nearby. He forced the women to undress with the intention of having sex with all of them. If they didn't strip, he told them, he was going to shoot them. He singled out one woman, telling her to 'boom, boom' him. She became hysterical and the other women panicked, yelling, screaming, and begging for mercy. Roschevitz decided to let them have it. He fired several rounds [of buckshot] and killed them all.

Later, as they were leaving…Gonzalez saw the young girl who had been raped. Once more she was without her pants, walking alongside some of the men. Gonzalez thought the girl figured that if she stuck close to them, they probably wouldn't kill her.[34]

The My Lai massacre was ordered by the officers and covered up by them later, all the way to general. When it was finally exposed in the US a year later, only one man, Lieutenant Calley, was convicted of any offense. He served four and a half months of his sentence before he was paroled.

The guerrillas tried to be different from the American army. Some-times their artillery hit village houses and killed people. Then the local commander would visit the bereaved family, stand before their eyes and their rage, and say he was sorry.

The National Liberation Front said, in all its talks and leaflets, that in a free Vietnam men and women would be equal. Men and women are not equal in Vietnam today. But what the guerrillas meant, what women like Vo Thi Mo understood when they went into the tun-nels, was that it would not be a carnival of rape and prostitution.

The landless peasants had gone to war for land. Now they were fighting for decency too. They had begun fighting for themselves. Now they were fighting for a vision of humanity.

In 1967 a 19 year old woman guerrilla was captured and tortured. Then the researchers from the American RAND corporation talked to her. She told them that the leader of the Village Liberation Women's Committee had recruited her to the Front 'against her family's wishes'. She had joined because the Front members she met were 'living embodiments of heroes of our legends; they are the men who stand up to fight the evil in order to protect the people'.[35] And if she was released she was going right back to join them.

# Washington

Meanwhile back in Washington, while the guerrillas were dying after Tet, the American ruling class was deciding it had to wind down the war. McNamara, the Secretary of Defense, realized his side was losing the war in 1967. He said so, directly to President Johnson and indirectly to Congress, and was kicked upstairs to run the World Bank.

His replacement at Defense, Clark Clifford, was confronted with Tet and a request from General Westmoreland in Vietnam for 206,000 more troops, to bring the total to 700,000. Clifford was a longtime member of the ruling class. The way he put that to his colleagues in March 1968 was:

> I make it a practice to keep in touch with friends in business and law across the land. I ask them their views about various matters. Until a few months ago, they were generally supporting of the war. They were a little disturbed about the overheating of the economy and the flight of gold, but they assumed that these things would be brought under control, and in any event they thought it was important to stop the Communists in Vietnam. Now all that has changed...the idea of getting deeper into the bog strikes them as mad. They want to see us get out of it. These are leaders of opinions in their Communities... It would be very difficult—I believe it would be impossible—for the president to maintain public support without the support of those men.[36]

This is the authentic voice of the ruling class: the light touch, the total assurance.

The 'overheating of the economy and the flight of gold' were a real worry. The war was costing the government a lot, and that produced a boom in America—full production and full employment. But because the war was so unpopular, it was impossible for Congress to raise taxes to pay for it. Without such taxes, and with full employment, Americans were using their extra income to buy goods from abroad and the American government was in effect borrowing from abroad. Both of these things made the American balance of payments worse. The dollar was the world's basic currency—since World War Two other countries had traded internationally in dollars—and the dollar was linked to the price of gold. By 1967, with America borrowing more money and buying more goods than it was lending, banks and traders in other countries were trading their dollars in for American gold reserves. Those reserves were shrinking, and the US government was approaching the point where the dollar could no longer be tied to gold.

This was a problem, but only because the war was unpopular and taxes couldn't be raised. There were other major problems. American economic dominance was steadily eroded as other economies grew faster, and all major industrial economies found that the rate of profit was falling after about 1966. But neither of these problems was caused by the Vietnam War, nor were they solved by ending the war. And when the dollar did eventually come off the Gold Standard under President Nixon, it still remained the world's major reserve currency.

This is why the economy and the Gold Standard were an important worry for American business in 1967, but not decisive. What was decisive was Tet.

But if Clark Clifford and the ruling class had turned against the war, Lyndon Johnson still wanted to win it.

In 1968, which was an election year, Senator Eugene MacCarthy ran against Johnson as a peace candidate in the first Democratic primary in conservative rock-ribbed New Hampshire. Johnson won, but only by 230 votes. Bobby Kennedy, JFK's brother, was waiting in the wings. Bobby had worked for Senator Joe McCarthy (of 'McCarthyism'), had been an early supporter of the Vietnam War and favored sending the troops in 1965. But unhappy with Johnson for many reasons, Bobby had turned against the war in 1967. After the New Hampshire primary he saw Johnson could be beaten and threw himself into the race for president. He was likely to win the Democratic nomination.

Clark Clifford was, he said later, 'more conscious each day of domestic unrest in our own country'. He called in the 'Wise Men'—the State Department's senior advisory group. The Wise Men spoke for the ruling class. They 'included men with close links to the world of finance, corporate law and big business',[37] a former chairman of the Joint Chiefs of Staff and a former Secretary of Defense. Dean Acheson, the liberal architect of the Cold War as Truman's Secretary of State, chaired the Wise Men.

The Wise Men had met with Johnson back in 1965, when he was balking at sending troops to Vietnam. Then they told him he had to intervene, for American power in the world. In 1967 they had met again and approved the war. Now they were unanimous for peace, and all had the same reason. As one said, 'The divisiveness in the country was showing with such acuteness that it was threatening to tear the United States apart'.

Dean Acheson went to that meeting with an editorial from the *Winston Salem-Journal* in his pocket. It said that because of the war Americans had 'lost sight of our national priorities, [and] the most crucial priority of all [is] of course, the home front'.

'I could have written it myself,' Acheson said.[38]

For the American ruling class, when push comes to shove, its central priority is control of America. And this was priority time.

# Chicago

Lyndon Johnson gave in to the Wise Men. He refused General West-moreland's request for 206,000 more troops in Vietnam, and announced on television that he would not run for a second term as president.

Four days later Martin Luther King was murdered in Memphis, Tennessee. Most black people assumed that the assassin had been hired by white power in some form, the FBI or white businessmen or the Ku Klux Klan. They did not expect a proper investigation of this death (and there has never been one).

King had carried his people's hopes. After his death, one black radical said to me, 'You know, I don't agree with Doctor King, you have to go further, but every time I listen to his speeches I cry.' Many felt that way. His murder had proved that his politics of non-violence and negotiation did not work. But his people honored him that weekend in the only way they could, in rage and sorrow, fire and riot. All over the country the black inner cities went up in flames—there were riots in more than 100 cities. Now the ruling class faced an anti-war movement and an enraged black movement.

But for the moment most of the war protesters assumed peace would come quickly. America had stopped bombing North Vietnam. Washington was talking to Hanoi. Bobby Kennedy was the peace candidate, and he was winning in the primaries. In June a Palestinian worker, a refugee in Los Angeles, shot Kennedy dead (because Kennedy was a Cold Warrior, because he supported Israel). Now Eugene MacCarthy was the anti-war candidate again, and the students and young liberals came back to him.

The nomination was to be decided at the Democratic Party convention in August in Chicago. The Yippies and some of the radicals in SDS called for a week of demonstrations outside the convention. Only a few thousand demonstrators showed up. This was partly because Mayor Daley and his Chicago police force had made it clear that the demonstrators would be met with force, issuing heavy warnings and shooting dead a Native American demonstrator the day before the convention. The liberal wing of the peace movement had also discouraged people from going to Chicago, saying it would make the Democratic Party look bad. But the main reason there were so few demonstrators was that most peace protesters now assumed the war would end soon.

The people had voted for peace in the primaries. The convention nominated Hubert Humphrey, Johnson's vice-president, a loyal supporter of the war. The few thousand demonstrators in Chicago broke through the police cordons and made it to Michigan Avenue, outside the convention and the delegates' hotel. The police gassed and beat them. The floor of the convention smelled of gas, and Senator Abraham Ribicoff of Connecticut told the convention on live television that the police were using 'Gestapo tactics on the streets of Chicago'.[39] Outside, the National Guard trucks patrolled the streets, guns ready. The demonstrators chanted, 'The whole world is watching! The whole world is watching!' And it was.

A year like any other, 1968 was becoming the year of 68. In America there were the riots for Martin Luther King and the Chicago demonstration. A mass student movement in Mexico was only broken when hundreds were gunned down in Mexico City. In May student demonstrations in France led to the largest general strike in world history. In Czechoslovakia a reforming wing of the ruling Communists tried to introduce 'socialism with a human face'. In August the Russian tanks rolled into Prague, and students and workers crowded round the tanks, protesting. In Pakistan student demonstrations and workers' strikes in Karachi brought down the military dictatorship. In Italy the two red years of strikes began. In Germany, Poland, Argentina, Japan, Thailand, Sri Lanka, Afghanistan, Iran, Turkey, Yugoslavia, Bolivia and Chile students demonstrated, workers went on strike, and revolution was in the air.[40]

And it had all started with Tet, with a world seeing that America, the greatest power on earth, could be defeated.

The American ruling class faced a contradiction. It wanted out of Vietnam. But it did not want the consequences of losing, of public humiliation in the atmosphere of 68. If Tet had begun all those struggles, TV pictures of the American troops leaving and the guerrillas marching joyously into Saigon would give heart to larger struggles inside America and all over the world.

So in 1968 the American government began peace negotiations in Paris with North Vietnam and the National Liberation Front. It stopped bombing North Vietnam. But it bombed South Vietnam, Laos and Cambodia for seven more years, and American troops stayed in South Vietnam for five more years.

And the American ruling class argued constantly among themselves.

They were all caught in a contradiction. They dared not fight and dared not lose.

So Johnson, and then Nixon, tried to talk peace and reduce troop levels enough to keep America quiet while making enough war to possibly defeat the Viet Cong. If that did not work, at least they could hurt Vietnam so badly nobody else would want to have that happen to their country.

They did not say that was what they were doing. But it is what they did.

They did it for the ruling class, not for political advantage. Richard Nixon, the Republican, campaigned for president in 1968 by saying he had a secret plan to end the war. Hubert Humphrey, the Democrat, knew he could win the election if he promised to end the war. Loyal to Johnson and the ruling class, Humphrey supported the war, and Nixon won the election. Voters preferred a man with a secret plan to end the war to one with a public plan to continue it. Once Nixon was elected, he faced the same problem as Johnson. Nixon had been a lifelong anti-Communist. He explained his plan to his aide Bob Haldeman:

> I call it the madman theory, Bob... I want the North Vietnamese to believe I've reached the point where I might do anything to stop the war. We'll just slip the word to them that, 'for God's sake, you know Nixon is obsessed about Communists. We can't restrain him when he's angry—and he has his hand on the nuclear button,'—and Ho Chi Minh himself will be in Paris in two days begging for peace.[41]

Nixon was trying to end the war without losing it. The White House began planning Operation Duck Hook—saturation bombing of Cambodia and North Vietnam, invasions of Cambodia and Laos, and nuclear bombing of North Vietnam if necessary.

Duck Hook was meant to be secret from the American people, but a clear threat to the North Vietnamese leadership. In 1969 most Americans waited for Nixon to make peace. When they realized he would not, and that the Paris peace talks were hopelessly stuck in arguments about the shape of the negotiating table, the protesters returned.

In November 1969 500,000 people demonstrated in Washington. It was bigger than Martin Luther King's civil rights March on Washington in 1963, the biggest demonstration in American history. For 30 hours a single file of people marched from the Arlington National

Cemetery, each one carrying a sign with the name of a destroyed Vietnamese village or an American who had died in Vietnam. Empty buses ringed the White House, bumper to bumper, with armed troops behind them as half a million demonstrators passed. The radicals demonstrated outside the Justice Department and the police in gas masks waded in, beating people, filling the air with gas. I was among the protesters, and the gas made me heave so hard I projectile vomited. Attorney-General John Mitchell watched from the window and felt it was like the Russian Revolution.[42] It wasn't. But it was more than Mitchell or I had ever seen.

Nixon wanted to quiet the protesters but not lose the war. On 20 April 1969 he announced he would withdraw 150,000 troops from Vietnam in the coming year. But at the same time Duck Hook continued. Ten days later Nixon invaded Cambodia. The Vietnam War had already engulfed all of Indochina. In both Cambodia and Laos Communist guerrillas fought the governments, and American planes supported the governments by bombing the people. The Viet Cong used areas of Cambodia near the Vietnamese border as a refuge, and North Vietnamese troops and supplies came down a dirt road, the 'Ho Chi Minh Trail', in Laos. The king of Cambodia, Sihanouk, had tried to keep his country out of the war, but quietly allowed secret American bombing of the Viet Cong and Khmer Rouge (Red Cambodians) on his land. This was not enough for the American government, which sponsored a coup by Sihanouk's defense minister, Lon Nol. The coup was not popular with Cambodians. The Khmer Rouge recruited and American bombing in Cambodia increased. Nixon's invasion of Cambodia was a message to Hanoi, but it was also an attempt to shore up Lon Nol.

Nixon, announcing the invasion of Cambodia on television, said, 'If, when the chips are down, the world's most powerful nation, the United States of America, acts like a pitiful helpless giant, the forces of totalitarian anarchy will threaten free nations and free institutions throughout the world'.[43] These words have been treated as a joke. Nixon meant them, and they expressed what half the ruling class were feeling. If they lost in Vietnam, free enterprise would be threatened by Communism and 'anarchy'—by which Nixon meant democracy from below.

Former ambassador to Indonesia Marshall Green came home from work after Nixon's speech on Cambodia. Green was in charge of the Far Eastern desk at the State Department, and by now a dove on Vietnam:

I came back to my house, and my son came into the room where I was talking to my wife. He denounced the position that the President had taken, and he said, 'I don't want to see you again.' And he left. And we didn't see him again for weeks... You were driven to brink of suicide, you really were.[44]

Student strikes and occupations swept the colleges. I was living in Knoxville, one of about 50 white radicals, hippies and dopers who had been holding a small anti-war movement together at the University of Tennessee. When Nixon announced the invasion we called a demonstration for the next evening, expecting a few hundred. The university plaza filled and overfilled, and there were thousands and thousands there. The men all seemed to have short hair, the women perms. The fraternities and sororities were there. Nixon had told us the 'silent majority' supported him. But he had promised peace and made war, and now the silent majority were with us.

Kent State University in Ohio was in a conservative area too. Two days after Nixon announced the invasion of Cambodia, on Saturday night, a crowd of 2,000 set fire to the Reserve Officers Training Corps building on campus. The governor sent in the National Guard. On Monday at noon there was a rally of 1,000 on campus. A few students threw rocks at the National Guard. The historian Kenneth Heineman takes up the story:

> The soldiers assembled, conferred among themselves, and marched away from the students and towards Blanket Hill. Arriving at the top of the hill near the pagoda, they turned and fired into the crowd. In thirteen seconds the Guardsmen expended sixty-one rounds. A few hundred feet away in the parking lot, Alison Krause fell mortally wounded. Danfora took a bullet in the wrist and Grace, shot in the foot, writhed in agony. Loaded onto an ambulance, Grace watched as medical attendants pulled a blanket over Sandy Scheuer's head... A young female runaway knelt beside Miller and, arms outstretched, wept.
>
> Stunned silence. Then hysterical crying. Marilyn Hammond frantically searched for her husband and, finding him unharmed, fainted. An antiwar student and Vietnam veteran, with blood all about him, stared into the distance. The students spontaneously sat down on the ground. When the Guard commander ordered them to move or be fired on again, freshman Mim Jackson stoically awaited death.

Glenn Frank, a conservative geology professor and World War Two veteran, had tried to defend the ROTC building from the students on Friday night. Now he saw the students shot, and about to be shot again:

> Glenn Frank pleaded with the officer to desist, but was curtly dismissed. With tears welling in his eyes and voice cracking, he urged students to leave the Commons: 'They're going to shoot us again. We're going to be slaughtered. They've got guns and the guns are at our throats.' Slowly, the students arose and dispersed. A colleague then helped the trembling professor home.[45]

In those few minutes Professor Frank had joined the protesters in his heart, saying 'they' and 'we'. Alison Krause, 19, Jeffrey Miller, 20, Susan Scheur, 20, and William Schroeder, 19, were dead. Schroeder was attending college on a Reserve Officers Training Corps scholarship.[46]

It was nothing, really, four people dead, compared to what was happening to the Vietnamese. Nothing even compared to what was happening to the American troops over there. Hardly anything compared to the blacks killed by police in the riots in Los Angeles and Detroit. But it was new. Nixon and the ruling class were raising the stakes. And at Kent State they had been protesting Cambodia, Vietnam, all that killing. Sometimes political killings are just atrocities, but sometimes they happen at moments when mass feelings are ready to change history. Roughly 4,350,000[47] students marched and protested at 1,350 colleges, and 536 colleges went on all out strike. In California the state governor, Ronald Reagan, closed the whole state university system. The American Federation of State, County and Municipal Employees came out against the war.

On a week's notice 150,000 people demonstrated in Washington. 'Those few days after Kent State were among the darkest of my presidency,' Richard Nixon wrote later. Henry Kissinger was effectively in charge of foreign policy. He wrote of those days:

> It was a time of extraordinary stress. Washington took on the character of a besieged city... The very fabric of government was falling apart. The Executive Branch was shell-shocked... Exhaustion was the hallmark of us all. I had to move from my apartment ringed by protesters into the basement of the White House to get some sleep... [Nixon], deeply wounded by the hatred of the protesters...reached a point of exhaustion that caused his advisers deep concern...[and seemed] on the edge of a nervous breakdown.

Duck Hook was finished. Nixon announced that all American troops would be out of Cambodia by the end of June. The protests had worked.

But all the way through the war many of the demonstrators did not think that their protests worked. Most of these were liberals who expected the system to work. They had been raised in the belief that America was a democracy where the government responded to the wishes of the people.

Instead the ruling class looked out the windows of the White House at the protests, and judged what it could get away with and when it would have to bow to the popular will. Even when it gave ground to the protestors and began to negotiate, it insisted that it was not influenced by the protesters.

The liberal protesters had expected some satisfaction, some truth, not an endless class struggle. And the war was still going on, with all the killing. So many of them switched from feeling you could reform a basically decent system to feeling you couldn't change anything at all.

They saw two alternatives—either the system was responsive to people or it was against them. They had no understanding of class struggle—that the people who run the system are always opposed to the majority of the people, but can be forced into doing things if that majority pushes them hard enough.

Many of them felt you could not change the majority of Americans. This came from a contempt for the working class. Abbie Hoffman, the Yippie leader, later put it this way, talking of Archie Bunker, a right wing working class character on TV:

> We deliberately chose to go for the children of the Bunkers because we could not get the Bunkers. It was kind of hard to appeal to…that class of Americans because many of them were beating us up and sending us to jail… Most Americans don't give a shit, period… I am convinced…that the dumping of tea in the Boston harbor alienated the majority of Americans at the time.[48]

At a small student rally in Knoxville in 1969 a refugee from the Hungarian workers' uprising in 1956 got up to speak. He suggested we go out to the factories at Oak Ridge and leaflet the workers against the war. We looked at him as if he was mad. The idea of leafleting scared us. We were sure, quite wrongly, that workers supported the war. When he suggested that we shop with small shopkeepers to support the little man, that was more on our wavelength.

But of course many students did not have contempt for workers. Many came from working class homes, many were working their way through college, and there were always individual workers on the demonstrations. The problem was political. Anti-Communism had broken socialism in the unionized working class. Millions of people were moving towards revolution in their heads, thinking, 'I am a revolutionary'. But they did not think that meant activity in the unions, or that American workers could change the world. This was true of workers too.

For instance, in the days after Kent State I was a teacher at Knoxville College, a black college across town from the mostly white University of Tennessee. The students at Knoxville College came from working class homes—the black upper middle class did not send their children to places like Knoxville College. Many of our students worked in the car plants in Detroit in the summer to pay their tuition. If they were lucky and they graduated, they hoped for jobs as local organizers for the Girl Scouts, parole officers in Georgia or cabin crew for an airline. They were workers.

After the shootings at Kent State they held back for a few days, saying, 'Its a white people's thing—we don't want to get involved,' but feeling inside they wanted to act. Finally there was a meeting in the gym. Out of about 810 students at the college, 800 came to the meeting. The student body president from the mostly white university came to speak. He was a black Vietnam veteran, which says something about how Tennessee was changing. He urged the Knoxville College students to strike over Kent State. They voted 800 to zero to strike.

Next morning 800 were on picket lines blocking every road into the college. They let the teachers cross on condition that we go to a meeting of our professional association, the American Association of University Professors, and vote on joining the strike. We voted two to one to strike. The governing board of the college met, 12 white Methodist ministers, and voted 12 to zero to join the strike.

They did so because everybody knew the students had guns in the dormitories. If the police or the National Guard were called onto campus, they would use those guns, and then the police or the Guard would slaughter us. (A week later the police opened fire on an unarmed crowd at Jackson, a black college in Mississippi, killing Philip Gibbs, 21, and James Earl Green, 17, a student at Jim Hill High School.[49] Even after Kent State, they could do that to black people.)

Our strike was far more militant and far more united than the white students across town, because the students at Knoxville College were working class, black, far more oppressed and far more angry about everything. But there was one weakness. The same picket lines that stopped the teachers allowed the catering workers through so they could cook and serve the students' meals. The legacy of the anti-Communist crusade was that working class black students on strike did not even think of mobilizing the working class (nor did I).

In an earlier chapter I quoted a firefighter whose son Ralph died in Vietnam. His wife, Ralph's mother, spoke to an interviewer in 1970:

> I think my husband and I can't help but thinking that our son gave his life for nothing, nothing at all... I told him I thought [the protesters] want the war to end, so no more Ralphs will die, but he says no, they never stop and think about Ralph and his kind of people, and I'm inclined to agree. They say they do, but I listen to them, I watch them; since Ralph died I listen and watch as carefully as I can. Their hearts are with other people, not their own American people, the ordinary kind of person in this country. I know when someone is worrying about me and my children, and when he says he is, but he's really elsewhere with his sympathy. Those people, a lot of them are rich women from the suburbs, the rich suburbs. Those kids, they are in college... They don't come out here and try to talk to us... I'm against this war too—the way a mother is, whose sons are in the army, who has lost a son fighting in it. The world hears those demonstrators making a noise. The world doesn't hear me, and it doesn't hear a single person I know.[50]

She was wrong in one way. There were many like her in the anti-war movement. But she was basically right. The voices of people like her were not heard.

But without the protesters, without all their class contempt or class confusion, without all their impatience and craziness and ego tripping leaders and bullshit and faction fights—without all that mess and all that energy she would have known that her son died for nothing and been unable to say it out loud.

The student revolt did not stop the war. But it limited the killing. Very few of us tried to organize workers. That was the legacy of anti-Communism. But we did make possible a working class revolt against the war in the armed services. That is the subject of the next chapter.

# Chapter 5

# The GIs' revolt

Ron Kovic's father was a checker at an A&P supermarket on Long Island in New York state. He worked hard long hours to take care of his family. The spring before Kovic graduated from high school, his father made him take his first job, stacking shelves in a supermarket. But:

> I didn't want to be like my Dad, coming home from the A&P every night. He was a strong man, a good man, but it made him so tired, it took all the energy out of him. I didn't want to be like that, working in the stinking A&P, six days a week, twelve hours a day. I wanted to be somebody.[1]

Ron Kovic joined the Marines out of high school and went to Vietnam. He made sergeant. American soldiers served one-year tours in Vietnam, counting the days, and very few volunteered for a second year. Kovic was one of the few. He was wounded the second time and was paralyzed from the waist down. Back in America he did physical therapy, tried hard and learned to live in a wheelchair. Later he wrote a book about it—*Born on the Fourth of July*.

In the book Kovic tells how he heard about a place for paralyzed American veterans in Guadalajara, Mexico, called the Village in the Sun. He went there and it was wonderful. Everybody else was in a wheelchair too. He didn't have to apologize for other people's discomfort there. He could go to prostitutes who were mostly polite and didn't show pity. He felt very lonely when one of them told him she had a child and was only doing this for the money. But it was good to play with another person's body, and good to have a woman hold him.

One night he went out with another Vietnam veteran named Charlie. They drank a lot and smoked some weed:

> In the last whorehouse [we] went to Charlie got in a wild fight with one of the whores. He punched her in the face because she laughed at him when he pulled down his pants and told her he couldn't feel his penis

anymore. He was crazy drunk and kept yelling and screaming, swinging his arms and his fists at the crowd… 'That goddamn fucking slut! I'm going to kill that whore for ever laughing at me. That bitch thinks it's funny I can't move my dick. Fuck you. Fuck all of you goddamn motherfuckers! They made me kill babies! They made me kill babies!' Charlie screamed over and over again.[2]

The owner of the brothel was furious, threatening Kovic and Charlie. Kovic was scared. But he couldn't move, because all he could think was that Charlie was saying things he'd been feeling for a long time.

Kovic thought a lot about one particular night in Vietnam. His unit had been sent out on patrol. They were afraid, and they thought they saw something, maybe the enemy, in a hut. Somebody opened fire, and then they were all firing madly. They stopped firing, and there was screaming from the hut. Sergeant Kovic and five men went to see what was in the hut.

Writing about it Kovic referred to himself as 'he':

Molina turned the beam of his flashlight into the hut. 'Oh, God,' he said. 'Oh Jesus Christ.' He started to cry. 'We just shot up a bunch of kids.'

The floor of the small hut was covered with them, screaming and thrashing their arms back and forth, lying in pools of blood, crying wildly, screaming again and again. They were shot in the face, in the chest, in the legs, moaning and crying.

He could hear the lieutenant shouting at them, wanting to know how many they had killed… A small boy…was still alive, although he had been shot many times. He was crying softly, lying in a large pool of blood. His small foot had been shot almost completely off and seemed to be hanging by a thread… He heard a small girl moaning now. She was shot through the stomach and bleeding out of the rear end…

The marines stared, stunned, and then Kovic took out his medical kit and started trying to bandage the spurting wounds. The other men helped him or stood around:

The lieutenant had just come up with the others. 'Help me,' he [Kovic] screamed, 'Somebody help!' 'Well, goddamn it sergeant! What's the matter? How many did we kill?' 'They're children,' he screamed at the lieutenant…

'Forgive us for what we've done!' he heard Molina cry.

'Get up,' screamed the lieutenant. 'What do you think this is? I'm ordering you all to get up.'

Some of the men began slowly crawling over the bodies, grabbing for the bandages that were still left. By now some of the villagers had gathered outside the hut. He could hear them shouting angrily...

The marines made the lieutenant call an evacuation helicopter to take the children to hospital:

The men in the hut were just sitting there crying. They could not move, and they could not listen to the lieutenant's orders...

'You men! You men have got to start listening to me. You gotta stop crying like babies and start acting like marines!' The lieutenant... was shoving the men, pleading with them to move. 'You're men, not babies. Don't you people understand—they got in the goddamn way!'

When the medical chopper came, he picked up the little boy... His foot came off and [Kovic] grabbed it quickly and bandaged it against the bottom stump of the boy's leg. He held him looking into his frightened eyes and carried him up to the open door of the helicopter.[3]

Looking back on that night, and other days, Kovic began to realize he had been used.

What made that clear was that he was still being used. He'd been born on the Fourth of July (Independence Day), and the American Legion put him up on the platform for the local Fourth of July parade, a disabled veteran in his wheelchair, a symbol. Then they wouldn't let him speak from the platform.

He started college, did his exercises, and while he was doing them he heard his leg break (he couldn't feel it). He went back to the Veterans Administration Hospital in the Bronx. He complained about the conditions there—there weren't enough staff and they didn't care. They couldn't afford to care, given the scale of suffering they were seeing. The American army in Vietnam had an emergency medical evacuation program that worked as none ever had before. In any previous war 200,000 men would have died, not 58,000. But that medicine meant many men were permanently wounded, and many of them were in the Veterans Hospital in the Bronx.

The American government doesn't spend enough money on its Veterans Hospitals. Doctors know it's not the elite end of medicine. Kovic kept screaming at the staff to clean up the vomit on the floor. He screamed for a bath: 'I asked to be treated like a human being.'

They put him in an isolation room.

His broken leg swelled up and the doctor suggested cutting it off. Kovic refused, so they operated instead. Afterwards they hooked tubes up to him in intensive care, pumping fluid into the wound and waste out, keeping the wound healthy. He wasn't going to lose his leg.

The pump stopped. The aide couldn't make it work. He got a doctor who explained that the pump was old and that they probably couldn't make it work. Kovic told them to get another pump. The doctor said the hospital didn't have another pump. Kovic couldn't believe it—a giant hospital in the Bronx with one pump. The doctor explained it was because of the war—all the money was going on the war, not the hospital. He was sorry, it wasn't fair, but it looked like Kovic was going to lose his leg.

A little more than an hour later the pump started all by itself for no reason anybody could see. Kovic didn't lose his leg. When he got out of the hospital he went back to college. Then Nixon invaded Cambodia and four students were shot at Kent State. There was a demonstration at Kovic's college. Back in Vietnam Kovic had always hated hippie protesters. Now he joined the protest. He was shy, maybe because of the politics, maybe because of his wheelchair, probably both. He sat in his car on the edge of the protest all day and didn't get out, but he honked his horn in support.

Three things got Kovic to that protest. The first was the war, what he'd seen and done in Vietnam. The second was the anti-war movement. The third thing was class. He went into the Marines because of what his family was, what his father did and the future he faced. Class was there in Vietnam too. It was why the lieutenant was the one trying to make them stop crying in the hut, telling them it didn't matter, trying to get them moving. That was class struggle, the lieutenant's struggle for his class and its orders. And the marines making the lieutenant call a medical helicopter for the children, that was their class struggle. Then, when Kovic came home, class was still there. It's why the hospital was the way it was. In America people like him didn't matter. He was there in his car honking his horn because he had put the war and class together in his mind.

After that he went down to the mass protest in Washington. Later he joined the Vietnam Veterans Against the War.[4] They were an organization of men like him, part of the peace movement. They went on the demonstrations with the rest, but they marched together and they held their own protests. From 1970 they were a growing part of the movement. In April 1971, a few days before the national demonstration in Washington, they set up a peace camp on the Mall. They wore fatigues and ran it like an army camp. The government told them they had to leave or they would be forcibly evicted. A delegation from the troops who would have to evict them visited the camp and promised the veterans they would refuse to do any such thing. The veterans refused to move. The government was bluffing. It knew the political cost of television pictures of clearing the veterans' camp, the screaming and the scuffling and some of the veterans disabled. At the last minute it let the veterans stay.

Roughly 2,000 veterans marched to the capital, dressed in old uniforms and combat fatigues, to return their medals to their congressmen. They found a fence had been put up in front of the steps of Congress to stop them. The police guarded the fence. One by one the veterans stepped forward and threw their medals over the fence at the Congress. Each man was supposed to say something as he stepped up:

'My name is Peter Branagan. I got a purple heart and I hope I get another one fighting these mother-fuckers.'

'I hope that time will forgive me and my brothers for what we did.'

'Second Battalion, First Marines—power to the people.'

Ron Ferizzi from Philadelphia: 'My wife is divorcing me for returning these medals. She wants me to keep them so my little sons can be proud of me. But three of my best friends died so I could get that medal.'

Another man, pointing at the steps of Congress: 'We're not going to fight anymore, but if we have to fight again it will be to take those steps'.[5]

It went on for three hours. Some men had a lot of medals to throw because their friends who couldn't make it had given them theirs to return too.

The next month, May 1971, the Vietnam Veterans Against the War in Massachusetts had a weekend protest to mark Memorial Day. They planned to march from Concord to Boston in honor of Paul Revere, who rode from Boston to Concord on the night of 18 April 1775 to warn the dissident American colonists that the British troops were coming to take away their arms. The first night of the protest 500 veterans camped by the Old North Bridge in Concord, where the revolution had started when the colonists opened fire on the British the morning after Revere's ride. The officials of the town of Concord refused permission for the camp and threatened to clear it. Phone calls and a local radio station mobilized supporters. There were 1,000 veterans and supporters when the police came late that night, and they arrested 485 people. Many of the 485 gave the police only their name, serial number and date of birth—19 April 1775.[6]

# The movement in the armed forces

The Vietnam Veterans Against the War were important for far more than their numbers. They gave the rest of the peace movement a feeling of legitimacy, that they weren't against 'our boys in Vietnam' but for them. But the VVAW was much smaller than the far bigger movement inside the armed forces.

That movement largely began with a few radicals who understood the importance of organizing in the army. A small group of Trotsky-ists, for instance, were important to *Vietnam GI*, a paper produced in Chicago with a print run of 15,000 and a mailing list of 3,000 in Vietnam.[7] The largest Trotskyist organization, the Socialist Workers Party, did systematic work around the bases from 1966 on. They also had a policy of not refusing the draft. They based this policy on the experience of the Russian Bolsheviks in World War One. Because the Bolsheviks were part of the working class, they had organized *inside* the army against the war, overturned the officers and taken their country out of the war. The SWP understood that was what had to be done in Vietnam too.

The SWP was a small organization, and the army began refusing to draft its members or keep them in the forces. But many went in and did good work. Joe Miles, for instance, was drafted to Fort Jackson in 1969 and started the movement there by 'inviting fellow black soldiers to listen to taped speeches by Malcolm X and discuss the need for GI organization'. Miles was transferred to Fort Bragg, North Carolina, at three hours notice, but the men he left behind founded GIs United Against the War. They got more than 300 signatures on a petition asking the base commander to allow them to hold a meeting on the base to discuss the war. He refused, so they got a lawyer and eight of them sued the army for denying their freedom of speech.

Meanwhile, at Fort Bragg, Miles had just recruited a second chapter of GIs United Against the War, most of them Vietnam veterans. They put out a newspaper, *Bragg Briefs*. This time the army transferred Miles to Fort Richardson, Alaska, where he formed a third chapter of GIs United, and they put out another paper, *Anchorage Troop*.[8]

But the organized socialist left was simply not that big. Most of the early organizing was started by radicals not in any party, who simply set up coffee houses in small cities near army bases. They provided coffee, a quiet and dignified atmosphere, and anti-war talk. A lot of GIs came and talked, and then the coffee house people and the GIs started to organize and put out an anti-war newspaper for the local base.

Once the coffee houses had set the example and the movement got going, servicemen and women on a lot of other bases founded organizations of their own and put out their own papers. There were about 300 such newspapers in the armed services over the course of the war.

Frank Cortright was part of that movement, and he later compiled a list of 245 papers. Most of them only came out for one or a few issues. The people who put them out were investigated, transferred, sent to Vietnam, court-martialed and given long sentences, dishonorably discharged and framed on other charges. But still the papers kept coming.

In the army and Marines there was the *Fatigue Press* at Fort Hood, Texas; the *FTA* (Fuck the Army) at Fort Knox, Kentucky; the *Last Harass* at Fort Gordon, Georgia; the *Pawn's Pawn* at Fort Leonard Wood, Missouri; the *Ultimate Weapon* at Fort Dix, New Jersey; the *Attitude Check* at Camp Pendleton, California; the *Green Machine* at Fort Greely, Alaska; the *Napalm* at Fort Campbell, Tennessee; the *Arctic Arsenal* at Fort Greely, Alaska; the *Black Voice* at Fort McClellan, Alabama; the *Fragging Action* at Fort Dix; the *Fort Polk Puke* at Fort Polk, Louisiana; *Custard's Last Stand* at Fort Riley, Kansas; *Whack!* produced by women at the Women's Army Corps School; and *Where Are We?* at Fort Huaracha, Arizona.

At bases overseas there were papers in, among other places, Paris, Kaiserlauthen, Baumholder and Stuttgart. There were several papers in Heidelberg, including *FTA With Pride*, several in Frankfurt, including the *Voice of the Lumpen*, 'affiliated with the Black Panther Party', several in Berlin including, at McNair Barracks, *Can You Bear McNair?* There was *Seasick* at Subic Bay, and other papers in the

Philippines, and *The Man Can't Win If You Grin* and other papers in Okinawa. There was the *Korea Free Press*, and many papers in Japan, including *Semper Fi*, produced jointly by marines and Japanese peace activists from the Hobbit Coffee House, and *Kill For Peace* at Camp Drake, Japan. In England there was the *Stars and Bars* and *Separated from Life*, which 'evolved out of the haircut defiance case of Sgt. Dan Pruitt'.

There were at least 84 papers in the Air Force and navy in the United States, including *Duck Power* in San Diego; *Harass the Brass* at Canute AFB, Illinois; *All Hands Abandon Ship* in Newport; Rhode Island; *Now Hear This* in Long Beach; the *Potemkin* on the USS Forestall; the *Star Spangled Bummer* at Wright-Patterson AFB in Ohio; *Fat Albert's Death Ship* in Charlestown; the *Pig Boat Blues* on the USS Agerholm; and three papers at Kirtland Air Force Base in New Mexico, *Special Weapons*, *I Will Fear No Evil*, and *Blows Against the Empire*.

The anti-war movement was everywhere, on almost every base of any size. In El Paso, Texas, for instance, GIs For Peace was founded in August 1969 at a meeting of several hundred soldiers, many of them from the Defense Language Institute at Fort Bliss. Their purpose was to 'promote peace, secure constitutional rights for servicemen, combat racism, improve enlisted living conditions, and provide aid to the local Chicano community'. Ten of the men involved were transferred in the next five months, and the editor of their newspaper, *Gigline*, was sent to Vietnam. But others took their places.

In November 1969 many of the soldiers at Fort Bliss were forced to march in the Veterans Day Parade in El Paso. A hundred GIs stood facing the reviewing stand, on the other side of the road, under a big banner saying 'GIs For Peace'. As the troops from Fort Bliss marched by, instead of saluting the reviewing stand, they saluted the protesters with peace signs and clenched fists.

Specialist 4 Paul Fuchs, section leader of his Vietnamese class at the Defense Language Institute, was told to spy on GIs For Peace. He did that, became an organizer for GIs For Peace, sent false reports to army intelligence and diverted their money to GIs For Peace. He and his friend Dennis Olney, locally referred to as the Fabulous Furry Freak Brothers:

> ...exhorted fellow classmates, all Army security trainees with top-level secret clearances, to resist orders to Vietnam. By the time Fuchs was removed as class leader (the Army finally realized something was wrong

when he filed for conscientious objector status), twelve of the twenty-one original members of the class had deserted, obtained discharges, or filed for conscientious objector status.[9]

Fuchs was discharged from the army by court order and Olney received a medical discharge after he told them, 'Someone injected LSD into my brain'.[10]

The army canceled reveille at Fort Bliss. Less than half the soldiers on base were turning up for the 6am parade. In January, 1970 some 80 GIs picketed a talk in El Paso by General Westmoreland, the army chief of staff and former commander in Vietnam, and 'to avoid an embarrassing public confrontation, the general was forced to sneak in the back entrance of his hotel'.[11]

And on 15 March 'approximately two thousand people, including more than eight hundred servicemen, came together for a festival of political speeches and rock music'.[12]

These meetings, organizations and newspapers were part of a much larger movement, a massive change in feeling. In the San Francisco Bay Area the student demonstrators had tried to block the local center for induction into the armed services in Oakland in 1967. They sat in the streets and they ran through the streets, and were gassed, clubbed and arrested. They failed to block the center. But awareness had been raised. From October 1969 to March 1970, 50 percent of the draftees ordered to report to the Oakland Induction Center failed to turn up, and 11 percent of those who did show up only did so to state they were refusing to be drafted.

During the whole war 206,000 people were reported to the federal Justice Department for refusing the draft.[13] I suspect that many of these people were middle class and upper class students. But between 1968 and 1975 over 93,000 people deserted from the American army alone. They were less educated than the average soldier. In one government survey 41 percent had less than nine years of education. They were working class people who didn't have a chance to refuse the draft.

Roger Williams did a survey of deserters in exile in Canada during 1969 and 1970. He found a few were political activists, often educated and opposed to or ambivalent about the war before they went into the services. But the majority were 'all-American boys' who 'knew that the war in Vietnam was wrong' and had deserted rather than work for the war. Another 30 percent were confused because 'the army which they had been taught was the noble defender of goodness and free-dom turned out to be ugly, brutal and evil.' Less than 5 percent had deserted because of personal reasons, family circumstances or crimi-nal trouble.[14]

Of course, American soldiers have always deserted. But the de-sertion rate tripled during the course of the Vietnam War, and at its height it was three times the rate of desertion at any point during the Korean War.[15]

In 1971 desertions (absences without leave for 30 days or more) ran 73 per 1,000 in the army and 56 per 1,000 in the Marines. That means 7 percent of soldiers and almost 6 percent of marines deserted. And it wasn't just that. That year 250,000 servicemen and women wrote to complain to their congressman or woman. In fiscal 1971, for every 100 people in the army, seven deserted, 17 went absent with-out leave, 12 complained to Congress, two received disciplinary dis-charges and 18 were punished without a court-martial. (The figures are a bit inflated because some people must have done several of those things that year—you could be punished, go AWOL, come back, complain to Congress and then desert.)[16]

At the beginning of the war basic training was what it had always been—boot camp, hell, the place men learned to obey insane orders. By the last years of the war boot camp was getting easier and easier and the drill sergeants were learning to negotiate with the men, be-cause the army was scared they would just walk away.

The unrest was part of the wider movement in America. The news-papers and organizations on the bases would not have happened with-out the civilian peace movement. That movement had won the argument against the war. By 1970 a solid majority of Americans were opposed to the war, and that majority was larger among work-ing class Americans, the people who went into the armed services.

The unrest took on the cultural forms of the wider movement. The movement in the States was full of dope, long hair, hippies and anarchism. In Vietnam the GIs painted peace signs on their helmets and wrote FTA (Fuck the Army) there and everywhere else. They smoked hash, opium and heroin, partly to escape. Many men counted the days and obliterated each day. But the drugs were a form of cul-tural rebellion too. Just smoking pot openly was a rebellion in itself. In one of the few open demonstrations by GIs in Vietnam, over 1,000 people came to Chu Lai beach to protest the war on 4 July 1971.

They didn't know what to do when they got there, so they had the largest pot party in the history of the war.[17]

Music was another way of expressing rebellion. In Vietnam and on bases in Germany people chose their music to express their attitude to the war. The white rebels, the majority, were called the 'juicers' and were into rock and roll. The blacks were into soul. The juicers and the blacks called the white career sergeants 'lifers', and the lifers liked country and western. Nobody fought over music in combat. They had to stick together there. And blacks never fought with white rock and roll fans. But in the rear in Vietnam, and especially in Germany, many felt that 'if blacks can account for up to twenty-two per cent of the dying they should have at least twenty-two per cent of the jukebox'.[18] There were arguments, bitter looks and sometimes fights.

Many of the black soldiers came from the big cities that had rioted in the 60s. They had seen it as teenagers. When Martin Luther King was murdered in 1968, the inner cities of America went up in flames. The historian James Westheider interviewed two black veterans who were in Vietnam when King died:

'Some of the younger guys were just angry and just wanted to hurt someone,' related Allen Thomas Jr, 'and there were some fights between whites and blacks, but most of the men were simply in shock. Several hundred men just sat down in a field, drank, smoked pot, but mostly just talked.' Serious violence was avoided because the black NCOs convinced the officers to 'back off' for a few days and let the men work through their anger and frustration. 'The unit was in stand-down anyway, and the last thing you wanted to do was set them off, you know, seasoned veterans with guns,' Thomas said. James Hawkins agreed that 'Dr. King's death changed things, it…made a lot of people angry—angry people with weapons'.[19]

The black people in the army came from the inner cities. They brought black nationalism into the army. Westheider again:

In Vietnam many blacks began to make and display black-power flags. Black marines in Da Nang designed one that would become a model for others. The flag had a red background to symbolize blood shed by African Americans in the war. A black foreground represented black culture. At the center were two spears crossed over a shield and surrounded by a wreath, meaning 'violence if necessary' but 'peace if possible'. Across the flag was a legend in Swahili proclaiming, 'My Fear is for You.' Variations of the flag appeared in South Korea and Germany as well as elsewhere in Vietnam.[20]

In 1966 an average of two thirds of black soldiers signed up again when their enlistment came to an end. It was a good job for a black worker compared to what was available in civilian life. By 1970 less than 13 percent of black soldiers were re-enlisting.[21] In 1970 there were black political or cultural groups on almost every base in Germany, like the Black Action Group at the Panzer Barracks in Stuttgart, the Black Dissent Group at Smiley Barracks in Karlsruhe, and the Unsatisfied Black Soldiers around Heidelberg. They had a central Defense Committee, and on 4 July 1970, nearly 1,000 US servicemen from all over Germany, mostly black but some white, attended a meeting in Heidelberg. That meeting demanded, among other things, equal promotions and family housing for black GIs, a committee of enlisted men which could veto sending any GI to the stockade, college preparatory classes for all GIs, and immediate withdrawal of all American forces from southeast Asia and all US interests from Africa.[22]

After that, black and white GIs together began organizing at Nelligen army base in Germany. A strict new commanding officer was trying to knock the base into shape. There was harassment, many disciplinary charges and unjust jailings. The soldiers replied with Molotov cocktails—firebombings on 21 July, 10 and 14 August. They phoned in bomb threats and they let down the officers' tires, again and again. On 21 September, 'following a weekend of growing friction and frustrated attempts to negotiate with officers, black and white GIs threatened to blow up the entire base.' Two more firebombs had gone off that morning, and the army declared a 6.30pm curfew and brought in truckloads of armed military police. But at 9pm about 100 GIs marched through the camp, despite the military police, shouting, 'Revolution', and, 'Join us': 'Several hours later they returned to barracks, but only after a pledge by provost marshal Lieutenant Colonel R McCarthy that no action would be taken against them.' Nobody was punished for that march either, although general harassment of activists continued. And the march had been black and white. One black soldier told *Overseas Weekly*, 'There is no racial problem between E-5s and below…that's one thing our demonstration has proved'.[23]

From 1970 on the fight against the war was moving from the campus to the barracks. The campus had to come first. A campus is an easy place to organize. Students are allowed to get away with a lot precisely because they are middle class.

Workplaces are harder. Workers, particularly manual workers, are constantly driven by their managers. The armed forces are the hardest of all. The ruling class needs the army to defend it from insurrection at home. It needs them to follow inhuman orders and risk their lives in war abroad. People won't die without asking questions, unless they are very scared. Any unrest in the armed services looks like mutiny, and mutiny threatens the whole rule of the rich over society.

This is not abstract. Industrial might and the ability to make war were the foundations of American power in the world. For big strikes, student protests and riots they call out the National Guard. In Berkeley, California, the students brought the National Guard over to their side three times during the Vietnam War. They knew those men were in the Guard to avoid the draft, and they talked to them.

Behind the National Guard is the army. In 1967 army units fighting to put down a democratic rising in the Dominican Republic were abruptly called back and sent onto the streets of Detroit to end the black uprising there. Many of those soldiers were black. At the same time, in Camp Pendleton, California, William Harvey and George Daniels organized a meeting among their fellow marines to discuss 'why black men should fight a white man's war in Vietnam'. Harvey was sentenced to six years and Daniels got ten.

At Fort Hood, in Killeen, Texas, the Oleo Strut anti-war coffee house held a love-in on 5 July 1968 that attracted 200 mostly white soldiers. In late August the troops of the 1st Armored Cavalry learned that they were about to be sent to control the anti-war demonstration at the Democratic Convention in Chicago. More than 100 black soldiers from the 1st Armored met all night to discuss 'army racism and the use of troops against civilians'. Their commander, General Powell, attended the meeting at one point, and the next morning 43 men were arrested for 'refusal to follow orders'. The Oleo Strut coffee house and the white and black soldiers organized a massive defense campaign for the Fort Hood 43, and most of them got off with short sentences. But Private First Class Bruce Henderson, a white man and the first editor of the Fort Hood *Fatigue Press*, was tried for possessing tiny traces of marijuana in the lint of his trouser pockets and got eight years hard labor (it was finally reduced to two years hard labor on appeal).[24]

These rebellions were important. When the army goes over to the crowd in any great national confrontation it is a revolution. That is what happened in Russia in 1917, in Germany in 1918, in Iran in 1981 and in the Philippines in 1985. It could happen in America. That, and the necessity to make people die for bad causes, is why discipline in all armed services is so tight. And that is one reason the revolt in the army came after the revolt on the campuses.

The second reason is that labor unions were alive in the working class in the 60s but political organization was dead. Most of the radicals and revolutionaries were in the student and civil rights movements, and they did not understand the importance of building in the armed forces. But the unrest in the army was not simply a reflection of civilian unrest. It was also driven all the time by the men coming back from Vietnam. It was what they said, the fact that so many of them joined the movement, and that everything about them told the other soldiers the war was wrong.

But the most important part of the soldiers' revolt was in Vietnam.

# Fragging

The GIs in Vietnam were working class people ordered to smash a revolt of poor peasants. They knew this. They were sent to a cruel war, and encouraged to kill and count bodies. The contradictions they were caught in, the pain and confusion of being on the wrong side, drove many of them into cruelty. But those same forces, at the same time, could and did drive men to revolt against the war. It is not a matter of some good, kind soldiers who loved peace, and some brutal monsters who loved war. Men in the same situation, in the same units, often the same men on different days, did terrible things and also refused to do them.

In 1968 Tim O'Brien was a GI in the 46th Infantry on the coast of central Vietnam, near Hue. He wrote a good book about it afterwards, *If I Die in a Combat Zone, Box Me Up and Ship Me Home*.[25] His unit patrolled a village called 'Pinkville' by the Americans. The year before, one of the hamlets in Pinkville had been the site of the My Lai massacre described in the last chapter.

A year later Tim O'Brien and Alpha company were still patrolling Pinkville, walking through My Lai. O'Brien, too, was terrified of mines all the time, watching every step, trying to outsmart the man who laid the mine, exhausted from fear. His unit did not talk about the fear much, but they all felt it all the time:

> Along the way we encountered the citizens of Pinkville; the nonparticipants in war. Children under ten years, women, old folks who planted their eyes in the dirt and were silent. 'Where are the VC?' Captain Johansen would ask, nicely enough. 'Where are all the men? Where is Poppa-san?' No answers, not from the villagers. Not until we ducked poppa's bullet or stepped on his land mine...
>
> In the next days it took little provocation for us to flick the flint of our Zippo lighters. Thatched roofs took the flame quickly, and on bad days the hamlets of Pinkville burned, taking our revenge in fire. It was good to walk from Pinkville and to see fire behind Alpha Company. It was good, just as pure hate is good.
>
> We walked to other villages, and the phantom Forty-eighth Viet Cong Battalion walked with us. When a booby-trapped artillery round blew two popular soldiers into a hedgerow, men put their fists into the faces of the nearest Vietnamese, two frightened women living in the guilty hamlet, and when the troops were through with them, they hacked off chunks of thick black hair. The men were crying, doing this. An officer used his pistol, hammering it against a prisoner's skull.[26]

And yet these same men were beginning to refuse the war. The first week O'Brien was with Alpha Company, they came under a mortar attack one night. O'Brien grabbed his rifle, his helmets, his boots and scrambled out of the barracks ready to fight:

> No one else came out of the barracks. I waited, and finally one man came out, holding a beer. Then another man, holding a beer.
>
> They sat on the sandbags in their underwear, drinking beer and laughing, pointing out at the paddies and watching our mortar rounds land.
>
> Later two or three more men straggled out. No helmets, no weapons. They laughed and joked and drank. The first sergeant started shouting. [He wanted them to fight.] But the men just giggled and sat on the sandbags in their underwear...
>
> A lieutenant came by. He told the men to get their gear together, but no one moved, and he walked away...
>
> The lieutenant hurried back. He argued with a platoon sergeant, but this time the lieutenant was firm. He ordered us to double-time out to the perimeter. Muttering about the company needed a rest and this had

turned into one hell of a rest and they'd rather be in the boonies, the men put on helmets and took up their rifles and followed the lieutenant past the mess hall and out to the perimeter.

Three of the men refused and went into the barracks and went to sleep.[27]

And nothing happened to them. The officers no longer dared to order men. They had to negotiate.

The first sergeant in Alpha Company was white. One of his jobs was to choose the men who would be transferred to support work, out of combat. The combat soldiers made fun of those men, called them 'Rear Echelon Mother Fuckers', but they dearly wanted those transfers. The first sergeant would not transfer black soldiers. Four men were killed in combat in one day, and the first sergeant came out on patrol to fill in. He was killed; it looked like a mine hit him:

> That evening we dug foxholes and cooked C rations over heat tabs. The night was hot, so instead of sleeping right away, I sat with a black friend and helped him pull his watch. He told me that one of the black guys had taken care of the first sergeant. It was an M-79 round, off a grenade launcher. Although the shot was meant only to scare the top sergeant, the blacks weren't crying, he said. He put his arm around me and said that's how to treat whitey when it comes down to it.
>
> In two weeks, a black first sergeant came to Alpha.[28]

Somebody up top had got the message.

'Fragging' was beginning. The word fragging meant taking a fragmentation bomb and throwing it into the tent of a gung-ho officer or sergeant who kept leading you out on dangerous patrols. It was a way of disciplining the officers.

Officers were usually warned. Lamont Steptoe was an officer with the 25th Infantry in Cu Chi in 1969 and 1970:

> Generally there was a pattern. If you were fucking with the men, they would generally warn you. When you came back to your bunk there would be a tear gas canister… The next time there would be a booby trap, which when you tripped it would let you know it could have been real. The third time would be the real thing. It's not like you weren't warned.[29]

Other officers were warned just by leaving a grenade pin on their bunk, or throwing a smoke grenade into their tent. The point was not to kill. It was to stop killing.

In *If I Die in a Combat Zone*, there is a description of the GIs' reaction to what appears to be a fragging. Alpha Company got a new colonel, Colonel Daud, who was gung-ho. He liked Combat Assaults, flying out in helicopters, landing scrambling out terrified, patrolling the villages:

> More Combat Assaults came in the next few days. We learned to hate Colonel Daud and his force of helicopters. When he was killed by sappers in a midnight raid, the news came over the radio. A lieutenant led us in song, a catchy, happy, celebrating song: Ding-dong, the wicked witch is dead. We sang in good harmony. It sounded like a choir.[30]

This was 1968. Already the officers had to negotiate with the men, and fragging was just beginning. Year by year it grew. According to one set of official figures, there were between 800 and 1,000 attempted fraggings in the armed services in Vietnam. According to the army there were 563 fraggings from 1969 to 1970, and from 1970 to 1972 there were 363 court-martials for fraggings. The great majority of these fraggings, 80 percent according to one set of figures, were directed at officers and NCOs. Most of them resulted in injury, not death. But the official figures miss most of the killings. They include only attempts with explosive devices, not with guns, which were easier to get. And in many cases nobody was prosecuted. The point had been made. To prosecute somebody was to keep up the struggle and possibly have more fraggings. A smart commander let it go. And if he didn't let it go, how was he to find out who did it?

Moreover, the usual way of killing officers in armies is to shoot them on patrol. This is doubtless what happened in Vietnam. It's what happened to the first sergeant in Alpha Company and it went on elsewhere. Miguel Lemus was in the 25th Infantry. Once his unit came back from a hard mission, scared and tired, and 90 of them smoked weed together:

> It was party time...and this officer tried to be a hero—bust ninety guys... We were along the trenches and they shot him. They threw him over a trench and shot him with a machine gun. No one said anything. Someone called on the radio and told them the captain had been shot by the gooks... Who saw it? Nobody saw it.[31]

The best guess is that over 1,000 officers and NCOs were killed by their own men. David Addlestone, an army lawyer, said that other army lawyers with the 173rd Airborne 'told of periods during 1970 and

1971 when violent attacks [on officers] were an almost daily occurrence'.[32] Lieutenant Colonel Herbert of the 173rd Airborne told *Playboy* that in his battalion in 1969:

> There had been two attempts on the previous commander's life. There had been quite a few fraggings in that battalion, of both officers and senior enlisted men. One man had both his legs blown off; seven people had been wounded by a grenade, and a Claymore mine had been thrown right at the tactical operations center—a mine to kill the staff, for Christ's sake.[33]

A lot of fragging was directed against the sergeants, the 'lifers' who were loyal to the corps and could get you killed. John Lindquist was in the 3rd Marines in 1969:

> One time they tried to frag the lifer's hootch, it didn't work because the grenade didn't go off. The lifers sat up there all night with a rifle waiting for somebody to try it again so they could blow them away...
>
> They tried to get this CID [Criminal Investigation Division] guy, but the grenade got a gunney [gunnery sergeant] who had nothing to do with it and he lost a leg... That rubbed me the wrong way.
>
> When I was down in Quang Tri they had three fraggings of first sergeants in 3rd Division... It got so bad that each battalion was concertinaed off from one another so they wouldn't fight...
>
> [We were] listening to Deep Purple and through the top of our hootch comes about five rounds of M16. They could have been lower... Somebody could be dead or wounded because somebody's fighting next door with other marines. The ground war was no longer really working.[34]

Another marine, in an anonymous account:

> We started having war calls, which is like at midnight everybody in the outfit starts screaming, 'Gooks in the wire'... And then you try to kill any of the lifers you didn't like.
>
> So we tried to get the CO a couple of times with a machine gun. One time his rack took nine holes. His cot, nine bullet holes...
>
> So one night this guy named H booby-trapped his tent. And in the morning when he woke up it wasn't the CO that got it. It was the executive officer Captain J... Captain K was the one we wanted to get. But J, it was good to get J 'cause he sucked too. They threatened to press charges against the whole outfit for mutiny. They were trying to figure

out a way they could keep it hush-hush. Nobody wants to know the Marine Corps mutinied.[35]

Mark Jury was an army photographer in Vietnam in 1969 and 1970. He traveled all over the country:

> Fragging is an institution in Vietnam. If the lifers make life unbearable, the kids will warn him with a CS (tear gas) grenade. If he persists, they'll 'frag' him with a real (fragmentation) grenade...
>
> In the field there're no problems. If and when a lifer is assigned to a combat company, he's put in shape quickly; the kids have the option to simply kill him during a fire fight. One unit's new first sergeant arrived when they were pulling 'palace guard'—security for headquarters. Usually it's a time for relaxation, but this guy was playing lifer, threatening punishment over 'unmilitary appearance' and dope smoking. The first day back in the field, one of the kids, a 6 foot 3 inch giant with long hair and peace symbols, said, 'Watch this.'
>
> He walked over to where the lifer was carrying an AK-47 (the NVA automatic rifle) and said loudly, 'Yeah, I'm gonna take my old AK with me tomorrow 'cause I think we are going to make contact.' Then he spun around and looked down at the sergeant, straight in the eyes, and slowly brought the barrel of the AK up and said, 'Sarge, if we make contact tomorrow, you better be real careful, 'cause the new guys are the ones that get scared and do stupid things and get themselves killed. And, Sarge, those AKs do one helluva job on you.'
>
> The next time out with the unit, I learned that the sergeant had become a helluva good guy until he couldn't take it any more and was shipped back to the States.[36]

GIs sometimes collected money to put on the head of a particularly dangerous officer. The man in charge at Hamburger Hill, so called because the GIs assaulting it were chewed into hamburger, had $10,000 on his head. He got out of Vietnam alive. Not everybody else did. Barry Romo commanded a platoon of the 196th Light Infantry Brigade. He remembered:

> My company commander had five hundred dollars on his head. And the reason was he was a coward... The North Vietnamese started an ambush on us. My company commander di-died [ran] out of the area— took the other two platoons behind me and ran down the hill and left us there. We had to fight our way back down... And after that my men collected five hundred dollars.[37]

There was another side to fragging. Ed Sowders was a medic at Cu Chi base hospital, on top of the tunnels, in 1968, and was organizing against the war:

> We've all heard of fragging. We know what it is, so I want to be honest about this. Fragging is a two-way street. It's not always the GIs in popular rebellion against their NCOs and officers. It's also a very convenient way to get rid of any troublesome lower ranking GI. I was afraid of that. Military intelligence is already on my ass. They already developed a file on me. They're already spying on me.[38]

Fragging spread from the combat troops to the rear. In one case:

> We banded together, blacks and white, we banded together and said, 'He's got to go, this sergeant's got to go... We can't let them continue to run this platoon.'
>
> We basically mutinied. At first we thought that murder was the answer... It was going to be draw straws and frag the motherfucker, right. Somehow that didn't happen. The next move was we'll go to the IG [inspector general] as a unit we'll lay out all these things we disagree with...making us stand formation, shine our shoes, and shit like that. Since we were NCOs, I was a sergeant, number of other sergeants, we'd present our case. That's exactly what we did. They sent in new people. It was a question of dealing with him one way or the more violent way.[39]

Fragging, and threats of fragging, were not acts of mindless revenge. They were ways of disciplining the officers, forcing them to negotiate. As Captain Barry Steinberg, an army judge, said, 'Once an officer is intimidated by the threat of fragging he is useless to the military because he can no longer carry out orders'.[40]

Yet fragging was not an attack on all officers. The senior officers, the brass, may have been intimidated by fragging, but stayed loyal to corps and career. The lieutenants and the sergeants split. Many of the junior officers had been in ROTC in college to avoid the war. Any great working class movement splits the middle class. Remember O'Brien's lieutenant, leading the men in singing 'the Wicked Witch is dead'. The Concerned Officers Movement was founded in Washington DC in 1970. It was especially strong among naval officers, but by 1971 it had 3,000 members in 20 chapters. The chapter at Keflavik Air Force Base in Iceland had its own anti-war paper, the *Stuffed Puffin*.[41] The pressure of fragging widened the split among the officers and NCOs. More and more simply cooperated in sandbagging.

O'Brien's unit was already doing that in 1968. They simply went down the road a bit when ordered out on patrol, camped out and made regular false radio reports.

The National Liberation Front had stated publicly at the peace negotiations in Paris that they would not fire on units who did not fire on them. They didn't always keep that promise. But many soldiers wore red armbands as a signal to the Viet Cong they didn't want to fight. And they simply refused to patrol, again and again and again, hundreds and thousands of times, all over Vietnam: 'During his year of legal defense work in Saigon, David Addlestone heard of literally dozens of combat refusals, with nearly every case ending not in punishment but in negotiations between commanders and GIs'.[42]

At Cu Chi, for instance, in November 1969, a 21-man platoon on patrol simply refused Captain Frank Smith's order to advance. They told a reporter they were all on short time, near the end of their year in Vietnam. They wanted to live. In April 1970 men of the 7th Cavalry refused Captain Al Rice's order to advance down a dangerous path. There was a TV camera along on the patrol, and American viewers got to see Captain Rice and the men negotiating, 'working it out', live. In December 1970 Lieutenant Fred Pitts of the 501st Infantry, his sergeant and his whole platoon all refused an order to advance.[43]

There were many other incidents. In the 1st Cavalry there were 35 combat refusals in 1970. Across the army and the Marines there were thousands during the war. In 1971 and 1972 troops were being withdrawn from Vietnam, but now there were more fraggings in an army of 200,000 than there had been in an army of 500,000. Nobody wanted to be the last American to die in Vietnam.

In 1971 an aerial photograph (see next page) of a giant peace symbol carved into the Vietnamese countryside was reproduced in many GI anti-war newspapers. It looked as if it had been made by a bulldozer. It had been carved in the fields of the village of Beautiful Waters, just south of Hue, by the men of the 101st Airborne.[44] By January 1972 the 101st were gone, part of the soldiers' revolt.

This David L Terry photograph first appeared in the *New York Times* in 1971 and was circulated widely in the GI press

# The fall of Saigon

The fragging and the combat refusals went together. Military discipline is fierce, and pacifism is not an option for soldiers in combat. If they don't fight they face the threat of being shot or court-martialed. Soldiers who want to stop a war and stay alive have to be prepared to shoot their officers, because their officers are prepared to shoot them. That is what the GIs did.

Nixon, Kissinger and the Pentagon were still trying to hold on in Vietnam. Main force units of the North Vietnamese Army remained in the jungles and mountains in strength. They were tired, thinned out and increasingly desperate, but they were still a fighting force. The Southern guerrillas were not, although they still had the political support of the majority of the villagers. If the Americans had stayed in some force, and the American troops had been willing to fight, then the United States could probably have won at the cost of 2 or 3 million more dead.

But from 1970 the GIs stopped fighting and the Pentagon grew desperate to get the troops out. In the *Armed Forces Journal* of June 1971 Col Robert Heinl, a Marine Corps historian, said what the officers were thinking:

> The morale, discipline and battle-worthiness of the U.S. Armed Forces are, with a few salient exceptions, lower and worse than at any time in this century and possibly in the history of the United States.
>
> By every conceivable indicator, our Army that now remains in Vietnam is in a state approaching collapse, with individual units avoiding or having refused combat, murdering their officers and non-commissioned officers, drug-ridden and dispirited where not near mutinous.
>
> Elsewhere than Vietnam the situation is nearly as serious...
>
> All the foregoing facts—and many more indicators of the worst kind of military trouble—point to widespread conditions among American forces in Vietnam that have only been exceeded in this century by the French Army's Nivelle Mutinies and the collapse of the Tsarist armies in 1916 and 1917.[45]

The revolt of the Tsarist troops in 1917 started the Russian Revolution—Col Heinl was sounding a warning of revolution. Note that he said that the situation in the armed forces outside Vietnam was almost as bad. The veterans were spreading the rot. And note that he was saying this in the official *Armed Forces Journal*. This was not a crank. This was the officer class making a public statement of what it felt.

Stewart Alsop, a right wing journalist close to the Pentagon, wrote a *Newsweek* editorial in December 1970. He described a 'growing feeling among the Administration's policymakers that it might be a good idea to accelerate the rate of withdrawal...[because] discipline and morale in the American army in Vietnam are deteriorating very seriously'. *Time*, writing on 'GI dissent' early in 1971, said that 'Officers from Chief of Staff William C. Westmoreland on down are known to be arguing that [the troops in Vietnam] are not being pulled out fast enough'.[46]

There was then no point in keeping the troops in Vietnam if they would not fight, and much danger. The last marines were pulled out in 1971. Negotiations dragged on between Hanoi and Washington. In March and April 1972 the North Vietnamese made main force attacks in strength in the north of South Vietnam—conventional warfare. The intention was to show Nixon what they could do and force him to negotiate seriously. The Viet Cong guerrillas were not part of this offensive, which was a sign of how weak they had become in the villages. The American government replied with massive bombing, to show what it could do. It was a sign of its weakness that they did not use American troops.

On 1 January 1972 there were 156,800 American troops in Vietnam. By 30 June there were 47,000. In those six months the Americans lost 178 dead and 809 wounded, and the South Vietnamese government forces lost 19,595 dead and 50,325 wounded. The American army was no longer fighting.

That left two cards in Nixon's hand—bombing and China. Nixon and Kissinger went to China in 1972 and made an informal agreement with the Chinese leaders. America would end its anti-Communist enmity to China and become China's ally against the Soviet Union. In return the Chinese government allowed the Americans to understand it had no objection to increased bombing of North Vietnam, and promised to lean on Hanoi to make peace with the Americans.

The other card was bombing. If the army and Marines would not fight, the planes could still bomb. But those bombs were delivered by human beings too. The peace movement spread to the big aircraft carriers. The USS *Constellation*, based in San Diego, was due to sail to bomb Vietnam in October 1971. The anti-war movement in San Diego organized its own referendum on whether the *Constellation* should go or not. Forty seven thousand civilians voted, 82 percent against the sailing. Six thousand nine hundred servicemen and women voted, 73 percent against the sailing. Nine sailors took refuge in a church and refused to go.[47]

The USS *Coral Sea* was to sail at the same time. Twelve sailors circulated a petition:

### TO THE CONGRESS OF THE UNITED STATES FROM THE BROTHERS OF THE CORAL SEA

In our opinion there is a silent majority aboard ship which does not believe in the present conflict in Vietnam. It is also the opinion of many that there is nothing we can do about putting an end to the Vietnam conflict. That because we are in the military we no longer have a right to voice our individual opinions concerning the Vietnam war. This is where we feel that the majority of the *Coral Sea* has been fooled by military propaganda. As Americans we all have the moral obligation to voice our opinions. We, the people, must guide the government and not allow the government to guide us. In our opinion this action is even more justified for the military man because he is the one who is taking personal involvement in the war. The *Coral Sea* is scheduled for Vietnam in November. This does not have to be a fact. The ship can be prevented from taking an active part in the conflict if we, the majority, voice our opinion that we do not believe in the Vietnam war. If you feel that the *Coral Sea* should not go to Vietnam, voice your opinion by signing this petition.[48]

Over 1,000 signed the petition, about a quarter of the crew. When the *Coral Sea* sailed from California, 1,500 civilians demonstrated and 35 sailors stayed behind. Once the ship reached Hawaii, several hundred crew members attended the anti-war entertainment put on by Jane Fonda and her FTA (Fuck the Army) Show. When the ship left Hawaii, 53 sailors stayed behind. The radicals who were left on board began publishing a newspaper on the ship, *We Are Everywhere*.[49]

Then the bombing escalated in 1972 and there was unrest on all the aircraft carriers involved. As the USS *America* left Norfolk, anti-war civilians in 13 kayaks and canoes sailed in front of the great ship to block its passage. The Coast Guard was sent to remove them, and hundreds of sailors stood along the rail of the *America*, throwing garbage at the Coast Guard. As the *Oriskany* left California, 25 sailors deserted. A week later ten of them surrendered to the navy with a public statement saying, 'The only way to end the genocide being perpetrated now in South East Asia is for us, the actual pawns in the political game, to quit playing'.[50]

On the munitions ship USS *Nitro* in New Jersey activists on board ship asked the local Vietnam Veterans Against the War to organize a similar flotilla. As the Coast Guard fought the kayaks, seven men jumped from the *Nitro* into the sea. One of them, William Monks, said:

I jumped from my ship because of my beliefs against the war and the killing in Vietnam… I also jumped for the many oppressed people in the military that think like myself, but because of the way the military functions, no one ever listens to these people… I see no reason why I should have to fight in Vietnam. I didn't start this war. I have nothing against the Vietnamese people; they never hurt me or my family.[51]

The sailors were also discovering how vulnerable hi-tech ships, especially aircraft carriers, were to sabotage. In fiscal 1971 the navy reported to Congress that there were '488 investigations on damage or attempted damage…including 191 for sabotage [and] 135 for arson'. In July 1972 a fire on the aircraft carrier *Forestall* did $7 million damage and stopped the ship sailing for two months. That same month somebody put a paint scraper and two 12-inch bolts into the gears on one engine and put the *Ranger* out of operation for three months.

Then, in October 1972, the carrier *Kitty Hawk* arrived in Subic Bay in the Philippines on the way home from bombing duty (the anti-war paper on the *Kitty Hawk* was called the *Kitty Litter*). Because sabotage had stopped the *Ranger* and *Forestall* sailing, the *Kitty Hawk* was ordered to turn around and go back to bomb. On shore black and white sailors fought. Back at sea only black sailors were questioned about it. A hundred black sailors met to protest, the Marines were sent in to break them up, and fighting between black sailors and marines 'with fists, chains, wrenches and pipes' lasted most of the night.

The same month, after a sit-in by black and white sailors on the *Constellation* supporting the demands of the ship's Black Front, 130 sailors were first given shore duty and then went on strike when ordered back onto the ship. None of them were punished and all were allowed to stay on shore.[52]

Throughout 1972 there were demonstrations on most US air bases in Japan, Germany and the US. In Thailand and Guam, where people were flying directly to bomb, it was harder to organize. But from Guam one man wrote to Congress, 'Ground crews no longer care whether or not their planes are safe and operational. Flights of crews do not wish to fly wasted missions and consequently abort when given the opportunity.' Another wrote, 'I for one, sir, do not wish to die as a mercenary for a foreign dictator'.[53]

In May 1973 the Air Force had to announce a 40 percent cut in bombing Cambodia. The *Washington Post* said it was because:

> …the Air Force is facing a deepening morale crisis among pilots, and especially among crews of the B-52s… High-ranking Defense Department sources say the morale situation at Guam has been poor for some time… The morale problem at U Tapao Air Base in Thailand is also growing worse daily.[54]

In December 1972 Washington began the round the clock, 24 hour 'Christmas bombing' of Hanoi and Haiphong by 200 B-52s. The

Chinese had assured the US there would be no retaliation. But in Thailand on 18 December Phantom fighter pilot Captain Dwight Evans refused to fly over North Vietnam. Captain Michael Heck refused to fly his B-52 on 26 December. He had flown over 200 combat missions, but he felt 'a man has to answer to himself first.'

The Vietnamese claimed they shot down 34 B-52s over Christmas. The Pentagon admitted 15 in public and more in private. The Air Force could not stand the losses.[55] Finally Washington folded and signed a peace deal in Paris in January 1973 agreeing to withdraw the last American soldiers from Vietnam. Although the US government refused to have a coalition government in South Vietnam, there would be a ceasefire. Both the Southern government and the guerrillas would hold what land they now controlled. North Vietnamese units would remain in the South, but the North Vietnamese government would hold back and not overthrow the Southern government. In return the Americans would give the North Vietnamese massive aid—$5 billion. American advisers and spies, but not soldiers, could remain in the South, and American aid to the Southern regime would continue. The American government would stop bombing North Vietnam, but could continue bombing South Vietnam, Cambodia and Laos.

The last American troops left. The peace held for a time, but few people expected it to hold forever. Everybody knew it was a victory for the Communists and a defeat for the American government. Almost everybody was surprised the Southern government lasted for two years afterwards. It lasted because the North Vietnamese government tried to observe the treaty and hold back its people. Perhaps it feared American bombing and perhaps it expected American aid. It was also under pressure from its Chinese allies, who wanted the peace deal to hold.

But President Thieu in South Vietnam knew he could not live with peace. He signed the peace agreement under American pressure, but the next day he announced that 'if Communists come into your village, you should immediately shoot them in the head'. And if anybody begins 'talking in a Communist tone', he said, kill them 'immediately'.[56]

Hanoi urged the guerrillas in the South to observe the cease-fire. But their leaders remembered how Diem had slaughtered them after the 1954 peace deal in Geneva. They stood their ground and fought Thieu.

The Americans refused to pay North Vietnam the $5 billion they had promised. The leaders in Hanoi seem to have been surprised.

In Saigon the economy was collapsing, as American aid was cut, and GIs and their dollars left. Unemployment rose and people grew increasingly desperate in the cities.

Hanoi had tried to observe the peace agreement. But the American ruling class simply wanted out and did not expect the deal to last. If they had, they would have supplied far more aid. Richard Nixon, the president, became increasingly isolated as the only important politician committed to President Thieu. Congress threatened to cut off all American aid to South Vietnam. Nixon was removed in the Watergate scandal, in part because of his continued support for Thieu. A new president, Gerald Ford, took his place.

In March 1975, the North Vietnamese army launched minor offensives north and west of Hue. President Thieu, his forces spread too thin, ordered them to pull back to Hue. As the retreat began, his army fell apart.

It was a conscript army. Seventeen percent of adult men in South Vietnam were in the army. They did not want to fight, and most of them had their families with them. As the retreat began, they left their units to look after their families. The army did not go over to the Communists. It collapsed and fled in fear, and suddenly the roads were clogged by an army of refugees.

In the end there was no final battle for South Vietnam. The soldiers, the uncommitted people in the South, looked at the Southern regime and said, 'They cannot support us. They are morally bankrupt. We will not die for them.'

Hue fell quickly, and the refugees, the landlords, the soldiers and their families, the urban supporters of the regime, headed for Danang. The Americans were frantically evacuating the consular, AID and CIA people the Paris peace deal had allowed them to keep in the country. An American on the last helicopter out of Nha Trang told a friend:

> As the pilot throttled the motors and prepared to pull off, an old Vietnamese man with a baby in his arms hobbled out of the crowd at the edge of the pad and lifted the child up toward the cabin, beseeching the Americans to take it aboard… [An American] moved to the edge of the open hatch and smashed the old man full in the face with the heel of his boot. The baby dropped to the ground, and almost at the same instant the chopper…soared skyward.[57]

When Hue fell there were 2 million refugees in Danang. There were

270 soldiers, two women, one child and a few Americans on the last plane out of Danang. An American reporter on the planes said that 'scores of people clung to the wings and the landing gear as the plane took off, and many were crushed under the wheels. Others fell off after it was airborne, and several bodies were later found mashed in the wheel wells themselves. The center aisle in the cabin glistened with blood'.[58]

Commercial and naval boats tried to evacuate the refugees from Danang. One CIA man made it out to the *Pioneer Contender*. He found:

> ...over 1,500 South Vietnamese troops were sprawled, lounging, fighting among themselves on the main decks and the bridge, and *practicing their aim* at the hapless Vietnamese civilians in their midst. Less than thirty yards away an ARVN trooper was in the process of raping a Vietnamese woman while another soldier held her male companion at gunpoint.[59]

The CIA man helped escaping refugees clamber onto the ship. More than 1,000 people from different small boats fell into the sea and drowned as they came aboard. In smaller boats refugees stood packed so tight that the living held the dead upright. One government soldier from Beautiful Waters was among them. He saw the other soldiers fight with guns and grenades in the surf to get to the boats ahead of each other, and the water ran red.

The soldiers were terrified of what would happen to them and their families. They expected the Communists would return the cruelty that had been done to them.

They did not. On 24 March 1975, as the Southern army disintegrated and the Northern tanks rolled on towards Saigon, the guerrillas walked openly on the paths of Beautiful Waters. They chatted with other villagers and told jokes, and they waved at the soldiers of the Southern government as they retreated in trucks down Highway One. A handmade cardboard sign on the road said, 'Victory without bloodshed'. An old peasant, a former Viet Minh, said in happiness, 'We have fought for 20 years, and our fight will end in a few days'.[60]

Three movements had defeated the American ruling class—the American peace movement, the GIs' revolt and the peasant guerrillas. The greatest of these was the peasant revolt. Hundreds of thousands of Communists and guerrillas had given their lives, and millions of peasants had died because they would not or could not leave their homes. Tens of millions had grieved for them. The Vietnam War is a history of horror, of rape and atrocity. But it is also a story of unimaginable, endless courage, of what men and women and children were capable of when they fought for a fair share of the rice they grew—and a world run by decency.

Chapter 6

# Vietnam and Cambodia
# after the war

In the spring of 1975 Communists took power in South Vietnam, Cambodia and Laos. All of Indochina, finally, was Communist. The American War was over. For the moment South Vietnam remained a formally separate state, but it was led by Communists and the leaders in Hanoi were the real power. Their mood that summer was quietly ecstatic. At the foreign ministry Indian journalist Nayan Chanda listened to a happy official recite a poem written when Chinese invaders were defeated 200 years before:

> There are no more sharks in the sea,
> There are no more beasts on earth,
> The sky is serene,
> Time now to build peace for ten thousand years.[1]

It didn't work out that way. The problem was rice. Before the war North Vietnam had been developing along a state capitalist model, following the example of Russia and China. But North Vietnam was poor—in 1954 roughly four working adults in 1,000 were in industry. Development had to start from the control of rice. In the late 1950s the government in North Vietnam persuaded most peasants into cooperatives. The state then took part of the rice in taxes, and took more through compulsory state purchases at very low prices. It is hard to find statistics for the exact amount taken. But one study of a village in the North found that during the American War roughly 30 percent of the crop went to the state. By contrast, a 1988 law promised peasants that the state would take no more than 60 percent of the crop. So we can assume a tax of 30 to 60 percent, but closer to 30 in the early years. In effect, the state had become the landlord.

In the cities the North Vietnamese government squeezed the workers. State employees, including workers in modern industry, saw their real wages fall by 25 percent. At the same time 25 percent of domestic product was being invested in industry, a very high rate, and the number of industrial workers grew to three people in 100. In other words, out of every 100 bowls of rice the peasants produced, 25 went to buying machinery abroad, and to building factories and machines, while three went to industrial workers.

The peasants' rice and the workers' labor were building an industrial economy. The war with America threw that out of kilter. North Vietnamese industry was dispersed to the countryside, and half of it was destroyed in the bombing. Russian arms and Chinese rice kept the Northern economy going during the war.

American money kept South Vietnam fed. But the war in the South forced the majority of Southern peasants to flee the countryside. By 1975, 74 percent of people in the South were living in towns, cities or refugee camps. Saigon had grown from 300,000 to 2 million people (the name was changed to Ho Chi Minh City in 1975, but most Vietnamese still call it Saigon).

With peace in 1975, the new government had to feed the cities of the North and South, and foreign aid was suddenly a problem. The North Vietnamese government was expecting massive aid from the US. Two years before Washington had promised to pay Hanoi $5 billion in reparations as part of the Paris peace agreements. But under presidents Nixon, Ford, Carter, Reagan, Bush and Clinton they refused to pay it. Hanoi had been counting on that money, but the US ruling class was not about to forgive its defeat. They punished Vietnam for 20 years, cutting off all aid and trade.

Where the American government led, the IMF and the World Bank followed. Where they led, most of the world's big banks followed. Vietnam attracted almost no Western or Japanese investment until 1990. During those years there was a boom in southeast Asia, based on foreign investment and production for export. Vietnam was shut out.

Chinese aid was suddenly a problem too. Since 1960 the Communists in Hanoi had been caught up in the larger rivalry between Russia and China.

The causes of this great power rivalry are complex. The Russian ruling class had treated China like another satellite economy to be exploited. Moreover, industrialization and class struggle were moving at different paces in the two countries. In Russia the economy and military capability had partly caught up with the West in the breakneck exploitation of the Stalin years. From 1953 onwards the rulers of Russia were trying to relax the brutal regime of prison camps. A more developed economy needed incentives, not slave labor. And they had seen most of the other bureaucrats of their generation packed off to those camps.

While the Russian leaders were trying to ease up on repression in the 1950s, the Chinese leaders were engaged in breakneck exploitation of their people. In China these were the years of forced industrialization in the 'Great Leap Forward', which led to a famine that killed 20 million. Any attempt to relax repression in China would open the floodgates of anger from below. So the Chinese rulers could not follow the Russian lead. Moreover, the Russian leaders were talking about 'peaceful coexistence' with the US. The Chinese leaders could see that the US government was still implacably opposed to them. So peaceful coexistence looked like a bloc between Russia and America directed at China.

In this context, China and Russia began to compete for leadership of the world Communist movement, and in the mid-1960s it seemed possible they would go to war along their long border. This was an enormous headache for the Vietnamese Communists. They needed the support of both Russia and China.

For much of the war they got it. Precisely because Russia and China were competing for leadership of the world's Communist states and parties, they had to be seen to be supporting the Vietnamese. After all, Vietnam was *the place* in the world where Communists were fighting American imperialism.

So the Vietnamese tried carefully to be neutral in the split between Russia and China. In this they largely succeeded. Both Russia and China aided Vietnam despite repeated squabbles over delays and looting on trains carrying Russian arms to Vietnam.

In 1972 this began to change. The Chinese ruling class had weathered the upheavals of the Cultural Revolution in the 1960s, and was now more firmly in control. They were beginning a turn towards market capitalism when President Richard Nixon approached them for an alliance that would help him to get out of Vietnam. The Chinese ruling class saw the possibility of an alliance with America against Russia, and they took it.

After the Communist victory in Vietnam in 1975, the Chinese leadership no longer needed to be seen to be supporting the Vietnamese.

With the war over Vietnam no longer made a difference in the international Communist movement. Neither Moscow nor Beijing any longer needed to be seen to be Vietnam's big brother.

So the Chinese government insisted on Vietnam taking its side, and the Vietnamese government refused. From 1972 onwards the Chinese had been worrying about a strong Vietnam, allied to Russia, on their southern flank. To cement their alliance with the US, and to keep Vietnam weak, they had urged the Vietnamese Communists to observe the Paris peace agreement and leave South Vietnam as a separate state. When Saigon fell in 1975 they were angry. The French diplomat François Missoffe reported from Beijing in early 1976, 'It does not matter whether there are two or three Vietnams, the Chinese say, but that there should never be one'.[2] When the Communists merged North and South Vietnam into one state in 1976, the Chinese leaders were furious.

China cut rice aid in 1976 and ended it completely in 1978. At the same time Russian aid was cut from $350 million to $200 million. Most Russian aid had been gifts. Now it was loans.[3]

The Vietnamese government faced a rice crisis. It had to feed the cities. The obvious solution, in its terms, was to get the peasants in the Mekong Delta in the south into cooperatives like the peasants in the north. The Mekong Delta had 48 percent of the rice fields in Vietnam.[4] The land was good and the Mekong had always been the rice basket of Vietnam. However, there was a problem.

In 1975 Saigon fell to North Vietnamese tanks and regular army troops, not the Viet Cong. The Southern resistance had been shattered after the Tet Offensive, so power now lay with Hanoi and the party leaders. But the Southern villages were still full of people who had fought on their own land for 20 years. Where they had not shared out the land before, they shared it out in 1975. According to one set of figures, 70 percent of the peasants now controlled 80 percent of the land. They knew about the taxes and cheap rice sales in the north. They did not want the cooperatives, and they would fight if they had to.

The government's first tactic was to try to win control of the rice trade by attacking the big Chinese capitalists in Cholon, Saigon's Chinatown. These big traders bought the rice from the smaller traders, who bought it from the peasants in the Mekong Delta. So in 1978 the government took over the big trading companies in Cholon. But the big traders had already signed over their trading networks on paper to relatives and small traders. The peasants continued to sell to any traders who came to the villages rather than to the government at low prices.

The peasants refused to form cooperatives despite the party's efforts. In Binh My village, near Saigon, the party cadres bullied people relentlessly. They went to some people's houses 20 times, one cadre said, so many times that the household dogs came to know them and stopped barking.[5]

There, around Saigon and Hue, the cadres had some success. But they found it much harder in the Mekong Delta. Ben Tre province is a good example. Way back in 1960 Ben Tre city had risen in a great unarmed insurrection against the Southern government. During Tet in 1968 the Viet Cong was so strong there that American bombers flattened the city. A decade later, in 1979, the new Communist government opened a model cooperative in Ben Tre province to encourage the peasants to join up. The peasants burned it down.[6]

By 1984, nine years after the end of the war, only 25 percent of the villages in the Delta were organized into cooperatives, and many of these were on paper only.[7] In 1987 the government admitted defeat. It announced that the drive for cooperatives was over because almost every village in the Mekong had joined up. They had joined what the Vietnamese called 'ghost cooperatives'.[8]

Nor did the state ever gain control of the trade in rice. Private traders continued to buy and sell almost all the rice in the delta and much of it in the rest of the country.[9]

The rice in the Mekong Delta was the central surplus in the Vietnamese economy. The government's failure to control that rice meant that state capitalism, the strategy of squeezing the workers and peasants to develop state industry, would not now work in Vietnam.

That failure was a victory for the peasants of the Mekong. They had defeated the French, the Americans and the Saigon government. Now they had stopped their leaders.

The government's first reaction was to try to squeeze more out of the cooperatives in the north. But the Red River Delta had less than half the land of the Mekong, more thickly settled and less fertile. The Northern peasants had been willing to make sacrifices during the war, when their sons were fighting and their homes were being bombed. With peace they expected to pay less, not more. They began to plant only enough to feed themselves, because the rest would all go to the government.

The peasants would not let the state have enough rice. Washington was shutting Vietnam out of world trade and China was refusing rice. The leaders in Hanoi felt they could not survive without more Russian aid. To obtain that they signed a mutual defense treaty with Russia late in 1978, and that pushed them into war with Cambodia and China.

# Cambodia

We have to double back now to what had been happening in Cambodia. The history of Vietnam after 1975 is very much bound up with Cambodia—the Cambodian tragedy was the last act and the worst consequence of the American War.

Everybody who writes about the killing fields in Cambodia between 1975 and 1978 speaks of madness. But just as with insane human beings, if you sit and listen to their story you can often understand them. So it is with the insanity of nations. Each insanity has its logic and its history. The leaders of Cambodian Communism may have been insane, or maybe not. But tens of thousands of Cambodians did their killing for them. Millions of Cambodian peasants supported their terror in the beginning. To understand why a whole society seems to go insane you have to understand the logic and the history, for madness has its roots in suffering.

Until 1970 Cambodia had been ruled by King Sihanouk, who tried to balance his interests between North Vietnam and America. The Viet Cong had bases on the Cambodian side of the border. The Cambodian Communists were called the Khmer Rouge—the Red Cambodians (Khmer is the word Cambodians use for themselves). They had bases in the jungle, and some support. King Sihanouk quietly allowed the Americans to bomb Communist bases on his territory.

In 1970 General Lon Nol deposed Sihanouk in a coup. Lon Nol took Cambodia into open alliance with the United States. Sihanouk went into exile in China and formed an alliance with the Khmer Rouge. Now both radicals and traditionalists in the countryside opposed Lon Nol's government. That is one reason President Nixon sent the American troops into Cambodia in 1970, but the protests at home forced Nixon to call the troops back. The only thing the American government could do to support Lon Nol was to step up the bombing of Cambodian villages that supported the Khmer Rouge.

Then came the Paris peace agreement in January 1973. This provided for an uneasy truce in both South Vietnam and Cambodia. The Khmer Rouge refused to abide by the truce. With the last American troops withdrawn from neighboring South Vietnam, they could see the writing on the wall. Lon Nol was weaker now. They had far more support in the countryside.

The North Vietnamese Communists told the Cambodian Communists not to fight. The fall of Phnom Penh, the Cambodian capital, would destabilize the whole Paris peace agreement. The Khmer Rouge ignored their Vietnamese comrades.

Now the only power that could stop the Khmer Rouge was American bombers. Lon Nol had an army that would not fight for him. In most places his government did not even have spotters, so the Americans just bombed, in B-52 raid after B-52 raid. The ground shook and the sky burned. In six months in 1973 they dropped one and a half times the tonnage of all the bombs dropped on Japan in the whole of World War Two. Cambodia was a small country, with 4 or 5 million people. The bombing affected most rural areas, because most of the countryside supported the Khmer Rouge.

Several hundred thousand people died in those six months, perhaps a tenth of the population, perhaps more. No country before or since has been subjected to bombing of that scale and intensity. And B-52 raids are terrifying.[10]

That suffering does not completely explain what happened afterward, but nothing of what happened afterward can be understood without knowledge of that suffering.

The bombing worked. The Khmer Rouge halted their advance. The bombing had been so fierce because Lon Nol and the Americans were so weak on the ground. Now it continued, not as fiercely but still on a larger scale than Vietnam had seen. And while the Vietnamese peasants had a way of understanding the bombing—it had grown out of years of their struggle, and it was a response by the oppressor to that struggle—for the Cambodians it was cataclysmic, senseless, the modern industrial world exploding onto them.

That bombing lasted until the end of the war in 1975. What the Cambodian peasants learned was that the Lon Nol regime and its middle class supporters in the cities were prepared to support anything the Americans did to them—anything.

The leadership of the Khmer Rouge decided that cities and all the people in them were the problem. They also decided they had to stand alone. When the Vietnamese Communists had made peace with the French in 1954 they had agreed to a separate South Vietnam, and told the Khmer Communists and nationalists to stop fighting. Just as the South Vietnamese Communists had to go North in 1954, so did most of the Cambodian Communist leaders. In 1961 a new leadership in Cambodia had launched a guerrilla war against Sihanouk, like the Viet Cong rebellion in South Vietnam. That time the Vietnamese Communists had urged them not to overthrow Sihanouk, whose neutrality Hanoi valued. Now, in 1973, the leaders of the Khmer Rouge interpreted the American bombing as a punishment because this time they had disobeyed Hanoi's orders not to fight.[11]

The leadership and the peasants had learned that the problem was the cities. The leadership had learned to beware of Vietnamese betrayal.

Then, in 1975, President Nixon was removed from office in the Watergate scandal. The US Congress was about to cut off all funds being used to fight in southeast Asia. The army of the Saigon regime began to melt, and the Khmer Rouge saw their chance. They took Phnom Penh, with almost no opposition.

The advancing Khmer Rouge fighters were now overwhelmingly peasants, mostly young people who had grown up under the bombs. When they took the city of Battambang they went to the airfield and destroyed those bombers.

Lon Nol's police, army officers and pilots were ordered to report to staging areas. They did so and were killed immediately. The leadership of the Khmer Rouge gave orders to send all the other city people to the countryside.

The people sent to the villages were 30 percent of Cambodians. They were now called the 'new people' in the villages. The peasants who had supported the Khmer Rouge were the 'old people'. The new people were expected to settle in the villages and work under the tutelage of the old people.

Most of the old people supported this policy. Kem Hong Hav was deported to Kong Pisei in the southwest. There:

> ...the real poor people liked the Khmer Rouge. They were not so intelligent, and happy to eat equally with the educated and rich people with whom they were angry. They liked the system and they really hated the Phnom Penh people, because we had not struggled for the revolution and equality alongside the Khmer Rouge.

You can hear an educated man's contempt for the peasants in that quote. But Kem Hong Hav also made it clear to the historian who interviewed him that the Khmer Rouge had no troops in that village. The village chief and the old people 'were the Khmer Rouge':

> Just as before, the base people [the old people] worked hard, in front of us, as models for the new people. They did not stop for wind or rain. They worked harder than us, on behalf of Angkar [the Communist Party]. For us, who were not yet tempered, it was hard. We were angry but dared not say so... The [most] ignorant ones had abandoned all their property and worked for Angkar; they had really forgotten the past, and were enthusiastic.[12]

Srey Pich Chnay, a student of fine arts in Phnom Penh, was sent to a village in the southwest. The peasants there told him: 'You used to be happy and prosperous. Now it's our turn'.[13]

The peasant hatred of the bombers lay behind the new regime in the village. When the war ended in 1975, the Khmer Rouge had already brought the peasants in most villages into collectives. Work was done together, in small teams, and the rice harvest was shared. Taxation was light.

It did not remain light. The leaders of the Khmer Rouge wanted a state capitalist development of Cambodia. This was the politics they had learned from Stalin in Russia, from Mao and the Chinese Communists, and from the Vietnamese. At the heart of this state capitalist politics, I have argued above, was the squeezing of peasants and workers to build a strong economy quickly. This required a police state—only a dictatorship can make the peasants give up their crops, and break workers' strikes.

But Cambodia was an underdeveloped country, with little industry, even compared to Vietnam, much less Russia or China. The people were not hungry. The land was lightly populated, with lakes and rivers full of fish. But industrial development would be a long, hard road. And Cambodia had far fewer people than neighboring Thailand and Vietnam. Moreover, the Khmer Rouge, and particularly their leader Pol Pot, distrusted the cities. Any forced development would be rural, on the backs of the peasantry.

Pol Pot and the Khmer Rouge leadership were trying to build state capitalism in the hardest possible circumstances. That meant working the peasants hard and policing them hard. There were precedents for such forced development. One was Stalin's terror in the

1930s. Another was the Great Leap Forward in China in 1958. That leap was fueled by the peasants' rice and work. It led almost immediately to famine. Nobody knows how many people died, but it was millions. The Chinese government then backed off. Pol Pot and his people sometimes spoke of their project as another Great Leap Forward. It was to have similar results.

What I am arguing here is that the killing fields of Cambodia have to be understood as a result of a state capitalist economy. This does not mean that state capitalism always causes such horror. After all, Nazi Germany in the 1930s, Sweden in the 1960s and the US in the 1980s were all private capitalist societies. But they differed enormously in the levels of repression and suffering. By the same token, Vietnam and Cambodia were very different places in 1978. But Nazi Germany can be understood as the madness of businessmen threatened by economic collapse, external enemies and the possibility of workers' revolution. Pol Pot's regime makes sense as a result of one way of trying to build state capitalism without industry.

Pol Pot and the Khmer Rouge leaders could not leap into an industrialized future. Given what modern American airplanes had done to them, they no longer wanted to. Yet Pol Pot was a nationalist. His vision was of a great agricultural country, harking back to a fantasy of a once great medieval Khmer Empire at Angkor Wat. The peasants would live in collectives, sharing small and equal rations of rice. Many of the new people from the city would be sent to work camps to build the great irrigation works Pol Pot thought were the glory of the old Khmer Empire. Symbolically, the name of the country was changed to Kampuchea, the land of the Khmers.

And much of the rice would go to the capital. Phnom Penh was almost empty. There were 20,000 civilians, many of them peasant girls of 12 and 14 who replaced the former workers in the factories. There were 20,000 soldiers. And there were Pol Pot and the leadership of the party, because this was still a dictatorship of the city over the country. The rank and file of the Khmer Rouge were peasants. The leadership came from the educated middle classes and the fringes of the ruling class in the city.

An awful lot of rice went to the capital. In 1977 the central government plan, for instance, provided for more than half of the expected crop in the southwest to be sent to the center. The same plan allocated none of the expected harvest in the northwest to the people there. It is not clear what they were expected to eat—probably nothing. The northwest was full of new people and more rebellious than the southwest.

It is unlikely that the government managed to actually corner all the rice in this way. But from the beginning there was hunger in most of the collectives. Where did the truckloads of rice that left the villages go?

Some of it probably went to China (the evidence is not conclusive).[14] The Chinese government was Pol Pot's one ally. It gave guns, planes, trucks, technicians, military advisors and diplomatic support. In return Cambodia was China's one ally in the region against Russia and Vietnam.

Wherever the rice went, the fact was it was gone, and yet the Khmer Rouge leadership kept squeezing the villages for rice. This was what produced the horror. The process moved at different paces in different places. It had a lot to do with the local leadership—some were kind and tried to protect the people under them. Some villages and regions were already hungry in 1975, and some not until 1978.

But everywhere the process went like this. There was not enough rice. In some places the new people, the city evacuees, got the same ration as the old people, in some places less. But with less and less rice, the old people were tempted to keep more for themselves. In three years about half of the new people died, in roughly equal numbers from starvation, disease and executions. Disease was caused by malnutrition and by overwork, because sick people who did not work did not eat.

This was a man-made famine (like all famines). In most places the dead were buried, but when there were too many they were left in the fields or thrown in the rivers. Seng Horl, a teacher sent to the southwest, said that famine killed 400 of the 1,100 people in his village in November and December 1976: 'There was not enough ground to bury people. Bodies piled up.' In Chen Leng's new village in the northwest rations fell to half a can of cooked rice a day in 1977, with 'less for children, and sometimes nothing for three days. People ate lizards and geckoes... Even some of the gravediggers died on the job.' In that village, as in much of Cambodia, all the women stopped menstruating.[15]

The less rice there was, the harder people were forced to work. They worked into the night. In certain lucky places there was one day off in ten for political education. Fishing and foraging were forbidden.

Tam Eng, an ethnic Chinese tailor in Phnom Penh, took her children to her Cambodian ex-husband's village in the south. They were sent to live in a special new village for Chinese people:

> We were not allowed to eat our own eggs. If my children were caught fishing or foraging at lunchtime, they were given planting to do before being allowed home again. And if they came back for work late, the… chief would complain, and they would disappear.

Eng saw one boy caught planting potatoes 'killed on the spot'.[16]

This seems insane, and so it seemed to the peasants. People complained to each other. The Khmer Rouge understood that in muttering lies the possibility of revolt. Seng was an 'old' person, a Khmer Rouge supporter and a teacher in the southwest. In his village:

> …the problems began in 1975… The work was demanding, and food inadequate. In some places it ran out, and people starved or swelled up… From early 1976, if you said the food was not tasty, or if you stole corn, you would be killed.[17]

This was everywhere. And the more people died or were killed, the more hatred people felt. They would not look the Khmer Rouge cadres in the eye—that might get them killed. But the cadres could still imagine what the people with downcast faces were thinking.

Many of the new people from the cities had relatives among the 'old' villagers. After all, the new people were 30 percent of Cambodia. Many of them had found their way to the villages their families originally came from. The regime understood quite quickly that the old villagers would grieve for their 'new' kin. So these old villagers were reclassified into reliable old villagers, and 'candidates'—those old villagers with kin among the new people. And as the candidates were killed or starved, and as the old people who spoke back or looked wrong were killed, the regime knew its enemies were multiplying.

Sen Osman said that in Takeo village from early 1977 there was 'a search for internal enemies and agents—enemies in words, enemies at work, inactive [people]… So if you said something a little wrong like "We are all tired," they would take you away and kill you'.[18]

As one of the Cham ethnic minority, Sen Osman was particularly vulnerable. Pol Pot's government began as extreme nationalists and therefore racists. Ethnic minorities were treated harshly from the beginning. Minority people who had supported the Khmer Rouge were still treated like Lon Nol's city people.

But as the regime found itself more and more unpopular, it began to look harder for ethnic enemies. There were several reasons for this. It knew it had enemies, but could not fully accept that its own people hated it, so it looked for foreign enemies and traitors. It was already nationalist, and an ethnic nationalism always carries with it a racism towards those not truly of the nation. And the regime thought that racism might unite the Khmers, who seemed to be dividing against it.

The regime was racist from the beginning. This made genocide possible. It is not clear whether it intended genocide from the beginning. What is clear is that mass ethnic killing escalated as the regime came under pressure from below.

The Chams, for instance, were Muslims, and therefore suspect as religious believers. From the beginning they were killed if they refused to eat pork. In some places pork was served twice a month to test the Chams, even when there was little other food. In places where there was no pork, they were simply asked if they would eat pork and killed if they said no.

Tep Ibrahim, a Cham, was exiled to the north. In 1977 the Chams in his village were told that Malaysia was sending gasoline to ransom them because they were fellow Muslims. Tep Ibrahim, like the others, was happy to go. But he was late when they loaded the trucks with Chams. He ran after the truck but could not catch it. Of those who went in the trucks, he said:

> …there are none of us left… Two days after they had left, their scarves and shirts were brought back and distributed to children… They were taken and thrown [into pits], killed off.

Later he cut bananas near where the trucks had been taken, and 'the whole district was smelling' of bodies.[19]

The Vietnamese minority were particularly suspect. They were villagers along the Vietnamese border and immigrant workers in the cities. The Khmer Rouge leaders felt Hanoi had betrayed them many times, and that the Vietnamese were 'ancient enemies' of the Khmer Empire. They began killing some, but not all, Vietnamese in 1975. Four hundred thousand ethnic Vietnamese then managed to flee to Vietnam. Many ethnic Cambodians (Khmers) fled with them across the border to escape the hunger and repression. At this point Vietnam was still an ally of Cambodia. The Vietnamese government accepted the fleeing Vietnamese Cambodians. But the Vietnamese army forced the ethnic Khmers back across the border into Cambodia and almost certain death as enemies of the regime there.

The Khmer Rouge raided across the border, slaughtering whole Vietnamese villages. The Vietnamese authorities forbade Vietnamese journalists to publish the photographs of the dead and the tales of the survivors. They did not want to anger the Chinese government, the ally of the Khmer Rouge.

Tension still grew between Vietnam and Cambodia. As the hatred grew in the villages, the Khmer Rouge leadership looked for enemies. On 1 April 1977 the order went out from Phnom Penh to arrest 'all ethnic Vietnamese, and all Khmers who spoke Vietnamese or had Vietnamese friends'.[20] People who were arrested were not taken to prison. Genocide had begun.

Heng Chor was an ethnic Khmer in Pursat. There in March 1977 a 'Khmer Rouge cadre killed his former wife, who was of Vietnamese descent, along with five of his sons, three daughters, three grand-children, his mother-in-law, eight from his sister-in-law's family, [and] seven from his brother-in-law's family'.[21] The cadre may have been trying to protect himself from the regime. He was, after all, a man with Vietnamese friends and relatives.

The Khmer Krom were suspect too. They were the ethnic Khmer minority in Vietnam. Some Khmer Krom had also migrated back into Cambodia. They spoke Cambodian with a Vietnamese accent. Pol Pot said they had Khmer bodies but Vietnamese minds, and they too were killed. Several times Khmer Rouge units raided across the border into Vietnam, rounded up Khmer Krom villagers and took them back into Cambodia because that was their real home. Once there, though, they became the Vietnamese enemy and were killed.

But the more killing, the more hatred from below. Then the regime took the children. Those over three, or sometimes over five, were taken to special children's centers, where their parents could see them only rarely. Those of ten or so were taken to special children's work camps, and their parents could not see them at all. This policy was tried in a few places in 1975 but did not become general until 1977 and 1978. This one policy, more than all the hunger and all the killing, turned the reliable 'old' villagers against the Khmer Rouge.

Even as they took the peasants' children away, Pol Pot and the other leaders appointed more and more of their own relatives to leading positions. Their kin were now the only people they could trust.

The people the government feared most, and killed most, were the cadres of the Khmer Rouge. These cadres were revolutionaries. They had joined the struggle out of a desire for equality and social justice. And they were the only people who commanded organizations with guns.

In place after place the Khmer Rouge cadres saw what was happening and were sickened by what they were ordered to do. They were also terrified. But because they were almost all spread out in villages they found it difficult to combine, difficult even to know if cadres in other areas felt the same. To plot a rebellion, a cadre had to talk to a lot of people. One of them, out of loyalty or fear, usually informed the central government. Moreover, it was difficult for the Communists to turn against their party, to fully admit to themselves what was happening.

So the cadre turned at different times, at different speeds. As they did so, one after another was taken away 'for study'. The Khmer Rouge leadership were justifiably terrified, because they knew they were hated. But the general fear meant that the rulers could not know precisely who hated them. It became a race between the regime trying to break rebellion and cadres trying to nerve themselves to rebel.

The regime usually won the race. But they had to send specially picked cadres into the northwest to exterminate almost all the cadres there. In the east the Vietnamese border provided a haven, and thousands of cadres and tens of thousands of villagers fought their way to safety. After that the regime launched a pogrom of the eastern cadres who had remained loyal.

When people were arrested in Cambodia they were usually killed, not sent to prison. But the senior cadres of the Khmer Rouge were the exception. The government had to find out what they were doing. Like many other governments, what the Khmer Rouge leaders feared most was Communists. So when senior cadres were arrested they were taken to Tuol Sleng prison, a former girls' school in Phnom Penh, where they were tortured and forced to write long confessions. Of the 20,000 people who went into Tuol Sleng, seven survived. The regime was afraid the relatives of these prisoners might take revenge, so it also executed their husbands, wives and children, and sometimes their mothers.

By the end of 1978 Cambodia was full of bitterness. Many people were imagining rebellion. The regime was imploding. It reacted by escalating raids into Vietnam and pogroms against the Vietnamese in Cambodia. Pol Pot's hatred for the Vietnamese was sincere enough, but this policy was also calculated to bring a disintegrating country together under Khmer Rouge leadership.

It didn't work. In December 1978 the Vietnamese army invaded Cambodia. Both the Vietnamese leaders and the Khmer Rouge leaders expected stiff Cambodian resistance to the Vietnamese. It didn't happen. The highway to Phnom Penh lay open, and within a week the Vietnamese army was in the capital. The Khmer Rouge troops had not fought to defend the Khmer Rouge regime. The Vietnamese installed a new government headed by two former Khmer Rouge commanders who had rebelled and fled to Vietnam, Heng Samrin and Hun Sen. Pol Pot and the leadership fell back into the countryside, counting on a prolonged guerrilla war. In a matter of weeks they were driven back into small enclaves in remote areas on the Thai border. The Vietnamese were about to smash them when the Americans stepped in.

The American government and media publicized the crimes of the Khmer Rouge. Pictures of the mass graves and the piles of skulls went round the world, proof of the evils of Communism. At the same time the military dictatorship in Thailand, the Chinese Communists and Jimmy Carter all worked together. The Khmer Rouge were allowed to rest in Thailand and then go back across the border. Under cover of humanitarian aid to refugees, the American and Chinese governments supplied food, money and arms to the Khmer Rouge. Without this support the Khmer Rouge would have gone under. At the same time the United States led successful fights at the UN, year after year, to keep Cambodia's UN seat for Pol Pot.[22]

The Americans were supporting Pol Pot to punish the Vietnamese for winning the Vietnam War.

# War with China

While the American and Chinese governments began to rebuild Pol Pot's tattered forces in 1979, the Chinese army invaded Vietnam along the northern border. The intention was to teach Hanoi a lesson and force it to retreat from Cambodia. Vietnamese resistance was fierce and the Chinese army had to withdraw.

The victims of this war were the Chinese minority in Vietnam. Already in 1978, the year before, the 'boat people' had begun to flee

Vietnam. At first they were the Vietnamese of Chinese ancestry in the south—the many businessmen and even more workers who had lost their jobs when the state took over the Chinese businesses in Saigon. After the Chinese invasion in the north, the Vietnamese government began a propaganda attack on Chinese people. More of the Chinese in the south fled, and the Chinese in the north, mostly peasants and fishermen, fled too.

The majority of the refugees crossed the northern border into China. But in the south many left by small coastal boats. The local bureaucrats took their gold in bribes, and individual officials took over the houses of the rich as they left. Many boat people drowned in storms. Many who pushed ashore in Thailand or Malaysia were pushed out to sea again. Those who reached Hong Kong were put in detention camps by the British. At first the American government refused to take any boat people. Pirates, mostly local fishermen in Thailand and Indonesia, boarded many boats, robbed the people, killed some and raped many women.

Then economic crisis hit in 1979 and 1980. Now most of the boat people were ethnic Vietnamese.

The economic crisis hit for four reasons. First, American and Chinese aid dried up. Second, the American boycott isolated the Vietnamese economy. Third was the cost of the Cambodian war and a standing army of 1.5 million. Fourth was the refusal of the peasants to grow more grain for the state.

As the crisis hit in cooperative after cooperative across the north, the local authorities instituted various local contract systems that allowed families to farm more of the land, and keep and sell more of the rice they grew. In 1981 this was formalized at a national level. A new law allowed individual peasant families to in effect rent land on a long term basis. The peasants then worked harder and grew more rice because they could keep more of what they grew. For the moment famine was averted.

# The occupation of Cambodia

Back in Cambodia the Khmer Rouge, with American and Chinese support, were gradually rebuilding their strength in the jungle. King Sihanouk was in alliance with them again, and they were helped by the way the Vietnamese government behaved after the invasion. The

Vietnamese had received a wary welcome. Anybody was better than the Khmer Rouge, and if ever an invasion of another country was justified the Vietnamese invasion of Cambodia was. But it was not simply a humanitarian operation. Had it been, the Vietnamese army would simply have turned power over to the Cambodian opponents of Pol Pot and left. Instead it kept 300,000 troops in Cambodia for ten years. Cambodians headed the government but Vietnamese made policy. According to the French anthropologist Marie Martin:

> All officials had a Vietnamese superior in the hierarchy who super-vised a single person or an entire department. At the head of each ministry was a Cambodian minister and a 'Vietnamese minister,' as the Khmers called them...
>
> Cambodians who held high positions...unanimously stated that each text written by a Khmer had to be approved by the Vietnamese authority in the department before circulation. All administrative, political and economic decisions had to have at least the endorsement of the adviser and were usually dictated by him.[23]

A Cambodian civil servant put it this way: 'In the ministries [the Vietnamese] used to be called advisors. Now they are administrators, making all the decisions. People leave for that reason. Those who stay work with clenched teeth'.[24] The advisors and the soldiers ate the Cambodian rice. Trucks of rice went north and east to Vietnam.

This occupation corrupted Cambodia. Everything was for sale—free care in public hospitals, for instance, and education. By 1991 the bribe for admission to medical school was $7,500 in gold.[25]

In this situation Pol Pot's Khmer Rouge managed to survive in the forests and mountains of the west. They would not have done so without American and Chinese money and guns, and refuges in Thailand. But they also would not have lasted without the distaste many ordinary Cambodians felt for their new rulers. They could not take power, but they could harass the government and kill.

Roughly 50,000 Vietnamese soldiers were killed in Cambodia in the ten years after the invasion, and 200,000 were wounded. Many of the wounded stepped on land mines supplied by America to the Khmer Rouge, and limbs had to be amputated. Moreover, in the American War the children of top Communist cadres had gone south to fight. In the occupation of Cambodia the Vietnamese troops were the conscript children of poor people, particularly peasants from the south. And with them went other poor Vietnamese, until the majority of prostitutes in Phnom Penh were Vietnamese.[26]

Advisors, prostitutes, a draftee army of poor boys, corruption and 50,000 dead—it reminds you of the Americans in Vietnam. The cruelty was not on the same scale. It did not have to be. Pol Pot did not have the popular support the Viet Cong had in Vietnam. But it was another colonial situation.

Why? Vietnam took rice and got Russian aid. But this in no way made up for the cost of the war over ten years. Moreover, Vietnam had to maintain a standing army of 1.5 million with modern weapons, an enormous drain on a poor economy. The Vietnamese army were in Cambodia as proxies for the Russians, just as the Khmer Rouge had become proxies for the Chinese and Americans.

One thing showed this clearly. When the Russian dictatorship fell in 1989 and Russian aid was withdrawn from Vietnam, the Vietnamese government promptly pulled its troops out of Cambodia.

Suddenly Washington faced the possibility of an American-backed Khmer Rouge victory in Cambodia, which would be appallingly embarrassing. The United Nations intervened, with American sponsorship but no American troops. Its official mission was to hold Pol Pot back and restore democracy. It organized elections. The party led by King Sihanouk's son beat the ruling party led by Hun Sen. Hun Sen then annulled the elections, and the United Nations continued to support him. Sihanouk and his son, ever the opportunists, formed a coalition with Hun Sen. Hun Sen began learning English. The end result was that a corrupt client regime of the Vietnamese had become a corrupt client regime of the United Nations. The Chinese and Americans then cut off aid to the Khmer Rouge, and they gradually withered.

The UN spent $2 billion to do this. UN civilian workers in Cambodia had an extra daily hardship allowance of $130 a day, 195 times the 67 cents a day paid to Cambodian teachers and civil servants. Cambodians saw that legal UN corruption far outstripped illegal Cambodian corruption. They began to steal whatever they could, led by Hun Sen and his government. Martin writes: 'Khmer summarize the life-style of their rulers in a short sentence: three wives, three villas, three cars'.[27]

# Meanwhile in Vietnam

The Vietnamese had troubles of their own. The rice supply in Vietnam had increased after 1981. But that increase was a one-off. By 1983 farmers were already working as hard as they could. The government then began raising rents on land and lowering the price they paid peasants for grain. The peasants began to react as they had in the 1970s, by growing only enough rice to feed themselves.[28]

What did the continuing economic crisis mean for people's lives? Some important things did get better for a while after 1954. By 1983 infant mortality was a third what it had been in 1960, and life expectancy had increased from 42 to 59 years. But after 1978 the weight of newborn babies began to fall, and in 1987 the Ministry of Health estimated that half of children were suffering from malnutrition. The average height of adults was getting shorter, and the real wages of city workers were falling. State employees had always counted on rations of rice and other staples at very low prices, but by 1979 a month's ration lasted only a few days. In 1976 city people spent 70 percent of their income on food. By 1980 it was 80 percent.[29]

Bui Tin was a senior Communist Party member, an editor and veteran of the French and American wars. In 1990 he went into exile in France at the age of 63. He wrote that on his street in Hanoi:

> There is a worker over forty years old with four children, three boys and a girl. He had been laid off from a state-run factory, his wife is a street sweeper and he survives as best he can. He does a bit of building work, carpentry, repairing bicycles or tailoring. In winter he even makes Western 'NATO' jackets according to a pattern which emanates from Thailand. In the evenings too, he takes a young son along to set up a stall selling tea and cigarettes outside the district finance office where they collect lottery tickets...
>
> Meanwhile an old lady of over eighty hawks titbits to the children. Also down the street, a retired colonel who specialized in anti-aircraft warfare now sells yoghurt [on the street]. A more junior officer who made a name for himself in 1954 at the time of the battle for Dien Bien Phu by sabotaging French aircraft before they took off from the airfield near Hanoi, now makes a living by pumping up bicycle tires. His problem is that even his pump is old and requires frequent repairs...

Such people are intent on surviving all these hardships on their own. They are accustomed to electricity and water cuts as well as the stinking environment. They even cheer when the light comes back on. But what do they really feel inside about human fate?[30]

In 1988 Duong Thu Huong, a Communist Party member and veteran of the Chinese and American wars, wrote a novel attacking the rulers of her society. The heroine of *Paradise of the Blind* is a worker. Here she thinks about the smiling faces of Japanese tourists:

Hundreds of faces rose in my memory: those of my friend, people of my generation, faces gnawed with worry, shattered faces, twisted, ravaged, sooty, frantic faces.

Our faces were always taut, lean with fear. The fear that we might not be able to pay for food, or send it in time, the fear of learning that an aged father or mother had passed away while waiting for our miserable subsidies, the fear that some embassy official just might not...

We had daring, calculating faces: You had to think of everything, weigh everything. All the time.

You had to think to survive, to feed your loved ones, to hustle for a day's wages sharecropping or sweeping on a train. You had to think too of the life that stretched out ahead, the pain that still waited for you, of a future as unsure and unfathomable as sea fog...

[I] have the eyes of a wild animal, darting about, razor sharp, ready to quarrel over goods at a shop counter or scuffle in a line for food. And there was the shame, the self-loathing, in the mirror of another's gaze. Life as one endless humiliation.[31]

The rice was not coming in from the countryside, and in 1988 the prospect of famine loomed in the north. The state capitalist model of development was not working in Vietnam. Russia under Gorbachev and China under Deng were adopting the market. In 1989 Russian aid stopped. The Communist ruling class in Vietnam knew they had to do something different.

What? The only ideas on offer in the world in 1988 were the ideas of the market. They had swept the West, Japan, Russia and China. And in Vietnam village after village and factory after factory had made unofficial free market deals that seemed to offer the only way to keep the enterprise going. There was a sort of creeping free market at the base of society—the Vietnamese called it 'fence breaking'.[32] And in 1988 the rulers at the top formally adopted Doi Moi, the 'New Change'. They hoped the market would solve their problems.

For the villagers, this meant that land was shared out. Each family got one share of the village land for each person in the family. In the cities the factories were *not* shared out. Instead foreign investment was welcomed. By one means or another state managers turned their enterprises into private companies owned by themselves. The government looked to the International Monetary Fund and the World Bank to tell it how to run the economy.

The new strategy was to make Vietnam a low wage economy exporting cheap goods. The model was the other southeast Asian economies, particularly Thailand, Indonesia and Malaysia.[33] Vietnam had the poorest people in southeast Asia. The government tried to attract foreign investment by promising its people would work harder, for less, for longer hours in less safe conditions than any workforce in southeast Asia. But trying to undercut Indonesian workers, for instance, meant squeezing labor very hard indeed.

The government also gave up trying to control the peasants' rice. Now private traders, with government support, bought the rice cheaply and exported much of it to China. Vietnamese still ate an average of just over 2,000 calories a day—not enough—but Vietnam became the third largest exporter of rice in the world.

In the countryside peasants could now sell land.[34] By 1990 official figures estimated that half the peasants were already in debt. Those who got too far in debt had to sell land. By 1993 the Vietnamese economist Dang Phong wrote that 'concentration of land is occurring quite strongly in the southern provinces and some central provinces'.[35] The new rich in the villages were mostly the old administrators of the cooperatives. When the land was shared out they took more than their share. As one villager said, the authorities could not stop this corruption. What could they do—'arrest themselves?'[36] And when the other villagers went too heavily into debt, these new rich were the people who could buy them out. In Vinh Hung district in the Plain of Reeds (the marshes south of Saigon) in 1993, while the district vice-president 'is kept busy with his work in the district, his wife runs the family business. In addition to their 100 hectares of land, they own a tractor and thresher, a pump, a petrol station which serves the entire area, and a truck'.[37]

This one family had 100 hectares while the average family farmed one hectare. This is an extreme example, but the same thing was happening all over the country, particularly in the south. And of course the only way such a rich household could farm the land was to rent to the newly landless or hire them as laborers.

A similar process was happening in the cities. The ministries, the army and the old factory managers now ran their own businesses. There was a complex mixture of state companies, private companies in partnership with state companies, and private companies paying state officials large bribes to get around the regulations those same state officials had constructed. The opportunities for profit, bribes and stealing were enormous. The old Communist cadre split in two. The majority became poorly paid minor officials or unemployed ex-officials. Now they took small bribes or made out the best they could with bicycle pumps. Their old ideals had been betrayed from the top, and now they had to betray those ideals to feed their families. They became empty men and women, hollowed out by corruption, ashamed and angry.

A minority of the officials became a new rich class of combined state-private capitalists. (They were more private than state—by 1997 private capitalist Malaysia had more of the economy in public ownership than Vietnam.) The Communists had always said they were servants of the people. Now the people sang a little verse about their 'servants':

> The servant travels in a Volga [car],
> The families of the masters wait at the station for a train.
> The servant has a nice villa,
> The families of the masters use oil paper to keep out the rain.
> The servant attends banquets, noon and night,
> The families of the masters eat greens and pickles every day.[38]

At the end of the American War Vietnam had been a poor country but a relatively equal one. There were rich and poor, but the gap was nothing like that in Indonesia or the US, and the village cooperatives and city workplaces provided free education and medical care. After 1988 people had to pay for medicine and schooling. They took sick children to the doctor less often and took more children out of school. Rationing had made sure that everybody got some food. Now that has largely gone.

An unequal society is unequal in every respect. One window on that inequality is what happens to women. The Danish anthropologist

Tine Gammeltoft did a study of IUD (birth control coil) use by women in one village in the Red River Delta near Hanoi in 1993-94.[39]

The population of Vietnam doubled between 1975 and 1994, and the government promoted birth control. The women of this village supported the campaign. They had to bear the children. Since the village cooperative had been divided, men looked for work outside the village while women did most of the farming, bending over or squatting all day long. Family incomes had risen because women worked harder. But their backs ached from work and their heads ached from worry. There was never enough money, and women worried about food for the children. The worry and the pain kept them awake at night. As one woman said, 'I often have headaches because of thinking a lot. When I don't think, there is no problem'.[40]

Another woman said, 'You go to work, come home tired in the evening, the children are a nuisance, the pig screams, you have to cook food for it. You go to sleep, already exhausted, so tired, the child has to be breastfed all night, the husband demands [sex]'.[41]

If the woman doesn't give the husband sex, they may fight. If she does, she often resents it. One woman put it this way: 'Women can't bear having a lot of sex. It makes you feel tired and worn out like a boiled vegetable.'

The women used birth control. Until the mid-1980s they had a choice of the pill, the condom or the coil. Most Vietnamese used the condom. But then the government decided that the health system would only supply the coil. Foreign exchange was short and a coil was cheaper. Moreover, women controlled their use of the pill and men controlled condoms. The state, through the nurses who put in the coils, controlled the coil.

So women used the coil. In America and Europe a large minority of women who use the coil have unbearable pain. Sometimes they put up with it, but usually they stop eventually. Three things are likely to increase pain with the coil—back pain, poor nutrition and anemia. The women in this Vietnamese village had all three. But the coil was their only choice, so they used it.

Some were all right on the coil but the majority were not. It hurt their bellies. It made their periods longer, so they bled more and became weaker and more anemic. It gave them headaches, and they lay awake at night, their muscles in pain, their backs in pain, their wombs in pain, worrying about their children and their husband's anger.

They endured, because they had few choices.

The women in this village were part of a far larger system. During the wars against the Americans and the French the government had encouraged women's rights because it wanted to mobilize women, wanted them to fight passionately for the cause. Now, as the whole society grew more unequal, the government cared less.

And many of the old ways linger. In the villages childless women still fear their husbands taking a second wife. Prostitution has not gone away either. In Saigon the government effectively encourages it as part of the tourist trade. During the American War the Rex Hotel in Saigon was famous among Vietnamese as a home of American debauchery. In 1998 I asked a rich American who had been to Vietnam several times in recent years what he recommended doing in Saigon. He said get a massage at the Rex Hotel.

But there is resistance among women too. In the Red River valley in the north there are many women without husbands because so many died during the war. The old moral code says they should not have sex or children. The government's new birth control policy says single women should not have children. But in all villages many single women have children anyway. They often pay men to have sex with them enough times to conceive, and then they pay a fine to the authorities when they have the child. But they refuse to be ashamed because they have suffered enough from the war.[42] And because so many have done it, it is now accepted.

# Resistance

The increasing inequalities in Vietnam have produced increasing resistance. The peasants had fought the French, the landlords and the Americans. Then they fought the collectives to keep their rice. Now they fight the market.

The land was divided in 1988. In the first two years 200,000 people filed official complaints about the way it was done.[43] In many cases old landlords in the south were trying to take back by force the lands they had before 1975—there were 976 reported cases of this in Ben Tre province alone in just the first half of 1993. Throughout the country local officials tried to take land by tricks or brute force. In other cases, a village claimed that local officials had given their land to a neighboring village. By 1990 this had happened in

6,000 villages nationwide, and in most cases people suspected bribery.

The peasants petitioned, demonstrated and marched in thousands of villages. In the four years to 1992 in Thai Binh province, for instance, there were 50 'serious clashes' over land. Benedict Kerkvliet summarizes a report in the newspaper *Nong Dan* about a village in Thanh Hoa province in the north:

> [The villagers] had been disgusted for some time with corruption by commune officials. Efforts to change the situation had brought no results. In fact, things worsened, as district officials pressured people to stop making allegations of misbehavior. In early 1989 villagers chose, by an election, the leaders of two production groups within the village.

The officials rejected their choices. The villagers 'refused to change their minds':

> Eleven investigators and public security officials [came] to arrest several villagers, including the two elected leaders… The officials were suddenly surrounded by a huge crowd of angry, shouting villagers, who prevented them from arresting anyone. Instead, the officers found themselves trapped. The crowd would not let them leave. When district and commune authorities sent in security police to rescue the eleven officers, 'thousands' of villagers fought back, using sticks, bricks, and anything else they could find. The security police found themselves overwhelmed; several were even disarmed by swarms of people. The security police retreated, leaving the villagers still with five 'captives'—three security police and two investigators.

In exchange for their hostages the villagers demanded that the authorities drop all criminal charges, dismiss several local officials, 'conduct a thorough investigation' and 'organize democratic elections by which trusted people are chosen to be village leaders'.[44] This is an extreme example and we do not know what happened next. But demonstrations were common—in 1988 farmers even marched on a provincial capital in the Mekong Delta.[45]

In the cities the workers went on strike. There is an official union, but it does not defend workers, only 12 percent of workers in private industry belong to it, and the government does not allow it to organize in foreign-owned companies. But, as Gabriel Kolko writes:

Since the worst abuses—from beatings, forced overtimes, and unsafe conditions to withholding pay—have occurred in joint ventures and foreign owned plants (especially Korean) that expect to make the most of Vietnam's promised comparative advantages, they have experienced the most labor disputes...

Strikes have varied greatly in size and duration. An initial official estimate of at least 214 strikes nationally from 1989 to March 1996 is too conservative. The union paper reported thirty-two strikes in the first ten months of 1994 alone. There were 'dozens' of unauthorized strikes in 1995, the party admits publicly, nearly double the number in 1994—and even more in 1996. These strikes technically are all independent of the official union.[46]

This is a very high rate of strikes in a small working class. In the 1990s Vietnamese workers have been far more militant than British or American workers. And, as Kolko points out, these strikes are illegal but they are reported sympathetically in the Vietnamese press and nobody is prosecuted. Leaders of peasant demonstrations have been arrested, and very occasionally sentenced to death. Strike leaders may lose their jobs, but the government does not dare to punish them.

This is because the rulers of Vietnam have some idea of what a mass strike in Hanoi or Saigon (Ho Chi Minh City) could do to them. Vietnamese independence started with the risings in Hanoi and Saigon in 1945. More recently they have seen the example of Tiananmen Square in China in 1989. Mass urban movements, largely composed of workers, have overthrown dictatorships in Iran, the Phillipines, Thailand and Indonesia. Vietnam's ruling class is frightened of attacking workers' leaders lest other workers rally round. It can live with a large demonstration of peasants marching on a provincial capital. A mass demonstration in one of the two big cities might change everything. A general strike could overthrow it.

So for the moment it allows the strikes to happen, and sometimes to win. But in the long run that gives workers a confidence that makes a rising from below more likely.

# Conclusion

The history of Vietnam after 1975 is a tragedy. The Vietnamese people fought for 30 years against French and American power and for a better world, with great courage and great losses. They ended up as the subjects of a new ruling class. That class was itself both the prisoner and agent of a world market and a world capitalist system. Vietnam today is a better place than it was under the Americans or the French. But it is not the kind of society all those people fought and died for.

The tragedy was that when those five men started meeting in the village of Beautiful Waters to talk about their village and how to change their country they could only see a choice between the private capitalism they lived under and a state capitalist 'Communism'.

This book has been written in the conviction that another way is possible—not inevitable, but possible. In Chapter 1 I quoted Ngo Van, who fought with a few dozen Trotskyist comrades in the rising of the Saigon working class in 1945. They marched in the great demonstrations that August under banners that called for peasants to take the land and workers to take the factories. They wanted to carry through what the Russian workers and peasants had tried to do in 1917. Most of them were killed, and the few survivors like Ngo Van were driven into exile. But what they fought for still remains, I think, the hope for humanity—democratic workers' power from below.

# Chapter 7

# America after the war

This chapter is about the consequences of the war for America.

The American ruling class lost the war in Vietnam. Three things made the defeat worse. First, America was a great power and Vietnam was a small peasant nation. Second, the whole world had watched the defeat. Third, the American people themselves had turned against the war and the American armed forces had refused to fight. The ruling class had lost the war to the Vietnamese *and* the Americans.

This gave heart to anybody who opposed American power in the world. It also demoralized every ruling class in the Third World that looked to America for support.

Moreover, the anti-war movement in America had been closely related to the black movement, the women's movement and the gay movement. The students had marched, the cities had burned and the soldiers had mutinied *at the same time*.

So after the defeat in Vietnam the American ruling class needed to reestablish their power. They tried to do this in several ways. First, as we have seen, they tried to isolate the Vietnamese economy and keep the Vietnamese poor as punishment for winning the war. Second, they supported Pol Pot and the Khmer Rouge in Cambodia because they were enemies of Vietnamese Communism. Third, they tried to blame the cruelty of the war on its own veterans. Fourth, they tried to rewrite history so the anti-war movement and the veterans became enemies. Fifth, they tried to persuade the American people to let their children fight ground wars for Washington again. Sixth, they tried to reverse the social gains made by the movements of the 60s, particularly by weakening unions and imprisoning black men.

All of these strategies can be summed up in one word—backlash. The rest of this chapter shows how this backlash worked, at home and abroad.

# The Vietnam syndrome

After 1975 the American ruling class faced what they called the 'Vietnam syndrome'. By this they meant the difficulty in getting American workers to risk their lives for American imperialism again. The liberals and the media spoke of this as if it were an illness, a 'syndrome', a bad thing. They also said the problem was that Americans were cowards—that the problem was body bags coming home. In fact the images that people remembered from the Vietnam War were not body bags. They were the photographs of the soldier with the empty thousand yard stare, the naked little girl covered in burning napalm running down the road screaming, the Saigon chief of police shooting a prisoner through the head up close, a marine using his cigarette lighter on the thatch of a house. These were images of cruelty, and of American and Vietnamese suffering. Americans had fought bravely enough in other wars. It wasn't that they were cowards. It was that they had learned not to trust people asking them to die for a cause that wasn't theirs.

By 1998 almost all liberal academics and public commentators argued that the Vietnam War had been a mistake. That same year 63 percent of the American public still felt it had been 'fundamentally wrong'.[1]

This was not acceptable to the media and government consensus, so they talked of syndromes and body bags. And from 1975 on the government tried to get Americans to agree to fight in foreign wars.

There is not space to examine all the American interventions after Vietnam, nor is there space to debate the rights and wrongs of interventions. The rest of this section looks at four situations where the American ruling class wanted to use ground troops—Angola in the 1970s, Lebanon in 1982, the Gulf War in 1990 and Kosovo in 1999—and how the memory of Vietnam in the American working class made that difficult for it.

The first example is Angola. The nationalist movement there won independence from Portuguese colonialism in 1975. Angola had a long border with South Africa. The blacks in South Africa could suddenly see the writing on the wall for their own white rulers, and there was a mass movement of school children's strikes in the townships and union strikes in workplaces. The South African apartheid government fought back by invading Angola. The Russians then cleverly sent Cuban troops to fight the South Africans.

Henry Kissinger, the American Secretary of State, quite correctly saw this as a major blow against America in the Cold War. Nelson Mandela's ANC in South Africa was at that time funded and supported by Russia, not the United States. South Africa was the most important concentration of private capitalism in the continent. And now the Russians, in the person of their Cuban clients, were able to use ground troops in Africa when the US could not.

Kissinger said in 1975, 'The United States will not accept further Communist military intervention in South Africa,' but Congress, haunted by Vietnam, 'voted 323 to 99 to ban covert military aid to Angola'.[2] Kissinger later asked the Pentagon to come up with a plan for fighting the Cubans in Angola. The Pentagon replied that it would take a very long time to come up with such a plan. Kissinger understood that the generals were preventing him from even thinking about fighting in Angola.[3] It is not hard to imagine what the generals might have thought about using an army with a lot of black soldiers to defend white racism in another Vietnam.

But this inability to intervene weakened American power. Then came the 1979-80 revolution in Iran.[4] Iran was a major oil producer ruled by an American-backed dictator, the Shah. Months of mass demonstrations and strikes in the banks and oilfields finally drove the Shah out.

Two different political trends led this mass movement. One was the left, and the other the Islamists under Ayatollah Khomeini. The Islamists are sometimes called Muslim fundamentalists, which is misleading. In fact, they are a political movement and a very modern one. They want a fairer world and are opposed to Western imperialism. They do merge religion and politics, but so did Martin Luther King and Malcolm X.

After the Shah was overthrown, the Islamists and the leftists competed for leadership of the revolution for over a year. The Islamists won in part by occupying the American embassy and keeping the white men hostage for months (they let the women and African-Americans go, on the grounds that they were oppressed in America). This massive humiliation for American power, the Islamist call for a more equal world, and the example of a successful revolution all encouraged strong Islamist movements in Iraq, Turkey, Syria, Bahrain, Saudi Arabia, Lebanon, Israel and Palestine, Egypt, Sudan, Tunisia, Algeria and Morocco. These movements were a challenge by tens of millions of people to the dictatorships in each country, but also to the American power that stood behind the dictatorships which controlled the largest source of oil in the world. The Middle East and its oil were important for profits, strategically crucial, and essential to the industries of Japan and Europe.

The US government reacted at home with a campaign to whip up anti-Muslim prejudice that lasted for years. Not just political Islamists but all Muslims were portrayed as sexist, terrorist, irrational medieval fanatics (unlike Christians and Jews). Official prejudice continued for so long, and so strongly, that now if you pick up almost any American newspaper article on Islamic fundamentalism and simply substitute the word 'black' or 'Jew' for 'Muslim', the racism will leap off the page at you.

In the Middle East itself American allies attacked the Islamists on two fronts. Saddam Hussein, the Iraqi dictator, supported by the US, led his people into a seven-year war with Iran (Hussein was barely a Muslim, and in no way an Islamist. His roots were in the Arab nationalist movement). And in 1982 the Israeli army invaded Lebanon, where the Islamists and Palestinians were winning a civil war. But the Israelis were unable to hold Beirut. They were replaced by a multinational force spearheaded by American marines, and American naval ships began long range shelling of Lebanese villages. An Islamist suicide bomber then drove a truckload of explosives into a US Marine base, killing 230 people, mostly marines. The Speaker of the US House of Representatives announced that America would not cut and run in the face of terrorism. But the marines were withdrawn.[5] One brave man in a truck had defeated American power.

Then the dictatorships in Russia and Eastern Europe fell in 1989. The US and the West had won the Cold War. US president Bush announced a 'New World Order'. Saddam Hussein, at this point still an American ally, invaded neighboring Kuwait. Hussein's army had just finished the seven-year war with Iran. The war had exhausted Iraq economically. The Kuwaiti royal family and their dictatorship had promised Hussein money for fighting Iran, and not delivered, and the Kuwaitis were increasing their own production of oil which was driving down the price of Iraqi oil. Kuwait fell quickly—the subjects of the Kuwaiti royal family did not fight for it. But Hussein's victory threatened Saudi Arabia, the major oil producer and American ally in the region. The people of Saudi Arabia hated the dictatorship of their royal family.[6] Hussein was not about to invade Saudi Arabia, but if the Kuwaiti royals went and the Americans did not defend them it would encourage the Saudi people. Something had to be done to protect the oil and the dictatorships.

Kuwait was a key test for American power, and US president Bush had to go to war. He organized a military coalition, based in Saudi Arabia, of most European powers and almost every dictatorship in the Middle East. When Hussein would not back down and was not allowed another way out, the coalition bombed massively and then sent in troops. The bulk of the allied fliers and soldiers were Americans.

The American government kept tight control of media coverage of the war, allowing only a few picked correspondents into Saudi Arabia and Kuwait. These correspondents had military minders at all times. The job of these minders was not to stop the journalists talking to Saudis, Kuwaitis or Iraqis. It was to stop them talking to American soldiers and pilots.[7] That was what the American military had learned from Vietnam.

The coalition bombing killed between 100,000 and 200,000 Iraqi troops. US bulldozers buried more alive in their trenches. The draftee Iraqi army were terrified by the bombing, and like most Iraqis they hated Hussein. They fled or surrendered.

The American troops rode into Kuwait with very few losses, many of them from friendly fire. Bush announced on American radio that he had finally buried the Vietnam syndrome. It was not that simple. Bush had said over and over again that the war was intended to overthrow Saddam Hussein, who was as evil as Hitler. Hussein's army was disintegrating, driving and running away as fast as they could. The Kurdish minority in the north and the people in the cities of southern Iraq rose in revolt against Hussein, expecting American help.

Yet the American army stopped at the Iraqi border and allowed Saddam Hussein to smash the revolts, when they could have overthrown him. There were two reasons. One was that the southern revolt was led by Islamists and a Kurdish victory in the north would have encouraged the Kurdish rebellion in Turkey, an American ally. But the other reason was that the American generals were not prepared to invade. General Colin Powell, chairman of the Joint Chiefs of Staff, had done two tours of duty in Vietnam. He was determined that such a thing would never happen to his army again.[8] When push came to shove, the generals were still terrified of fighting on the ground.

An American-organized economic boycott over the next ten years cut off medical supplies, cut back the food supply and pulverized the economy. Infant mortality soared, and over 1 million Iraqi children died as a result of the boycott.[9] But Hussein remained in power, exposing to all the limits of American power.

Our last example of American intervention is the Kosovo war in 1999. There is not space here to fill in the complex background to that war.[10] To put it very simply, the fall of Communism in Eastern Europe shattered the old Communist dictatorship in Yugoslavia. The old Communist bosses reinvented themselves as new elected nationalist leaders of the different provinces and ethnic groups in Yugoslavia. In a series of wars the armies of these new leaders drove out members of rival groups in ethnic cleansing, burning their homes and killing some people to make the others flee. This began with Croatian atrocities against Serbs, which were then followed by Serbian atrocities against Croats. Then the Serbian and Croatian leaders agreed to divide the province of Bosnia between them. This led to a three-cornered war between Serbs, Croats and Muslims in Bosnia, with ethnic cleansing and atrocities on all sides. The war ended when America brokered a division of Bosnia into three ethnic statelets under the supervision of a UN governor, producing in effect three UN colonies.

These wars left the old Yugoslav state a shadow of its former self. Where there had been six provinces there were now two—Serbia and Montenegro. And within Serbia there was a restive minority in the south, in Kosovo. The 1.8 million people in Kosovo were mostly Albanian speakers, with some Serbs and Gypsies. The Albanian nationalists in Kosovo saw their chance to set up their own state, as the Bosnian nationalists had done. First they tried peaceful non-cooperation with the Serb government, and then an Albanian nationalist Kosovo Liberation Army (KLA) launched a guerrilla struggle against Serbia. At first the American government said the KLA was terrorist. The Serbian army and police fought the KLA guerrillas, killing some 2,000 people in 1998 and making roughly 200,000 people into refugees.

The American government wanted to keep control of what was happening in Yugoslavia and the neighboring countries. It was worried about the local wars spreading to its allies in Turkey and Greece. It also wanted to establish the United States as the dominant power in Eastern Europe. And oil was being discovered in great quantities in central Asia, in the newly independent countries of what had been the Soviet Union. It looked like there was more oil there than in the Middle East, and it was not clear who would control the new oil—Russia, China, the US or Turkey. For all these reasons the American government decided to take control of Kosovo and insisted that Serbia allow American-led UN troops into Kosovo and Serbia.

The Serbian government refused to let this happen, and the American government threatened to bomb Serbia. At this point, in late 1998, the American government also began bombing Iraq. But Hussein defied them publicly, and American bombing did not bring him to heel.

The Serbian government saw what had happened in Iraq and decided that it too could defy American bombing. Humiliated by Iraq, the American government could not afford to be humiliated by Serbia too. So it began bombing Serbia and Kosovo. This bombing had the support of other NATO powers, although most of the planes were American.

In the year before the American bombing of Serbia the Serbian army had killed 2,000 people in Kosovo. But the Serbian army reacted to the bombing by killing more and thus forcing over half the Kosovan Albanians to flee as refugees. The numbers of dead are disputed. For the moment all that can be said for sure is that the Serbian army killed at least a thousand Kosovans, and the American bombing killed several thousand Serbs and Kosovans.

The American government and its NATO allies had expected the Serbian government to crumble in the face of bombing. Milosevic, the Serbian leader, had retreated in the face of bombing threats before, there had been mass internal movements of opposition in Serbia and there was a strong feeling for peace. But at first the bombing united the Serbian opposition behind Milosevic. The bombing went on week after week.

America was using bombs, of course, because it still did not dare use American ground troops. The British general in charge of NATO thought ground troops would be needed. Many people in the American government now thought they would be needed. It began to look as if Serbia might hold out and American power would suffer a very public defeat that would weaken American influence in all of Eastern Europe—and beyond, in places like Palestine, Indonesia and Colombia.

The Pentagon said that it would take many months to get American troops in a position to fight in Kosovo. This was a transparent lie. America had bases over the border in Albania. For 40 years NATO forces had been prepared to fight Russian troops in Europe at a few hours notice. The idea of a superpower that could not fight for many months was ridiculous. What was happening was that the Pentagon was still looking over its shoulder at Vietnam.

So were President Clinton and the American government. Public opinion in America was split roughly half and half over the bombing of Serbia. But a majority was clearly against ground troops, and by the end of the war 80 percent of Americans were in favor of a bombing pause to allow negotiations. Moreover, most Americans who supported the bombing said, when you talked to them, that their main feeling was confusion. Probably it was necessary to support the Kosovan refugees, but they weren't really clear what was happening.

This was not a situation where the American generals wanted to risk another Vietnam, and President Clinton felt unable to press them. The NATO command did insist that the American army send Apache helicopters. These were the most modern and expensive helicopters the Americans had. They could fly low over Kosovo and engage the Serbian army up close and personal. The American generals saw this as a bridge to using ground troops. They allowed Apache helicopters to go to bases in Albania, but then announced that the helicopters could not be used in Kosovo because the weather was bad, there were clouds, the pilots were not properly trained and it would take months to get everything right. The generals were prepared to trash talk one of their most treasured and expensive weapons to prevent any possibility of another Vietnam.[11]

In the end opposition to the war grew in Serbia. There were protest demonstrations in several cities, and the Serbian government gave up. America and NATO sent occupying troops into Kosovo and the war was over.

The lesson the American government drew was that bombing worked. This makes it more likely that it will bomb elsewhere in future. It also makes it more likely that eventually it will bomb an opponent with more support than Milosevic had in Serbia. Then it will be faced again with pressure to use ground troops.

The Kosovo war ended with America more powerful. But there is still a limit on that power. During the Kosovo war Vietnam veterans in their fifties all over America, in truck stops and at family dinners, right wingers and liberals, were saying to the younger people that, whatever the rights and wrongs in Kosovo, their experience should not be repeated. They were right. The 'Vietnam syndrome' is not a sickness, in the way that the American ruling class talks about it. The 'syndrome' is what American workers learned from the Vietnam War. One thread that has run all through this book is that limits on American power in the world are good for the world *and* for ordinary Americans.

# Veterans

The ruling class backlash against the Vietnam War was not simply a matter of trying to use ground troops abroad. It involved rewriting history as well. Central to this were the American veterans of that war. What happened to them was taken from them and made into something else.

Hollywood generally portrayed veterans as dangerous and violent men.[12] The most famous examples are *Taxi Driver*, *Rambo: First Blood* and *Coming Home*, but dozens of B movies portrayed the same dangerous veterans. These men were suffering from psychosis produced by flashbacks on screen well before psychiatrists discovered 'post-traumatic stress syndrome' and decided to call men's memories 'flashbacks'. And the point Hollywood was making was the same point as the psychiatrist in the VA hospital—the violent wishes of GIs were the cause of the violence in the Vietnam War.

The blaming of veterans for the cruelty of the war went in the face of the facts that they had been ordered to do it, that they had been rewarded for doing it, that attrition had been the strategy, and that they had finally refused to fight. It also went in the face of the fact that far more people were killed by planes than guns.

But Hollywood had to blame somebody for the cruelty of the war, because Americans had not forgotten that it was a cruel war. The majority of them were still saying so in public opinion surveys 20 years later.[13] The truth was that liberals were responsible for Vietnam—John Kennedy, Robert Kennedy, Lyndon Johnson and Robert McNamara. Now that most people knew the war was a mistake *and wrong*, the blame was being dumped on the GIs.

At the same time the history was rewritten to divide GIs and the anti-war movement. First, the soldiers' refusal to fight was forgotten.

But then, ten years after the war ended, there began to be many sto-ries of anti-war protesters or hippies spitting on returning veterans. Jerry Lembcke began researching these spitting stories at the time of the Gulf War. Lembcke was a Vietnam veteran and a former activist in Vietnam Veterans Against the War, and he didn't remember any spitting. He remembered that most veterans had been against the war and that people had behaved decently to them when they came home—especially the anti-war protesters. So Lembcke went back and looked for reports of spitting on veterans by anti-war types or hippies in the 1960s and 1970s. He found none at all anywhere in the papers or the magazines. He found no accounts of it at the time in right wing magazines. He found no accounts for many years afterwards, and he found opinion surveys of veterans at the time who said they had been well received by people their own age. The only accounts of spitting on veterans Lembcke found were pictures and news stories of anti-war veterans protesting against the war and being spat on by supporters of the war.

Lembcke also found that returning veterans were spat on in the movies *first*, before there were any other accounts of spitting. And he pointed out that the movie *Coming Home* showed an anti-war crowd protesting against returning soldiers at an airport, something which never happened. Instead the peace movement protested at induc-tion centers, ports and airports against soldiers having to go and fight.

So the media and the politicians tried to blame the soldiers for the war and separate them in retrospect from the anti-war move-ment. In the 1980s politicians, particularly Reagan and Bush, began insisting that they were the true friends of the veterans. The trouble, they said, was that America had not honored its veterans properly (the liberals spat on them). The symbols of this were the 'prisoners of war/missing in action', Americans captured during the war and still held by Hanoi. There could be no proper diplomatic relations with Viet-nam until these men were returned.

These prisoners did not exist. There were men the Pentagon had listed as missing in action and never accounted for. As the Viet-namese government kept insisting, they were dead.

But their non-existence made them the one group of veterans the right could really support. They could not support the men who were actually still dying from the war, the victims of Agent Orange.[14] The men who had worked on Operation Ranch Hand, dumping pesticides from planes, were particularly badly hit. But many other GIs had been exposed. More and more of them became sick and listless, depressed and unable to work or do anything much. They got rashes, they began to come down with cancers, and more and more of their children were born with terrible birth defects.

The federal Veterans Administration (VA) hospitals told them over and over that it was in their heads—they were suffering from 'post-traumatic stress'. And indeed they were stressed, for they felt themselves dying, they were unable to work and they had no explanation for what was happening to them.

Gradually they realized. What made their medical condition obvious was that very much larger numbers of people in Vietnam were suffering from the same thing, and that hundreds of thousands of children had been born there terribly deformed (now a third generation are being born with the same defects). But the government and the politicians fought as hard as they could to resist any compensation or treatment for the Agent Orange victims in America. To do so would be to admit what had been done in the war. It would open the question of whether the Vietnamese children, unborn when the war ended, should be compensated. And it would allow pictures of those children on American TV screens. That would make another war far harder to wage.

So the politicians supported veterans who did not exist, blamed the living veterans and ignored the dying. They did so because they wanted to be able to go to war again.

# Stress

Most Vietnam veterans coped, as people do, and got on with building their lives. Although the great majority were not psychopaths, some did suffer greatly afterwards. Vietnam Veterans Against the War had left a legacy of political organization, and the veterans were able to insist something had to be done. The Veterans Administration was already responsible for the medical care of all veterans. In the 1980s it began to offer help to people suffering from what psychiatrists now called 'post-traumatic stress disorder'. Allan Young, an anthropologist, spent a year watching and listening to staff and resident patients in one such VA psychiatric center in 1986-87.[15]

What happened in that hospital is interesting for two reasons.

First, it shows how the veterans were blamed for the cruelty of the war. But it also shows the class struggle in miniature, in one hospital, between psychiatrists and working class patients. The backlash in America was not simply a campaign in the media. It was something that was pushed and fought through in the details of people's daily lives.

One man was both manager of the center staff and director of the treatment offered. He had a model of post-traumatic stress the staff had to use. It went as follows.

Men with post-traumatic stress disorder are split between their aggressive and sexual sides. At one moment in the past they did one wrong thing, and they did it because they enjoyed it. After they enjoyed that thing they were overwhelmed with guilt. So they split their desire from their aggression. The cure for them is to recall that moment in group therapy. When they have returned to that moment, and accepted that they wanted to do evil, they can leave the guilt behind and become whole people.

Note carefully—they did *one* wrong thing. Terrible things that were done to them and terrible things they saw did not count. It had to be an atrocity they wanted to commit, and only one atrocity. A lot of time in therapy was spent trying to find that one event.

It was all nonsense, as Allan Young shows clearly in his book on the VA clinic, *The Harmony of Illusions*. But the nonsense served a function. This center treated men wounded by the war, but it was a government center. It could not say, 'The officers and the government are to blame.' It could not say, 'What was done to you in Vietnam is of a piece with what has been done to you since.' And it could not allow the patients to say these things. So the psychiatric theory blamed the men—they wanted to kill.

The men kept trying to talk about what had been done to them. Young quotes from a group therapy session where 'Henry' explains some of why he is upset:

> HENRY: Maybe I am crazy. I was raised a Baptist. I went to church every Wednesday and Sunday, and I went to Bible camp. By the time I was eighteen I was in Vietnam. After I was in-country for only three days, I killed a sixteen-year-old boy. I began questioning my religion. I was asking myself what kind of god would put me in a position like this and let me do this. At first, I felt sad. But then people started telling me, 'Way to go,' and the captain and the sergeant congratulated me for having a kill after such a short time. After a while, I fell into the program. I'd see

guys lose legs and other shit happen, and it didn't bother me anymore. I began to enjoy it and went back for a second tour. I wanted to get revenge, and I wanted to do as much destruction as possible.[16]

Here is part of group therapy a week earlier. Lewis, a junior psychologist, explains the theory:

LEWIS: Forgetting traumatic events originates in a conflict. You don't want to remember. Your conflict is always driving you back to the original event, but you don't want to go back to it. Stress responses do two things for you. First, you don't have to face your conflict, and second, you punish yourself... One of the jobs of combat training is to remove some of the conflict over aggression, so that you can be aggressive...
MARTIN [another patient]: Well, I can tell you we had no problem being aggressive in Vietnam.
LEWIS: OK, Martin. Give us an example, but use the word 'I' instead of 'we'.

Two weeks later Carol, a counselor, shuts Henry up in group therapy:

CAROL: Yesterday you were wearing all black, Henry, a black shirt, black jeans. And what was Paul's response? He said the clients are like troops being shot at by [Vietnamese] people in black pajamas.
HENRY: Listen, the people who were shooting *at me* in Vietnam weren't wearing black uniforms. Black clothes don't mean anything to me. There was *no* aggressive intent. After the session, when I realized my clothes produced a stress response, I went to my room and changed, and I came to lunch in different clothes.
CAROL: Even if it were not your conscious experience right now, its meaning will come to realization. Same thing about the meaning of your remark yesterday, about the Vietcong not being *your* enemy.
HENRY: Well, that's right. The Vietcong were acting the same way we would have acted in their place. I had no anger against them. My anger's against the people who sponsored the war.
CAROL: Which is equivalent to saying, 'My anger is against all Americans'.[17]

Which shut him up and forced him to blame himself.

The class struggle in therapy went on all day, every day, in this clinic. The therapists, controlled by the managing psychiatrist, tried to make the veterans responsible for the war. The veterans fought back:

CAROL: Say to yourself, I've been punishing myself and people around me for twenty years. Say, Jack, you can choose to stop!

JACK: Listen, Carol. On some nights, I feel anxiety going through my body like electricity. It started in Vietnam. It wasn't just a feeling. It was an anxiety together with terrible chest pains and difficulty breathing. Just like having a heart attack. They sent me over to the field hospital to get an EKG. The doctors told them there was nothing wrong. They said I was just hyperventilating. They told me to breathe into a paper bag when I got those feelings, and they gave me a supply of Valium to take back. But I got those attacks anyway. And I'm still getting them...

CAROL: The model says that we're dominated by two drives, aggression and sex, and that—

JACK: Listen, Carol. When I got those attacks, I sure didn't want to get fucked, and I can't believe it was my aggression.[18]

The staff had a way of explaining away the patients' anger towards them. They said anger is a defense. The patient gets angry so he doesn't have to get in touch with his feelings of guilt about what he did. He seems to be angry with me. Actually, he's angry with me because I'm pushing him to reveal his guilt.

Sometimes patients tested the 'limits' set by the staff. They threatened violence or left the room during group therapy to have a piss. They wore dark glasses in the group or disagreed with the therapists too effectively. If they broke these limits, they faced a 'panel'.

This panel was made up of all the staff the patient had told his intimate secrets to. They discussed everything about him behind his back. Sometimes they threw him out of the hospital. The other patients regarded this as a punishment—just like the army. The staff disagreed. They felt they were only setting limits.

And the center Allan Young studied was one of the best in the Veterans Administration. It was Freudian, progressive, and the patients were encouraged to talk. Many of these men had been to other hospitals before, where they were drugged to the eyeballs, shot full of thorazine, strapped to tables for weeks, given electric shocks over and over, given electric shocks even while they were awake.

These were men without jobs whose median income—except for Veterans Administration disability benefits—was less than $1,000 a year. If they did not get a good report from the staff, they could lose those benefits. If the staff decided that they had 'post-traumatic stress disorder' they could get $40,000 to $60,000 in back benefits. So there was a lot of pressure on them to be good. But not too good—if they were cured they might lose benefits and still not have a job.

In that situation it's hard to be honest and open in therapy. Yet these men often were. They tried desperately. They had suffered for years and it was the only help available.

And so they waited days or weeks for each man to gather the courage to say what he did and what was done to him. As each man told the group his worst 'event' they sat silent, leaning forward, willing him on to tell the truth. They wanted to tell and hear the truth. They had seen enough lies. But they also hoped the therapists were right and this would cleanse them.

The men told the truth. It did not cure them. The therapists said that once a man had returned to that moment and owned his responsibility he would be whole. But he was not. He was ashamed. And in the eyes of the men who were there too he was right to be ashamed.

The therapists said he could put his guilt behind him. But he could not. Somebody had to bear that guilt. It should be the guilty—not the working class boys sent to hell, but the rich and powerful men who sent them there.

It would have helped those veterans in pain to be angry with the men who sent them there—titanically angry, encouraged in their anger, supported in their anger, honored for their rage. Instead they were silenced, so those who ruled America then could still rule it now, and hope to send other men to other Vietnams.

# The backlash in America

America's rulers were also trying to break the power and memory of the movements of the 1960s in America. Weakening movements against the ruling class at home would make it easier to allow American intervention abroad. And the class struggle at home was still what mattered most to the American ruling class.

In the 1960s and 1970s it had been shaken by the anti-war movement, the black movement, and the women's and gay movements. At every level, in every cranny of American society, opposition from below had grown stronger. From 1975 on, all American governments and employers tried to reverse this. They were helped in their efforts by the political confusion of American radicals.

The movements of the 1960s and 1970s were massive. Most of the millions of people involved were blue collar workers or lower level white collar workers. These were the majority of the marchers in the civil rights movement, the rioters in the Northern cities and the soldiers in revolt in Vietnam. Many of the students in the anti-war movement came from these backgrounds, and opposition to the war was strongest in the working class.

But these movements were led by middle class professionals. More important, they saw themselves as sectional movements, fighting for blacks or women or peace. Most of the people involved did not see the possibility of a united movement of all the oppressed, trying to unite all workers and concentrate their struggle against the corporations at work. The few organized revolutionaries they met looked to the example of Russia or China or Cuba, places where workers were ruled by dictatorships and oppressed in their daily working lives much as American workers were. Because these organized revolutionaries looked to the example of dictatorships, their own organizations also had unpleasant internal regimes that repelled people who were looking for more democracy.

So the most radical elements in all the movements looked not to the whole working class but to some more radical version of their own sectional struggle. Some of the peace activists became terrorist bombers. Many of the most radical women became separatists, and many of the radical blacks became separatist nationalists. All of these movements stalled because the great majority of women, black people, gays, lesbians and people who wanted peace had to continue living and working in a system run by the corporations. By the end of the 1970s almost all these radical separatists realized they had trapped themselves in dead ends. They felt defeated but did not know why.

As these movements ran into the sand, the American ruling class was making a space for the professional class which had led the movements. Job and educational opportunities opened up for women and blacks. By 1990 a sixth of black households made over $50,000 a year. This was not riches, but it did create a black middle class with some feeling of a stake in the system. Many of them got jobs as congressional representatives, junior diplomats, army officers, police chiefs, judges, and other administrators and defenders of the system.

Women too saw a rise in their wages. But most of this rise was concentrated in the top 20 percent of women earners, and really large gains only happened for the top 10 percent. These women still faced all sorts of 'glass ceilings', but they too could, and often did, feel they had a stake in the system.

So when the American ruling class started to push a domestic backlash after 1975 the radicals felt defeated, and many of the liberal leaders workers had looked to, and still looked to, were now reluctant to really fight the ruling class.

The backlash reached into every corner of American life. Susan Faludi, in her excellent book *Backlash*, has detailed the attack on women's rights.[19] A central fight there was over abortion. But gays too suffered as the Reagan and Bush governments refused to do anything about AIDS and blamed gay men for their own suffering.[20] In the universities there was a sustained attack on the ideas of the 60s. But the two main weapons in the backlash were an attack on the unions and the imprisonment of blacks.[21]

Two important things mark America between 1975 and 1999 as very different from the rest of the industrialized world. In America and Eastern Europe the real take-home hourly wages of workers fell. In the rest of the industrialized world they rose. And in 1971 there were 200,000 prisoners in America. By 2000 there were over 2 million— a tenfold increase. No other country except Rwanda imprisons anything like that proportion of its population, and such a thing had never happened in America before. Both the fall in wages and the rise in prisoners were treated in the American media as if they were normal events. Both weakened the American working class.

The fall in wages was made possible by a sustained attack on the unions.[22] The key battle here was a national strike by air traffic controllers in 1981. The air traffic controllers were federal employees, and President Reagan fired all of them, hired scab labor and refused to let the strikers have their jobs back. The leaders of the other unions in the airline industry, frightened of massive government fines, told their members to cross the air traffic controllers' picket lines.

Because there was no radical network in the unions and workplaces to organize people not to scab, the airline workers felt helpless without the backing of their leaders and went into work. That broke the strike. After that workers in other industries realized that if the government and employers could do that to the airline controllers, they could do it to anybody.

At the same time there were large-scale layoffs and plant closures in heavy industry, the traditional heart of the union movement. Here again the union leaders told their members they could not fight the logic of the capitalist market, and if they did not agree to work for less in worse conditions then the jobs would simply go to workers in Third World countries. Again there was no socialist network in the unions to argue that the enemy was the corporations, not workers in other parts of the world.

That led to a rash of give-back contracts accepting cuts in wages and job conditions. Because the unions were not fighting, people in the new service industries did not join unions and the unions did not lead the fights necessary to recruit them. Labor unionism was not abolished, but union membership shrank and the unions were weaker.

Most people still had full time jobs. But the men who lost jobs in industry had to take jobs at lower wages in the service sector, and an increasing minority had to work one or more part time jobs with lower wages and often no health benefits. Real hourly wages for blue collar and routine white collar workers fell, and work got harder and more dangerous. Family incomes stayed more or less steady, because many more women went out to work and both men and women worked longer hours. But families were running harder and harder to keep up. Without unions, or with weaker unions, and with the threat of losing the job they had, people got more scared of standing up for themselves at work.

From 1997 on, with almost full employment, real hourly wages did begin to rise again a bit. But during the 1990s the main corporate attack was on workers' health care. Most of the big strikes in the 1990s were in defense of what little health care insurance workers had, and many had none at all. The corporations increasingly forced their employees into health plans run by HMOs, health care organizations that were cheaper for corporations because they rationed the treatment workers could get.

The attack on workers as workers was one big weapon in the backlash. The other was prison. Any major social policy has to be understood in terms of its consequences. What is important is not what the people at the top say is their motivation. It's what their policies do that matters. What mass imprisonment did was pulverize the lives of black workers and subdue them as a political force.

By 1999, 45 percent of prisoners were black, mostly men. The number of women prisoners was rising more rapidly than ever, but they were still a small minority of prisoners. At any one time over a third of black men between the ages of 18 and 30 were in prison, on probation or awaiting trial. In the black working class, and in the inner cities, the proportion was even higher. Behind the almost 2 million people in prison were the many millions more who had been to prison in the previous 20 years. And behind those men were their parents and wives and children, tens of millions of them. Almost every black worker had some relative who had been to prison.

Prison destroys relationships. It brutalizes people, weakens and frightens them so they come out harder on the surface and more terrified inside. Prison management often relied on the more criminal and brutal prisoners to control the rest, and so prisons became factories for rape. A society that babbled about post-traumatic stress built mass factories for trauma. And because even rape could not control so many men, there were more and more special units with men locked down for 23 or 24 hours a day for years.

With the mass imprisonment went increases in police numbers, in 'zero tolerance' daily harassment on the streets, in torture in police stations, and in paramilitary police SWAT teams with body armor, automatic weapons, grenade launchers and helicopters. Under the pressure of the movements of the 1960s, the Supreme Court had suspended the death penalty in 1972. As the backlash gained force, the Supreme Court reversed itself in 1976. The number of executions increased steadily over the next 20 years. By the end of 1999, 598 Americans had been executed. That same year all the countries of Western and Central Europe insisted that Turkey could not join the European Union until it abolished the death penalty, because no country could be considered civilized if it executed even one prisoner. And the American media still talked as if there was nothing odd about America.

What was happening was both breaking and demonizing the black working class. This did white workers no favors. The proportion of black prisoners was rising, but the number of white prisoners was rising too. Millions of Latino and white families went through the same suffering. This made everybody more frightened.

It also divided black and white workers. There is little evidence that white workers became more racist. However, black workers had been at the heart of the movement of the 60s and 70s. Anybody who wanted to fight back in those years looked to the black movement as an example. When white workers thought of black workers, they saw in their minds a grandmother in a Southern city leading her church choir out of church, down the road to the courthouse, singing their defiance at the police dogs. Or they saw a black man in a Northern city riot with a Molotov cocktail in his hand. By 1999, when many white and black workers thought of the inner cities the images that came to mind were likely to be junkies and street gangs.

This was the result of the policy of mass imprisonment. A beacon of hope had been turned into an object lesson of what could happen to you. The American ruling class had reacted to the mass union movement between 1938 and 1946 with a persecution of Communists that jailed a few hundred and lost less than 20,000 people their jobs. In the 80s and 90s they reacted to the civil rights movement and Vietnam with a persecution of blacks that sent millions to prison.

This was only possible because the leadership of the black middle class did not organize against it. The centerpiece of the prison drive was the war of drugs. This was not actually a war on drugs but a war on drug takers. And Jesse Jackson, the leader of the black middle class, was part of that war on drugs. The black mayors, police chiefs, and spokesmen and women joined in too. Some of them said we have to clean up our cities by imprisoning our children. Others, to their credit, did not say that, but were still far enough into the system that they did not organize mass resistance to the war on drugs and imprisonment.

But by 1999 this was changing. Some middle class black leaders were campaigning hard against police brutality. The union leaders, too, were looking for ways to fight back. In both cases this was happening because there was widespread bitterness among both black and white American workers about their lives, and an increasing hatred of class injustice. That feeling of bitterness was beginning to break through into action.

The bitterness had been building a long time. Mostly you noticed it if you talked to people, and the mood on demonstrations was both angry and hopeful. It was not much reported in the newspapers, but it kept breaking through.

In 1992 Los Angeles saw a riot against police brutality when police were caught on video beating a black man, Rodney King, and were then acquitted. The riot was on the scale of the black riots in the 60s, but this time it spread to Latin and Anglo white neighborhoods.

There were supporting demonstrations in many cities, made up of mixed black and white crowds chanting, 'No justice, no peace!' This was new.

In 1997 the Teamsters union members at United Parcel Service (UPS) went on a national strike. UPS was well known as a corporate pioneer in part time and casual work. The central demand of the strikers was more full time jobs. There was support for them right round the country. This time, unlike other strikes in the 1990s, UPS could not use scabs. The one place it tried, in Massachusetts, UPS and other workers fought the police on the picket line and stopped them. The UPS workers won.

The Clinton administration promptly removed the reforming Teamsters union president, Carey, on a technical violation of union finance laws. Other union leaders took fright. Not all of them were corrupt, but most of them, like Carey, were sitting on somebody else's dirty books in their organization. For the moment the union leaders were careful.

Then in 1999 there were weeks of demonstrations in New York after the police shot down an unarmed and innocent African immigrant, Amadou Diallo, on the street. There were thousands on each demonstration. At one point they blocked the Brooklyn Bridge, and the crowds were both black and white. Over 2,000 people were arrested in civil disobedience.

These demonstrations were in effect against Mayor Guiliani of New York, the apostle of 'zero tolerance' policing. They gave the unions of the people who worked for New York City the confidence to call a rally for a decent wage for all working families. 50,000 people came. This too was new.

And then came the demonstration in Seattle against the World Trade Organization (WTO) in December 1999. The WTO meeting was supposed to be one more milestone in American and capitalist dominance of the world economy. The demonstrators came with many agendas. Some were brought by labor leaders to protest the loss of American jobs. Some were protesting the effects of the world market in the Third World. Some were against sweatshops. Some were defending sea turtles. Some of them wanted to reform the WTO, and some wanted to abolish it. The union leaders talked of America while young radicals talked of capitalism.

The union leaders told their members to march separately from the environmental and political campaigners. Rank and file Teamsters refused, and forced their way through police lines to join the 'turtle kids'. Together the union members and the left stopped the opening day of the WTO conference. The police waded into them with gas and rubber bullets. Some of the demonstrators replied by breaking windows of corporate chainstores, starting with Starbucks, home of the $5 cup of coffee, that symbol of yuppie arrogance. When the first Starbucks window broke on television a shout went up in living rooms across America.

A riot followed. President Clinton had to react to this riot by saying the demonstrators had a point, because he knew ordinary people all over the country supported them. The delegates of the other big and little capitalist powers gathered for the WTO said to themselves Clinton can't even control his own people—why should we do what he tells us? The conference ended with nothing decided and no agenda for the next one.

It was a very public victory for the demonstrators. They had arrived supporting many causes. But it turned out that what united them was a hatred of capitalism. They kept saying so to the reporters, and the word 'anti-capitalism' was suddenly part of the mainstream media vocabulary. The America Federation of Labor had never been part of a national demonstration against capitalism. Now suddenly it was.

The wind changed in American politics. After Seattle every struggle in America will be a little bit easier. The oppressed will be a little more confident, the ruling class a little more wary. For the first time in 60 years, there is a mass movement in America which calls itself anti-capitalist.[23]

That movement has a resonance around the world. In 1989 students in Saigon protested against their course content and conditions by holding meetings and seminars at their university. They called this form of protest a 'teach-in'—Madison, Wisconsin, had come to Saigon.

In 1999 Vietnam was in Seattle. The memory was there as the police attacked the crowd and they chanted, 'The whole world is watching,' as they had chanted in Chicago in 1968. And the present was there as many demonstrators came as part of the movement against sweatshop conditions in the Third World, the same thing the workers in Saigon were striking against through the 1990s. The American workers in Seattle were also fighting corporations which wanted a low wage, non-union economy. In Seattle and Saigon the enemy was the world market. As one anonymous demonstrator said to a reporter, 'Our parents had Vietnam. This is our Vietnam.' *Newsweek* reported:

> Two young men stood chest to chest, screaming in each other's faces, both tear-stained from the pepper gas wafting along Sixth Avenue in downtown Seattle. One wanted to smash the Nike window, the other to stop him. 'How do you think they stopped Vietnam?' demanded the one with the rock.[24]

It wasn't that simple in the 1960s and it won't be that simple this time round. You could say that tens of thousands of union members marching make far more difference than a few people with rocks. And you would be right. But if you worked in one of the Nike sweatshops in Vietnam, you would know that the man with the rock was your brother.

# Further reading

There are a very large number of good books on the Vietnam War. The books listed below are just some of the places to begin reading on that topic. Full citations are given in the bibliography.

**General:** A moving and funny collection of contemporary documents from all points of view: John Pratt, *Vietnam Voices: Perspectives on the War Years 1941-1982*; and Marilyn Young, *The Vietnam Wars: 1945-1990*.

**Vietnamese Communism:** Gabriel Kolko, *Anatomy of a War: Vietnam, the United States and the Modern Historical Experience*, which is also a very good history of the whole war; David Marr, *Vietnam 1945: The Quest for Power*; and James Trullinger, *Village at War: An Account of Revolution in Vietnam*, about the village of Beautiful Waters.

**The air war:** James Gibson, *The Perfect War: Technowar in Vietnam*.

**GIs:** Christian Appy, *Working Class War: American Combat Soldiers and Vietnam*; and then, among many good memoirs, Micheal Clodfelter, *Mad Minutes and Vietnam Months: A Soldier's Memoir*.

**North Vietnamese soldiers:** Duong Thu Huong, *Novel Without a Name*.

**Viet Cong guerrillas:** Tom Mangold and John Pennycate, *The Tunnels of Cu Chi*.

**Washington policy makers:** David Halberstam, *The Best and the Brightest*.

**The anti-war movement in America:** Tom Wells, *The War Within: America's Battle Over Vietnam*, which is also good on the policy makers; and Fred Halstead, *Out Now!: A Participant's Account of the American Movement against the Vietnam War*.

**Vietnam Veterans Against the War:** Ron Kovic, *Born on the Fourth of July*; and Richard Stacewicz, *Winter Soldiers: An Oral History of the Vietnam Veterans Against the War*.

**The soldiers' revolt:** Joel Geier, 'Vietnam: the Soldiers' Rebellion', *International Socialist Review* 9, 1999; Richard Cortright, *Soldiers in Revolt: The American Military Today*; and Richard Moser, *The New Winter Soldiers: GI and Veteran Dissent during the Vietnam War*.

**My Lai:** Michael Bilton and Kevin Sim, *Four Hours in My Lai: A War Crime and its Aftermath*.

**American veterans:** Jerry Lembcke, *The Spitting Image: Myth, Memory and the Legacy of Vietnam*; and the second half of Allan Young, *The Harmony of Illusions: Inventing Post-Traumatic Stress Disorder*.

**Vietnamese veterans:** Bao Ninh, *The Sorrow of War*, a great novel.

**Cambodia:** William Shawcross, *Sideshow: Nixon, Kissinger and the Destruction of Cambodia*; and Ben Kiernan, *How Pol Pot Came to Power: A History of Communism in Kampuchea, 1930-1975*.

**Thailand:** Daniel Fineman, *A Special Relationship: The United States and the Military Government in Thailand, 1947-1958*; and Ji Ungpakorn, *The Struggle for Democracy and Social Justice in Thailand*.

**China and Vietnam:** Quiang Zhai, *China and the Vietnam Wars, 1950-1975* and Nayan Chanda, *Brother Enemy: The War After the War*.

**Vietnam after 1975:** start with Gabriel Kolko, *Vietnam: Anatomy of a Peace*; and then a novel by Duong Thu Huong, *Paradise of the Blind*; and two anthropology books, Tine Gammeltoft, *Women's Bodies, Women's Worries: Health and Family Planning in a Vietnamese Rural Community* and John Kleinen, *Facing the Future, Reviving the Past: A Study of Social Change in a Northern Vietnamese Village*.

**US politics today:** the journal *International Socialist Review*, available from PO Box 258082, Chicago IL 60625.

**State capitalism:** Tony Cliff, *State Capitalism in Russia*; Tony Cliff, *Revolution Besieged: Lenin, 1917-1923*; Chris Harman, *Class Struggles in Eastern Europe, 1945-1983*; and Charlie Hore, *The Road to Tiananmen Square*.

**The Russian Revolution of 1917:** Leon Trotsky, *History of the Russian Revolution*.

**The Chinese Revolution:** Harold Isaacs, *The Tragedy of the Chinese Revolution*, on the 1920s; and Jack Belden, *China Shakes the World,* on the 1940s.

# Notes

## Introduction

1   I take the phrase from Appy, 1993.

## Chapter 1

1   Trullinger, 1980.
2   Trullinger, 1980, p11.
3   Trullinger, 1980, p36.
4   Trullinger, 1980, p36.
5   Kolko, 1985, p15.
6   Trullinger, 1980, pp24-25.
7   Trullinger, 1980, p24.
8   Lacoutre, 1968, p14. For Ho Chi Minh's life see also Chapter 3 of Marr, 1995.
9   For the background to the view taken here, see Cliff, 1974; and Cliff, 1987. Also very useful in understanding the period are Lewin, 1968; Rees, 1997; Deutscher, 1959; and Ciliga, 1979.
10  See two very good books: Harman, 1982; and Isaacs, 1961.
11  I am simplifying a complex story. For the full details, see Isaacs, 1961.
12  Trullinger, 1980, p29.
13  Young, 1991, p5.
14  Trullinger, 1980, p42.
15  Trullinger, 1980, p43.
16  Marr, 1995, pp208-209. For the famine as a whole, see Marr, 1995, pp96-107, 207-210.
17  Marr, 1995, pp392-401.
18  Young, 1991, p11.
19  Halberstam, 1983, p104.
20  Ngo, 1990, p23.
21  Ngo, 1995; and articles by various people in *Revolutionary History* 3:2 (1990), pp8-43.
22  Trullinger, 1980, pp45-46.
23  Young, 1991, p29.
24  Luong, 1992, p157.
25  Luong, 1992, pp63-64.
26  See, for instance, Bui, 1995, pp23-31; and many passages in Duong, 1993. For an intermediate position, see Luong, 1992, pp186-200; and, for a more sympathetic account, Moise, 1983.

27   Eisenhower, 1963, p372.
28   Thayer, 1989, pp2-3; Young, 1991, pp38-39.
29   Trullinger, 1980, p75.
30   Race, 1972, p35.
31   Race, 1972, p34.
32   For capitalism in the South, see Kolko, 1985, pp208-230.
33   Young, 1991, p56.
34   The most detailed source for the passionate arguments in the party is Thayer, 1989. Kahin, 1986, is also very good.
35   Race, 1972, pp99-100.
36   Race, 1972, p110.
37   Race, 1972, pp113-116.
38   Kolko, 1985, p104.
39   Chanoff, 1986, quoted in Bergerud, 1991, p18.
40   Race, 1972, pp129-130.

# Chapter 2

1    The answer to this question is complex, but again relates to the broader picture of US foreign policy interests. See German, 1999.
2    Halberstam, 1983, pp10-13. For more on the American ruling class see Domhoff, 1967, Aldrich, 1988 and Munkirs, 1985.
3    For American foreign policy after 1945 the best places to start are Kolko and Kolko, 1972; and Ambrose, 1993.
4    The account of anti-Communism that follows leans particularly heavily on Schrecker, 1998; Caute, 1988; and Navasky, 1980. Three books are very useful for the causes of anti-Communism: Lipsitz, 1981; Fones-Wolf 1994; and Harris, 1993.
5    Fine, 1969; Preis, 1964, pp3-85; and Dubofsky and Van Tine, 1977, pp181-279.
6    Preis, 1964, pp257-286.
7    Lipsitz, 1981, p129.
8    Lipsitz, 1981, p126.
9    Powers, 1987.
10   Schrecker, 1988, p285.
11   Navasky, 1980, describes the process in detail.
12   For Hollywood, see Ceplair, 1980; and Schwartz, 1982.
13   Schrecker, 1988, pp267-269.
14   Schrecker, 1988, p276.
15   Schrecker, 1988, p144.
16   Schrecker, 1988, p363, estimates that 10,000 to 12,000 who lost their jobs can be counted, but more would have gone quietly and disappeared from the statistics.
17   Zhai, 2000, pp133-139.
18   Kahin, 1986, p131. Knute Rockne was a famous American football coach at Notre Dame University.
19   For the full argument on Kennedy's complicity, see Chomsky, 1993.
20   Kahin, 1986, p296. This discussion of the coup relies on Kahin, 1986, pp121-235, though we disagree on the possibility of a neutralist solution working.

21  McCoy, 1991, pp193-261.
22  Kahin, 1986, p226, his emphasis.
23  For Johnson's role, see Kahin, 1986, p347-402.
24  McNamara, 1995, p31.
25  McNamara, 1995, p32.
26  Pratt, 1984, p194.
27  Robinson, 1995, pp235-272.
28  Kolko, 1988, p181.
29  Kolko, 1988, p181.
30  Kolko, 1988, p181; Robinson, 1995, pp273-303.
31  Brackman, 1969, p192.
32  Brackman, 1969, p197.

# Chapter 3

1   Gibson, p319.
2   Pratt, 1984, p243.
3   Appy, 1993, pp164-167.
4   Caldwell, 1971, pp123-124.
5   Young, 1991, pp129-130.
6   Young, 1991, p191.
7   Gibson, 1986, pp374-375.
8   Pratt, 1984, p227.
9   Burchett, 1966, p19, quoted in Gibson, 1986, p376.
10  Broughton, 1969, p113, quoted in Gibson, 1986, p377.
11  Clodfelter, 1995, p228.
12  Truong, 1985, pp168-170.
13  Bao, 1993. Here and elsewhere in the book I quote novels as evidence. I do this
    when they seem based on the author's own experience. Many of the people
    who fought in Vietnam chose to write of their experiences in novels partly
    because it was the way they could best tell the truth. Novels are particularly
    good sources for North Vietnamese society, and for North Vietnamese soldiers.
    For the class prejudices involved in not using novels as sources, see the
    excellent discussion in Gibson, 1986, pp461-476.
14  Chapelier, 'Plain of Jars: Social Changes Under Five Years of Pathet Lao
    Administration', Asia Quarterly, 1971, pp18-19, 36, quoted in Branfman, 1972,
    p19.
15  Branfman, 1972, p97.
16  Branfman, 1972, p116.
17  Young, 1991, p130.
18  Gellhorn, 'Suffer the Little Children', Ladies Home Journal, January 1967, p109,
    quoted in Wells, 1994, p84.
19  Tuso, 1990, pp186-187.
20  Tuso, 1990, p182.
21  Appy, 1993, pp17-38. This section and the next lean heavily on Appy's
    magnificent book.
22  Coles, 1971, p131.

23  Appy, 1993, pp25-26.
24  Bergerud, 1991, p128.
25  Appy, 1993, p124.
26  Appy, 1993, pp16-17.
27  Baker, 1981, pp77-78.
28  Bergerud, 1991, p133.
29  Bergerud, 1991, p133.
30  Halberstam, 1983, p268.
31  Halberstam, 1983, pp305-306.
32  Appy, 1993, p156.
33  From a manuscript by Micheal Clodfelter reprinted in Pratt, 1984, pp651-652. For a more detailed version of Clodfelter's experiences, see the excellent Clodfelter, 1988.
34  Pratt, 1984, p653.
35  Pratt, 1984, pp653-655.
36  Pratt, 1984, p656.
37  Caputo, 1977, pp xvii-xviii.
38  Appy, 1993, p156.
39  This account of life in the tunnels is based on Mangold and Pennycate, 1985. See also Bergerud, 1991; Bergerud, 1993; and Schell, 1967, reprinted in Schell, 1987.
40  Mangold and Pennycate, 1985, p74.
41  Bergerud, 1991, pp200-201.
42  Bergerud, 1991, p229.
43  For the clearing of Ben Suc, see Schell, 1967.
44  P Marin, 'Coming to Terms with Vietnam', Harpers, 1980, quoted in Appy, 1993, p296.
45  Vietnam Veterans Against the War, The Winter Soldier Investigation: An Inquiry into American War Crimes (Boston, 1972), quoted in Appy, 1993, p294.
46  Winter Soldier Investigation, quoted in Appy, 1993, pp294-295.
47  Trullinger, 1980, p117.
48  Appy, 1993, p295.

# Chapter 4

1   Wells, 1994, p23. This chapter relies heavily on Wells and Halstead, 1978.
2   Wells, 1994, p24.
3   Wells, 1994, pp36-37.
4   DeBeneditti and Chatfield, 1990, p158.
5   For the whole story, see Marqusee, 1999.
6   Moser, 1996, p41.
7   Halstead, 1978, p265; and Wells, p129.
8   Westheider, 1997, pp12-13.
9   Wells, 1994, pp107-111, 411.
10  Young, 1991, p203.
11  Wells, 1994, p112.
12  Marqusee, 1994, pp164-165.

13  Loewen, 1996, 133.
14  Wells, 1994, p133.
15  Wells, 1994, p191.
16  Wells, 1994, pp107, 197.
17  Wells, 1994, pp107, 373.
18  Halberstam, 1983, p779.
19  Wells, 1994, p112.
20  Halberstam, 1983, p786.
21  Shea, *Vietnam Simply*, quoted in Pratt, 1984, pp273-274.
22  Truong, 1985, p236.
23  And there certainly were unions and strikes in South Vietnam, many not led
    by Communists. For an acount of one industrial dispute, see Wesseling, 2000,
    pp56-61.
24  Bao, 1993, pp170-171.
25  Young, 1991, p223.
26  Bergerud, 1991, p218.
27  The best book on Phoenix is Valentine, 1982.
28  Snepp, 1977, pp42-43.
29  Snepp, 1977, p316.
30  Duong, 1995, pp2-3.
31  Griffiths, 1972, p41.
32  Bilton and Sim, 1992, p82.
33  Bilton and Sim, 1992, pp130-131.
34  Bilton and Sim, 1992, pp131-132.
35  Young, 1991, p189.
36  Young, 1991, p229.
37  Kolko, 1985, p319.
38  Wells, 1994, pp250-251.
39  Farber, 1988, p201.
40  For 1968 see Harman, 1998; Ali and Watkins, 1998. For Chicago see Farber,
    1988.
41  Young, 1991, p237.
42  Wells, 1994, p395.
43  Karnow, 1984, p609.
44  Wells, 1994, p422.
45  Heineman, 1993, pp248-249.
46  Halstead, 1978, p539.
47  The figure is from Heineman, 1993, p249. It is perhaps a little too exact.
48  Kissinger, *White House Years*, pp509-514, quoted in Wells, 1994, p430.
49  See Spofford, 1988.
50  Coles, 1971, pp133-134.

# Chapter 5

1  Kovic, 1976.
2  Kovic, 1976, p111.

3   Kovic, 1976, p191-194.
4   For the Vietnam Veterans Against the War, see Stacewicz, 1997; Kovic, 1976; Moser, 1996.
5   All of the above quotes are from Moser, 1996, pp113-114.
6   Moser, 1996, p117.
7   Cortright, 1975, p55.
8   Cortright, 1975, p60.
9   Cortright, 1975, p26.
10  Cortright, 1975, p26.
11  Cortright, 1975, p65.
12  Cortright, 1975, p66.
13  Cortright, 1975, p5.
14  Quoted in Moser, 1996, p79.
15  Cortright, 1975, pp10-15.
16  Cortright, 1975, pp10-15, 24-25.
17  Cortright, 1975, p34.
18  Terry, 'Bringing the War Home,' *Black Scholar*, November 1970, p14, quoted in Westheider, 1997, p76.
19  Westheider, 1997, p98.
20  Westheider, 1997, p88.
21  Westheider, 1997, p78.
22  Cortright, 1975, p95.
23  Cortright, 1975, p97.
24  Cortright, 1975, pp56-57.
25  O'Brien, 1973.
26  O'Brien, 1973, pp120-122.
27  O'Brien, 1973, pp79-80.
28  O'Brien, 1973, p173.
29  Moser, 1996, p49.
30  O'Brien, 1973, pp113-114.
31  Trujillo, 1990, p35.
32  Cortright, 1975, p44.
33  Cortright, 1975, p45.
34  Moser, 1996, pp50-51.
35  Moser, 1996, p51.
36  Jury, 1986, p40.
37  Moser, 1996, p49.
38  Moser, 1996, p50.
39  Moser, 1996, p49.
40  Moser, 1996, p50.
41  Cortright, 1975, pp108-110, 295.
42  Cortright, 1975, p39.
43  Cortright, 1975, pp36-37.
44  Moser, 1996, p64.
45  Geier, 1999, p38.
46  Cortright, 1975, p489.
47  Cortright, 1975, pp11-12.

48   Halstead, 1978, p641.
49   Cortright, 1975, pp112-113.
50   Cortright, 1975, p115.
51   Cortright, 1975, p118.
52   Cortright, 1975, p122.
53   Cortright, 1975, p136.
54   Cortright, 1975, p137.
55   Young, 1991, pp278-279.
56   Young, 1991, p280.
57   Snepp, 1977, p271.
58   Snepp, 1977, p257.
59   Snepp, 1977, p249.
60   Trullinger, 1980, pp200-201.

# Chapter 6

1    Chanda, 1986, p24.
2    Chanda, 1986, p133.
3    Porter, 1993, p137.
4    Ngo, 1993, p163. The following account of cooperatives in the Mekong leans heavily on Ngo.
5    Porter, 1993, pp170-171.
6    Porter, 1993, p161.
7    Ngo, 1988, p165.
8    Fforde and de Vylder, 1996, p183, put it more diplomatically: the cooperatives were 'weak and informal' and the figures should be treated 'with caution'.
9    Official statistics for the whole country in the 1980s said that the state's share of the trade in staples fluctuated between 14 and 21 percent, see Fforde and de Vylder, 1996, p94. These figures suggest that the state controlled less than 10 percent of the trade in rice in the Mekong. Of course, one has to be careful with official figures in Vietnam for several reasons. Sometimes the authorities massage the figures, but in recent years corruption and local deals mean that they often cannot really count accurately anyway, and the accounting conventions for national statistics assume a state controlled economy that has never fully existed. For some of the problems with statistics, see in particular Kimura, 1989, especially chapters 1 and 2.
10   For the bombing, see Shawcross, 1979.
11   For the history of Cambodian Communism the best book is Kiernan, 1985.
12   Kiernan, 1996, pp172-173. This section on Cambodia leans heavily on Kiernan's book, the only one I have found which makes sense of what happened. I have pushed his argument further than he would in some places, and I disagree with Kiernan about the motives of the Vietnamese government, but that is not central to his argument.
13   Kiernan, 1996, p175.
14   See Kiernan, 1996, pp235-236.
15   Kiernan, 1996, pp235, 239.
16   Kiernan, 1996, pp183-184.

17  Kiernan, 1996, p203.
18  Kiernan, 1996, p274.
19  Kiernan, 1996, p274.
20  Chanda, 1986, pp86-87.
21  Kiernan, 1996, p297.
22  The whole sorry story is best told in Shawcross, 1984.
23  Martin, 1994, p217.
24  Shawcross, 1984, p418.
25  Martin, 1994; and Kamm, 1998.
26  Bui, 1995, p124; Martin, 1994, p271.
27  Martin, 1994, p273.
28  Le Cao Dan, 1995, pp114-119.
29  Fforde and de Vylder, 1996, pp55, 80, 233-234; Porter, 1993, pp55-57.
30  Bui Tin, 1995, pxvi.
31  Duong, 1993, p229.
32  This a theme throughout Fforde and de Vylder, 1996.
33  For a positive view of this strategy see Hiebert, 1966. For a negative view, and the best explanation of what was happening, see Kolko, 1997.
34  In theory the state still owned the land, but in practice everybody was sure the state would never take it back and they could effectively sell it, so they did.
35  Dang, 1995, p167.
36  Kerkvliet, 1995.
37  Dang, 1995, p167.
38  Bui, 1995, p109.
39  Gammeltoft, 1999. Her picture of women's lives is largely confirmed by the Vietnamese sociologist Pham, 1999.
40  Gammeltoft, 1999, p146.
41  Gammeltoft, 1999, p163.
42  Pham, 1999, p190.
43  Kerkvliet, 1995, p74.
44  Kerkvliet, 1995, pp78-79.
45  Porter, 1993, p162.
46  Kolko, 1997, p117.

# Chapter 7

1  Chomsky, 1999, pp119-120, footnote 33, p180.
2  Ambrose, 1993, pp276-277.
3  Kissinger, 1999, pp803-808, pp829-832.
4  The best short introduction to the Iranian revolution is Marshall, 1988. Bayat, 1987, is also very useful.
5  For the Lebanese civil war and the Israeli and American interventions, see Fisk, 1990. For how the marines felt, see Petit, 1986.
6  For Saudi politics and the long standing links between the royal family and America, see the excellent Aburish, 1995. The same author's 1997 book is good on the whole region.
7  See MacArthur, 1991.

8  This is a recurring theme in Powell's memoirs: Powell, 1995. See also Woodward, 1991.

9  Simons, 1998; and Arnove, 2000.

10  For the detail, see Chomsky, 1999; Glenny, 1996; German, 1999; and the articles in *International Socialist Review* 7 and 8, 1999.

11  For the Apache saga see Priest, 1999.

12  The following discussion of films and spitting on veterans is based on Lembcke, 1998. There is also a good discussion of films in Appy, 1993, pp310-314.

13  Chomsky, 1999, p180.

14  The best account of Agent Orange and US government policy towards its victims is Wilcox, 1983.

15  Young, 1995.

16  Young, 1995, p247.

17  Young, 1995, p251.

18  Young, 1995, p245.

19  Faludi, 1991.

20  See the magnificent Shilts, 1988.

21  The following discussion of imprisonment relies on Taylor, 1999; Tonry, 1995; and Parenti, 1999. The discussion of wages, incomes and unions relies on Smith, 1992; and Mishel, Bernstein and Schmitt, 1999.

22  Moody, 1988.

23  For more on this see Geier, 2000.

24  *Newsweek*, 13 December 1999, p32.

# Bibliography

Aburish, Said *The Rise, Corruption and Coming Fall of the House of Saud* (New York, 1995)

Aburish, Said *A Brutal Friendship: The West and the Arab Elite* (New York, 1997)

Aldrich, Nelson Jr *Old Money: The Mythology of America's Upper Class* (New York, 1988)

Ali, Tariq and Susan Watkins *1968: Marching in the Streets* (New York, 1998)

Ambrose, Stephen *Rise to Globalism: American Foreign Policy Since 1938* (New York, 1993)

Appy, Christian *Working Class War: American Combat Soldiers and Vietnam* (Chapel Hill, 1993)

Arnove, Anthony (editor) *Iraq Under Siege: The Deadly Impact of Sanctions and War* (London, 2000)

Baker, Mark *Nam: The Vietnam War in the Words of the Men and Women Who Fought There* (New York, 1982)

Bao Ninh *The Sorrow of War* (London, 1993, first published in Vietnamese 1991)

Bayat, Assef *Workers and Revolution in Iran: A Third World Experience of Workers' Control* (London, 1987)

Belden, Jack *China Shakes the World* (London, 1973)

Bergerud, Eric *The Dynamics of Defeat: The Vietnam War in Hau Nghia Province* (Boulder, 1991)

Bergerud, Eric *Red Thunder, Tropic Lightning: The World of a Combat Division in Vietnam* (Boulder, 1993)

Bilton, Michael and Kevin Sim *Four Hours in My Lai: A War Crime and its Aftermath* (London, 1992)

Brackman, Arnold *The Communist Collapse in Indonesia* (New York, 1969)

Branfman, Fred *Voices from the Plain of Jars: Life Under an Air War* (New York, 1972)

Bui Tin *Following Ho Chi Minh: The Memoirs of a North Vietnamese Colonel*, translated and adapted by Judy Stowe and Do Van (London, 1995, first published in Vietnamese 1991)

Caldwell, Malcolm 'Report from North Vietnam', in Ken Coates, Peter Limqueco and Peter Weiss (editors), *Prevent the Crime of Silence: Reports from the International War Crimes Tribunal founded by Bertrand Russell* (London, 1971)

Caputo, Philip *A Rumor of War* (New York, 1997)

Caute, David *The Great Fear: The Anti-Communist Purge under Truman and Eisenhower* (New York, 1978)

Ceplair, Larry and Steven Englund *The Inquisition in Hollywood: Politics in the Film Community, 1930-1960* (Garden City, NY, 1980)

Chanda, Nayan *Brother Enemy: The War after the War* (New York, 1986)

Chomsky, Noam *Rethinking Camelot: JFK, the Vietnam War and US Political Culture* (Boston, 1993)

Chomsky, Noam *The New Military Humanism: Lessons from Kosovo* (London, 1999)

Ciliga, Ante *The Russian Enigma* (London, 1979, first published in French 1938)

Cliff, Tony *State Capitalism in Russia* (London, 1974, first published 1948)

Cliff, Tony *Revolution Besieged: Lenin, 1917-1923* (London, 1987)

Clodfelter, Micheal *Mad Minutes and Vietnam Months: A Soldier's Memoir* (Jefferson, NC, 1988)

Clodfelter, Micheal *Vietnam in Military Statistics: A History of the Indochina Wars, 1772-1991* (Jefferson, NC, 1995)

Coles, Robert *The Middle Americans: Proud and Uncertain* (Boston, 1971)

Cortright, David *Soldiers in Revolt: the American Military Today* (Garden City, NY, 1975)

Cortright, David 'GI Resistance during the Vietnam War', in Melvin Small and William Hoover, *Give Peace a Chance: Exploring the Vietnam Antiwar Movement* (Syracuse, 1992)

Dang Phong 'Aspects of Agricultural Economy and Rural Life in 1993', in Benedict Kerkvliet and Doug Porter (editors), *Vietnam's Rural Transformation* (Boulder, 1995)

DeBeneditti, Charles and Charles Chatfield *An American Ordeal: The Antiwar Movement of the Vietnam Era* (Syracuse, 1990)

Deutscher, Isaac *The Prophet Unarmed: Trotsky, 1921-1929* (New York, 1959)

Dubofsky, Melvyn and Warren Van Tine *John L Lewis: A Biography* (New York, 1977)

Domhoff, G William *Who Rules America?* (Englewood Cliffs, 1967)

Duong Thu Huong *Paradise of the Blind* (London, 1993, first published in Vietnamese in 1988)

Duong Thu Huong *Novel Without a Name* (New York, 1995, first published in Vietnamese in 1990)

Eisenhower, Dwight *The White House Years: Mandate for Change, 1953-1956* (New York, 1963)

Faludi, Susan, *Backlash: The Undeclared War Against American Women* (London, 1992)

Farber, David *Chicago '68* (Chicago, 1988)

Fforde, Adam *The Agrarian Question in North Vietnam, 1974-1979: A Study of Cooperator Resistance to State Policy* (Armonk, NY, 1989)

Fforde, Adam and Stefan de Vylder *From Plan to Market: The Economic Transition in Vietnam* (Boulder, 1996)

Fine, Sidney *Sit-Down: The General Motors Strike of 1936-1937* (Ann Arbor, 1969)

Fineman, Daniel *A Special Relationship: The United States and Military Government in Thailand, 1947-1958* (Honolulu, 1997)

Fisk, Robert *Pity the Nation: Lebanon at War* (London, 1990)

Fones-Wolf, Elizabeth *Selling Free Enterprise: the Business Assault on Labor and Liberalism, 1945-60* (Urbana, 1994)

Gammeltoft, Tine *Women's Bodies, Women's Worries: Health and Family Planning in a Vietnamese Rural Community* (Richmond, UK, 1999)

Geier, Joel 'Vietnam: the Soldiers' Rebellion', *International Socialist Review* 9, 1999

Geier, Joel 'Nader 2000: Challenging the Parties of Corporate America', *International Socialist Review* 13, 2000.

German, Lindsey (editor) *The Balkans: Nationalism and Imperialism* (London, 1999)

Gibson, James *The Perfect War: Technowar in Vietnam* (Boston, 1986)

Glenny, Misha *The Fall of Yugoslavia: The Third Balkan War* (London, 1996)

Griffiths, Philip Jones *Vietnam Inc* (London, 1972)

Halberstam, David *The Best and the Brightest* (London, 1983, first published 1972)

Halstead, Fred *Out Now!: A Participant's Account of the American Movement against the Vietnam War* (New York, 1978)

Harman, Chris *The Lost Revolution: Germany 1918 to 1923* (London, 1982)

Harman, Chris *Class Struggles in Eastern Europe, 1945-1983* (London, 1988)

Harris, Howell *The Right to Manage: Industrial Relations Policies of American Business in the 1940s* (Madison, 1993)

Harris, Nigel *The Mandate of Heaven: Marx and Mao in Modern China* (London, 1978)

Heineman, Kenneth *Campus Wars: The Peace Movement at American State Universities in the Vietnam Era* (New York, 1993)

Hersh, Seymour *The Price of Power: Kissinger in the Nixon White House* (New York, 1983)

Hiebert, Murray *Chasing the Tigers: a Portrait of the New Vietnam* (New York, 1996)

Hore, Charlie *The Road to Tiananmen Square* (London, 1991)

Isaacs, Harold *The Tragedy of the Chinese Revolution* (Stanford, 1961, first published 1938)

Jury, Mark *The Vietnam Photo Book* (New York, 1986, first published 1971)

Kahin, George *Intervention: How America Became Involved in Vietnam* (New York, 1986)

Kamm, Henry *Cambodia: Report from a Stricken Land* (New York, 1998)

Karnow, Stanley *Vietnam: A History* (New York, 1984)

Kerkvliet, Benedict 'Rural Society and State Relations', in Benedict Kerkvliet and Doug Porter (editors), *Vietnam's Rural Transformation* (Boulder, 1995)

Kiernan, Ben *How Pol Pot Came to Power: A History of Communism in Kampuchea, 1930-1975* (London, 1985)

Kiernan, Ben *The Pol Pot Regime: Race, Power and Genocide in Cambodia under the Khmer Rouge, 1975-79* (New Haven, 1996)

Kimura, Tetsusaburo *The Vietnamese Economy 1975-86: Reforms and International Relations* (Tokyo, 1989)

Kissinger, Henry *Years of Renewal* (New York, 1999)

Kleinen, John *Facing the Future, Reviving the Past: A Study of Social Change in a Northern Vietnamese Village* (Singapore, 1999)

Kolko, Gabriel *Anatomy of a War: Vietnam, the United States and the Modern Historical Experience* (New York, 1985)

Kolko, Gabriel *Confronting the Third World: United States Foreign Policy 1945-1980* (New York, 1988)

Kolko, Gabriel *Vietnam: Anatomy of a Peace* (New York, 1997)

Kolko, Joyce and Gabriel Kolko, *The Limits of Power: The World and United States Foreign Policy* (New York, 1972)

Kovic, Ron *Born on the Fourth of July* (New York, 1976)

Lacoutre, Jean *Ho Chi Minh: A Political Biography* (New York, 1968)

Le Cao Dan 'Agricultural Reforms in Vietnam in the 1980s', in Irene Norlund, Carolyn Gates and Vu Cao Dam (editors), *Vietnam in a Changing World* (Richmond, UK, 1995)

Lembcke, Jerry *The Spitting Image: Myth, Memory and the Legacy of Vietnam* (New York, 1998)

Lewin, Moshe *Lenin's Last Struggle* (New York, 1968)

Lewin, Moshe *Russian Peasants and Soviet Power: A Study of Collectivization* (Evanston, 1968)

Lipsitz, George *Class and Culture in Cold War America: 'A Rainbow at Midnight'* (South Hadley, Mass, 1981)

Loewen, James *Lies My Teacher Told Me: Everything Your American History Textbook Got Wrong* (New York, 1996)

Luong, Hy Van and Nguyen Dac Bang *Revolution in the Village: Tradition and Transformation in North Vietnam, 1925-1988* (Honolulu, 1988)

MacArthur, John *Second Front: Censorship and Propaganda in the Gulf War* (New York, 1991)

McCoy, Alfred *The Politics of Heroin: CIA Complicity in the Global Drug Trade* (New York, 1991)

McNamara, Robert with VanDeMark, Brian, *In Retrospect: The Tragedy and Lessons of Vietnam* (New York, 1995)

Mangold, Tom and John Pennycate *The Tunnels of Cu Chi* (New York, 1985)

Marqusee, Mike *Redemption Song: Muhammad Ali and the Spirit of the Sixties* (New York, 1999)

Marr, David *Vietnam 1945: The Quest for Power* (Berkeley, 1995)

Marshall, Phil *Revolution and Counter-Revolution in Iran* (London, 1988)

Martin, Marie *Cambodia: A Shattered Society* (Berkeley, 1994)

Mishel, Lawrence, Jared Bernstein and John Schmitt *The State of Working America 1998-99* (Ithica, 1999)

Moise, Edwin *Land Reform in China and North Vietnam: Consolidating the Revolution at Village Level* (Chapel Hill, 1983)

Moody, Kim *An Injury to All: the Decline of American Unionism* (London, 1988)

Moser, Richard *The New Winter Soldiers: GI and Veteran Dissent During the Vietnam War* (New Brunswick, 1996)

Munkirs, John *The Transformation of American Capitalism: From Competitive Market Structures to Centralized Private Sector Planning* (Armonk, NY, 1985)

Navasky, Victor *Naming Names* (New York, 1980)

Ngo Van 'On Vietnam', *Revolutionary History* 3:2 (London, 1990)

Ngo Van *Revolutionaries They Could Not Break: The Fight for the Fourth International in Indochina 1930-1945* (London, 1995)

Ngo Vinh Long 'Some Aspects of Cooperativization in the Mekong Delta', in David Marr and Christine White (editors), *Postwar Vietnam: Dilemmas in Socialist Development* (Ithica, 1988)

O'Brien, Tim *If I Die in a Combat Zone, Box Me Up and Take Me Home* (New York, 1973).

Parenti, Christian *Lockdown America: Police and Prisons in the Age of Crisis* (New York, 1999)

Petit, Michael *Peacekeepers at War: A Marine's Account of the Beirut Catastrophe* (Boston, 1986)

Pham Van Bich *The Vietnamese Family in Change: The Case of the Red River Delta* (Richmond, UK, 1999)

Porter, Gareth *Vietnam: The Politics of Bureaucratic Socialism* (Ithica, 1993)

Powell, Colin with Joseph Persico, *My American Journey* (New York, 1995)

Powers, Richard *Secrecy and Power: the Life of Edgar J Hoover* (London, 1987)

Pratt, John *Vietnam Voices: Perspectives on the War Years 1941-1982* (New York, 1984)

Preis, Art *Labor's Giant Step: Twenty Years of the CIO* (New York, 1964)

Priest, D 'How Fear of Losses Kept Super-Copters from Kosovo Action', *International Herald Tribune* 30 December 1999.

Race, Jeffrey *War Comes to Long An: Revolutionary Conflict in a Vietnamese Province* (Berkeley, 1972)

Rees, John 'The New Imperialism', in Alex Callinicos and others, *Marxism and the New Imperialism* (London, 1994)

Rees, John 'In Defence of October', in John Rees and others, *In Defence of October: A Debate on the Russian Revolution* (London, 1997)

Robinson, Geoffrey *The Dark Side of Politics: Political Violence in Bali* (Ithica, 1995)

Schell, Jonathan *The Village of Ben Suc* (New York, 1967), reprinted in Jonathan Schell, *The Real War: The Classic Reporting on the Vietnam War* (New York, 1987)

Schell, Jonathan *The Military Half: an Account of the Destruction of Quang Nga and Quang Tin* (New York, 1968), reprinted in Jonathan Schell, *The Real War: the Classic Reporting on the Vietnam War* (New York, 1987)

Schrecker, Ellen *Many are the Crimes: McCarthyism in America* (Boston, 1988)

Schwartz, Nancy *The Hollywood Writers Wars* (New York, 1982)

Shawcross, William *Sideshow: Kissinger, Nixon and the Destruction of Cambodia* (New York, 1979)

Shawcross, Willliam *The Quality of Mercy: Cambodia, Holocaust and the Modern Conscience* (New York, 1984)

Shilts, Randy *And the Band Played On: Politics, Plagues and the AIDS Epidemic* (New York, 1988)

Simons, Geoffrey *The Scourging of Iraq: Sanctions, Law and Natural Justice* (New York, 1998)

Smith, Sharon 'Twilight of the American Dream', *International Socialism* 54, 1992.

Snepp, Frank *Decent Interval: An Insider's Account of Saigon's Indecent End Told by the CIA's Chief Strategy Analyst in Vietnam* (New York, 1977)

Spofford, Tim *Lynch Street: the May 1970 Slayings at Jackson State College* (Kent, Ohio, 1988)

Stacewicz, Richard *Winter Soldiers: An Oral History of the Vietnam Veterans Against the War* (New York, 1997)

Taylor, K 'Racism and the Criminal Injustice System', *International Socialist Review* 8, 1999.

Thayer, Carlyle *War by Other Means: National Liberation and Revolution in Vietnam* (Sydney, 1989)

Tonry, Michael *Malign Neglect: Race, Crime and Punishment in America* (Oxford, 1995)

Trotsky, Leon (translated by Max Eastman), *History of the Russian Revolution* (London,1977)

Trullinger, James *Village at War: An Account of Revolution in Vietnam* (New York, 1980)

Truong Nhu Tang with D Chanoff and Can Toai Doan, *A Vietcong Memoir* (San Diego, 1985). British edition, *Journal of a Vietcong* (London, 1986).

Tuso, Joseph *Singing the Vietnam Blues: Songs of the Air Force in South-east Asia* (College Station, Texas, 1990)

Ungpakorn, Ji *The Struggle for Democracy and Social Justice in Thailand* (Bangkok, 1997)

Valentine, Douglas *The Phoenix Program* (New York, 1982)

Wells, Tom *The War Within: America's Battle Over Vietnam* (Berkeley, 1994)

Westheider, James *Fighting on Two Fronts: African Americans and the Vietnam War* (New York, 1997)

Wesseling, Louis *Fuelling the War: Revealing an Oil Company's Role in Vietnam* (New York, 2000)

Wilcox, Fred *Waiting for an Army to Die: The Tragedy of Agent Orange* (New York, 1983)

Woodward, Bob *The Commanders* (New York, 1991)

Young, Allan *The Harmony of Illusions: Inventing Post-Traumatic Stress Disorder* (Princeton, 1995)

Young, Marilyn *The Vietnam Wars: 1945-1990* (New York, 1991)

Zhai, Quiang *China and the Vietnam Wars, 1950-1975* (Chapel Hill, 2000)

# Index

A&P: 117

Aburish, Said: 210

Acheson, Dean: 106

Addlestone, David: 133-134, 137

Afghanistan: 108

Africa: 8, 21, 128

African-Americans, *see* race relations, US

African National Congress (ANC): 55, 177

Agency for International Development (AID): 144

Agent Orange: 70, 184-185

*Agerholm*, USS: 124

AIDS: 191

Airforce, US
  101st Airborne: 77-79, 98
  173rd Airborne: 133-134
  Canute Air Force Base: 124
  Kirtland Air Force Base: 124
  Wright-Patterson Air Force Base: 124

air traffic controllers, US: 191

air war, *see* bombing

Alabama: 123

Alaska: 123

Albanians, in Kosovo: 35, 180-182

Aldrich Jr, Nelson: 204

Algeria: 55, 177

Ali, Muhammad: 86

Ali, Tariq: 207

Alsop, Stewart: 139

Ambrose, Steven: 204, 210

America, *see* United States

*America*, USS: 141

American Association of University Professors: 114

American Declaration of Independence: 20

American Federation of Labor (AFL): 42, 196

American Federation of State, County and Municipal Employees: 112

American Legion: 119

American Red Cross
  blood segregations: 45

American Revolution: 121-122

Angkar *see* Khmer Rouge

Angkor Wat: 156

Angola: 176-177

anti-capitalism: 196

anti-Communism in the US: 2, 35-60, 61, 109, 114, 115, 140, 194

anti-war movement: 5, 55, 69, 78, 89, 90, 107, 111-115, 122-130, 140, 141
  *see* also protests

anti-war newspapers: 122-124, 126, 129, 136-137, 141-142

Apache helicopters: 182

Appy, Christian: 199, 203, 205, 206, 211

Arbenz: 51

Argentina: 108

Arizona: 123

Arlington National Cemetery: 109-110

*Armed Forces Journal*: 139

Army of the Republic of Vietnam (ARVN): 33, 50-51, 62, 140

Army, US
  196th Light Infantry Brigade: 135-136
  1st Cavalry: 137
  25th Infantry: 72, 75, 81, 132, 133
  46th Infantry: 130-132
  501st Infantry: 137
  Nelligen Army Base: 128
  *see also* GIs, draft, combat refusals, basic training, soldiers' revolt

Arnove, Anthony: 211

artillery, *see* firepower
atomic bomb, *see* nuclear weapons
attrition: 3, 63, 73, 79, 99
   *see also* body count
Australia: 60
Austria: 55

B-52s: 65-67, 96-97, 142-143
backlash in US after 1975: 175-194
Bahrain: 177
Baker, Mark: 206
Bali: 57
Ball, George: 54
Bao Ninh: 66, 96, 200, 205, 207
basic training: 71-72, 126
Batista: 56
Baumholder: 123
Bay of Pigs: 57
Bayat, Assef: 210
Beautiful Waters: 9, 10, 11, 16, 18, 23-
   25, 26, 28, 29, 30, 84, 93, 98, 137-
   138, 145, 174, 199
Beirut: 178
Belden, Jack: 201
Bengal: 19
Ben Suc village: 82
Ben Tre province: 33, 93, 95, 151, 171
Bergerud, Eric: 204, 206-207
Berkeley, University of California: 85,
   129
Berlin: 123
Bernstein, Jared: 211
Bilton, Michael: 103
Binh My: 151
birth control: 169-171
Black Action Group: 128
Black Dissent Group: 128
Black Front: 142
Black Panther Party: 123
Black Power: 88
blacks in the United States, *see* race
   relations
boat people: 162-163
body count: 63, 73, 76-80, 99
Bolivia: 108
Bolsheviks: 13-14, 122
bombing, US: 2-3, 62-71, 99, 140, 142

of Cambodia: 4, 62, 108, 110, 142,
   143, 152-154
of Hanoi: 89, 91, 142
of Iraq: 35, 181
of Japan: 153
of Laos: 62, 108, 143
of North Vietnam: 53, 54, 62, 63,
   109, 110, 143-144, 153, 200
of South Vietnam: 50, 62, 63, 108,
   153, 200
of Yugoslavia: 35, 181
boot camp, *see* basic training
*Born on the Fourth of July*: 117
Bosnia: 180
Boston: 121
   Tea Party: 113
Brackman, Arnold: 205
Branagan, Peter: 121
Branfman, Fred: 67-68, 205
Britain
   government: 21, 23, 39, 43, 60
   army: 21, 23
   colonialism: 19, 21, 55, 163
   Labour Party: 23, 39, 60
Bronx: 119
Broughton, Jack: 65, 205
Buddhists: 23, 51-52, 94, 95
   protests: 51-52, 95
buffaloes: 68, 79, 98
Bui Tin: 166-167, 203, 210
Bulgaria: 40, 55
Bundy, MacGeorge: 92
Bunker, Archie: 113
Burchett, Wilfred: 65, 205
Bush, George: 184, 191

C rations: 84, 132
Caldwell, Malcolm: 63, 205
California: 112, 123
Call, Michael: 75
Calley, Lieutenant 'Rusty' 103
Cambodia: 4, 7, 13, 21, 25, 27, 67, 96,
   110-113, 120, 143, 155, 158-160, 200
   after 1975: 3-4, 147, 152-161
   bombing of: 4, 62, 108, 110, 142,
   143, 152-154
   strikes: 155

Cham minority: 158-159
Khmer Rouge: 152-161
US invasion of in 1970: 110-113, 120
Camp Drake: 124
Camp Eagle: 98
Camp Pendleton: 123, 129
Canada: 60, 125
Canute Air Force Base: 124
Cao Dai religion: 51
capitalism: 8, 14, 20, 28, 30, 40, 63, 76,
  149, 156, 169, 174, 177, 195, 196
  *see also* anti-capitalism and state
  capitalism
Caputo, Marine Lieutenant Philip: 79,
  206
Carey, Teamsters union president: 195
Carmichael, Stokely: 86, 88
Carter, Jimmy: 148, 162
Castro, Fidel: 56-57
casualties
  Indonesia: 58-59
  Iraq: 179
  Korea: 49
  Kosovo: 180
  South Vietnamese government
  forces: 140
  US: 74-76
  Vietnamese: 62, 65, 96-97, 164-165
Catholics 28, 51-52
  refugees 51
Caute, David: 204
Central Intelligence Agency (CIA):
  18, 50-51, 56, 58, 67, 73, 91, 97, 99-
  100, 144, 145
Ceplair, Larry: 204
Chanda, Nayan: 147, 200, 209-210
Chanoff, David: 204
Chapelier, George: 67, 205
Charlestown: 124
Charlie, *see* National Liberation Front
Chatfield, Charles: 206
Chen Leng: 157
Chicago: 107-108, 122, 129, 196
Chicano community, *see* Latino
children: 10-68, 69, 82-84, 98, 118-
  119, 131, 146, 158, 160-161, 166,
  169-171, 180, 185

Chile: 108
China
  government and Communists: 1-2,
  4, 7, 14, 15-16, 24, 27, 28, 36, 39-
  40, 49-50, 61, 140, 143, 147-150,
  155, 162-165, 174, 200
  aid to Vietnam: 148-150
  Red Army: 40, 48-49, 51
  support for Pol Pot: 157, 162-165
  Tiananmen Square: 174
  *see also* state-capitalism,
  Guomindang and Sino-Soviet split
Chinese minority
  in Cambodia: 158
  in Vietnam: 31, 150-151
Chinese Revolution: 40, 55, 201
Cholon: 150-151
Chomsky, Noam: 5, 204, 210, 211
Christians: 114, 177-178, 186
Christmas bombing: 142
Chu Lai beach pot party 126-127
  *see also* drugs
Churchill, Winston: 21, 23
CIA, *see* Central Intelligence Agency
Ciliga, Ante: 203
civil rights movement: 2, 3, 59, 61,
  86-88, 109, 130, 190, 194
class struggle
  and international relations: 2-4, 35-
  36, 39, 148-150, 175-183
  in Cambodia: 3-4
  in China: 148-149
  in Russia: 148-149
  in the US: 2-4, 40-47, 59, 71, 83-84,
  129, 175-179, 185-189
  in the US military: 61, 113-115,
  117-146
  in Vietnam: 2-4, 24-25, 61-62, 147-
  148, 151-152, 172-179
  in the Vietnamese Communist
  Party: 16-17, 25, 26-27, 30-33
  *see also* ruling class and working class
Cliff, Tony: 4, 201, 203
Clifford, Clark: 104-105, 106
Clinton, Bill: 148, 182, 195-196
Clodfelter, Micheal: 77-79, 98, 199,
  205-206

cluster bombs: 64
Coast Guard: 141
coffee houses: 123, 124, 129
Colby, William: 97
Cold War: 2, 27, 61, 177-178
see also peaceful coexistence
Coles, Robert: 205, 207
Colombia: 181
colonialism: 51
   British: 19, 21, 55, 163
   French: 1-12, 17-28, 30, 55, 61, 80,
   93, 98
   Portugese: 55, 176
combat refusals: 130-132, 137
Coming Home: 183-184
Communist International
   (Comintern): 13, 15, 32, 149
Communists/Communist Parties
   Cambodia: 110, 147, 152-155, 161,
   162
   China: 15, 24, 40, 48, 49, 155, 162
   Czechoslovakia: 108
   Eastern Europe: 180
   France: 13, 18, 21, 24
   Greece: 48
   India: 30
   Indonesia: 57-59
   Iran: 48
   Laos: 67, 110, 147
   North Korea: 48, 49
   Philippines: 51
   South Korea: 50
   Russia: 13, 14, 56
   US: 41-47, 86, 88, 194
   Vietnam: 1, 2, 4, 9, 12-17, 19, 20,
   22-35, 47, 49, 50, 53, 61, 62, 65, 77,
   79, 80-82, 94, 96, 97, 99, 100, 105,
   143, 144, 145, 147, 148, 149, 150,
   151, 153, 154, 164, 166, 167, 169,
   174, 175
   Yugoslavia: 180
Communist Youth Brigade: 100
Concerned Officers Movement: 136
Concord: 120-121
Congo: 51
Congress, US: 54, 104, 105, 121, 126,
   142, 177-178

Congress of Industrial Unions (CIO):
   42
conscription see draft
Conservative Party, Britain: 39
Constellation, USS: 140, 142
cooperatives see land
Coral Sea, USS: 140-141
Cornell University: 85-86
corporations: 38, 41, 190
   see also Nike, Dow, Ford, General
   Motors, Starbucks, RAND
corruption: 165, 168-169
Cortright, Frank: 123
Cortright, Richard: 200, 208-209
Croatia: 180-181
Cu Chi: 133, 136, 137
   tunnels: 80-82, 93, 97, 99
Cuba: 56-57, 176-177
Cultural Revolution: 149
Czechoslovakia: 40, 55, 108

Daley, Mayor: 107
Danang: 72, 76, 79, 127, 144-145
Danfora at Kent State: 111
Dang Phong: 168-169, 210
Daniels, George: 129
Dartmouth College: 89
Daud, Colonel: 133
De Gaulle, Charles: 18, 21, 24
Dearborn, Michigan: 89
death penalty, US: 193
DeBeneditti, Charles: 206
Declaration of Independence, US: 20
Deegan, Richard: 72
Deep Purple: 134
Defense Language Institute: 124-125
Defense, Department of, see Pentagon
Defense, Secretary of, see McNamara,
   Robert
Demilitarized Zone (DMZ): 92-93
democracy: 16, 29, 39, 47, 55, 88, 110,
   112, 165, 174, 190
Democratic Party: 37, 40, 45, 48, 86,
   87, 106, 107, 109, 129
demonstrations, see protests
desertions, US armed forces: 125-126
Detroit: 112, 114

Deutscher, Isaac: 203
de Vylder, Stefan: 209, 210
Diallo, Amadou: 195
Diem, Ngo Van: 30, 31, 32, 34, 51-52, 143
Dien Bien Phu: 27, 166
Disney, Walt: 44
Doi Moi: 167-168
dollar and Gold Standard: 105-106
Domhoff, G William: 204
Dominican Republic: 129
domino theory: 54-56
dope, *see* drugs
Dow Chemical Company: 69
Dowd, Doug: 85-86
draft
   Iraq: 179
   riots: 125
   US: 5, 71, 86, 122-123, 125
   Vietnam: 144, 164-165
drugs: 126-127
Dubofsky, Melvyn: 204
Duck Hook: 109, 110, 113
duck test: 45
Duong Thu Huong: 100, 101, 167, 199, 203, 207, 210
Dutch in Indonesia: 51

Eastern Europe, fall of Communism: 178-180
economy
   Indonesia: 57
   North Vietnam: 4, 8, 30, 147-148
   Russia: 14
   South Vietnam: 8, 144, 148
   Vietnam after 1975: 163, 165-169
   US: 47, 105-106, 191-192
education
   US: 89
   Vietnam: 16, 25
   *see also* students and universities, US
Egypt: 55, 177
Eisenhower, Dwight: 27, 204
El Paso, Texas: 124-125
elections
   Cambodia: 165
   US: 106

   Vietnam: 22-23, 27-31, 172
Electrical Workers Union, US: 42
Evans, Captain Dwight: 143

Fabulous Furry Freak Brothers: 124-125
fascism: 43
Faludi, Susan: 191, 211
famine: 19-20, 157
   Bengal: 19
   India: 19
   North Vietnam, 1945: 18-20
   Cambodia: 157-158
   China: 149, 156
   threat of, in Vietnam 1981-88: 163, 167
Farber, David: 207
Federal Bureau of Investigation (FBI): 40, 43, 86, 107
Ferizzi, Ron: 121
Fforde, Adam: 209-210
Fine, Sidney: 204
Fineman, Daniel: 200
firepower: 2, 61-84
Fisk, Robert: 210
Flint, Michigan: 40
Fonda, Jane: 141
Fones-Wolf, Elizabeth: 204
Ford Motor Company: 38, 76
Ford, Gerald: 148
*Forestall*, USS: 124, 142
Fort Bliss: 124-125
Fort Bragg: 122-123
Fort Campbell: 123
Fort Dix: 123
Fort Gordon: 123
Fort Greely: 123
Fort Hood: 123, 129
Fort Huaracha: 123
Fort Jackson: 122
Fort Knox: 123
Fort Leonard Wood: 123
Fort McClellan: 123
Fort Polk: 123
Fort Richardson: 123
Fort Riley: 123
Fourth of July parade: 119
fragging: 130-136, 139

France
  government: 18, 21, 39, 49, 60, 108
  army: 23, 24, 26, 139
  colonialism: 1-12, 17-28, 55, 61, 80,
    93, 98
  war in Indochina: 17-27, 54-55, 61,
    166
Frank, Glenn: 112
Frankfurt: 123
Free French: 18
French Communist Party: 13, 21, 24
French Foreign Legion: 24
French Socialist Party: 13
Front, see National Liberation Front
FTA (Fuck the Army) Show: 126, 141
Fuchs, Paul: 124-125

Gammeltoft, Tine: 170-171, 200, 210
Garvey, Marcus: 88
Gates, Bill: 38
gays and lesbians: 4, 13, 191
Geier, Joel: 200, 208, 211
Gellhorn, Martha: 69, 205
General Motors: 40
Geneva peace negotiations: 1, 27-28,
    29, 49, 67, 143
Georgia, US: 123
German, Lindsey: 204, 211
Germany: 14, 17, 18, 21, 24, 27, 29,
    39-40, 43, 48, 55, 108, 127, 128,
    130, 142
ghetto uprisings, see riots
Giap, Vo Nguyen: 17
Gibbs, Philip: 114
Gibson, James: 199, 205
Girl Scouts: 114
GIs: 62, 63, 71-84, 96, 143, 199 62
  admiration for NLF: 80-83
  revolt: 3, 117-146, 183-184, 200
  troop withdrawals: 139-140, 143
GIs for Peace: 124-125
GIs United Against the War: 122-123
Glenny, Misha: 211
Gold Standard, see dollar
Goldwater, Barry: 53, 85
Gonzalez, Leonard: 102-104
Gorbachev: 55

Grace, at Kent State: 111
Great Leap Forward: 149, 156
Greece: 180
Greek Civil War: 48
Green, James Earl: 114
Green, Marshall: 58-59, 110-111
Griffiths, Philip Jones: 100, 101, 102,
    207
ground war: 2-3, 54, 71-84, 118-119
Guatemala: 51, 57
guerrillas: 1, 2, 3, 18, 24-26, 31, 50-51,
    56-57, 61, 67, 70, 73-75, 77-78, 80-
    82, 85, 92-99, 104, 108, 110, 138,
    140, 143, 145, 147, 154, 162, 180
  see also Viet Cong and National
    Liberation Front
Guiliani, mayor of New York: 195
Gulf of Tonkin, incident: 54
Gulf War, second: 178-179 189
Guomindang: 14, 15, 18, 48, 21

H-bomb: 47
Halberstam, David: 76, 199, 203, 204,
    206-207
Haldeman, Bob: 109
Halstead, Fred: 90, 199, 206-207
Hamburger Hill: 135
Hammond, Marilyn: 111
Hanoi: 7, 20, 22, 89, 91, 93, 95, 107,
    138, 140, 142, 143, 144, 166-167
  bombing of: 89, 91, 142
  'Hanoi Hilton': 65
  insurrection: 20-22, 173
Harman, Chris: 201, 203, 207
Harris, Howell: 204
Harvard Unversity: 37, 71
Harvey, William: 129
Hau Nghai province: 80-82
Hawaii: 141
Hawkins, James: 127
Heck, Michael: 143
Heidelberg: 123, 128
Heineman, Kenneth: 111, 207
Heinl, Colonel Robert: 139
Helms, Richard: 90-91
Henderson, Bruce: 129
Hendricks, John: 72-73

Heng Chor: 160
Heng Semrin: 162
Herbert, Lieutenant Colonel: 134
heroin trade: 53
Hiebert, Murray: 210
Hiroshima: 20, 39, 62, 91
Hitler, Adolf: 37, 40, 43, 103
Hmong minority: 67
Ho Chi Minh: 12, 13, 15-16, 23, 24,
    26, 28, 55, 109
Ho Chi Minh City, see Saigon
Ho Chi Minh Trail: 110
Hoffman, Abbie: 113
Hollywood: 44-45 183-184
    unions: 44-45
Hong Kong: 163
Hoover, J Edgar: 40, 43
Hore, Charlie: 201
hospitals, see Veterans Administration
    hospitals
Hue: 7, 9, 10, 11, 12, 16, 50-51, 151,
    93, 144
Huk guerrillas, Philippines: 51
Humphrey, Hubert: 45, 108, 109
Hun Sen: 162, 165
Hungary: 14, 40, 48, 55
    workers: 113
Hussein, Saddam: 35, 178-179, 181
Huynh Tan Phat: 52

Iceland: 13
imperialism: 23, 61, 176
    see also colonialism
International Monetary Fund (IMF):
    148, 168
India: 19, 55
Indochina: 7, 15, 21, 25, 147
Indonesia: 51, 55, 57-59, 163, 168,
    173, 181
    Communist Party (PKI): 57-59
international relations: 2, 4, 15, 35
    see also class struggle and
    international relations, and United
    States foreign policy
International Socialist Review: 200
Iran: 48, 51, 55, 108, 130 173, 177-179
Iraq: 178-180, 181

bombing by the Americans: 35, 181
    casualties:179
    draft:179
Isaacs, Harold: 201, 203
Islam: 57, 86, 159
Islamists: 55, 177-179
Israel: 107, 177-178
Italy: 55

Jackson State: 114
Jackson, Mim: 111
Japan
    government: 18, 19, 20, 30, 59, 108,
    124, 142
    army: 17-21, 23
    tourists: 93
Java: 57-58
Jim Hill High School: 114
Johnson, Lady Bird: 90
Johnson, Lyndon: 62, 67, 76, 85, 91,
    92, 93, 104, 106, 107, 109, 183
Joint Chiefs of Staff: 49
Jordan: 55
journalists, see media, US
Jury, Mark: 135, 208
Justice Department: 125

Kahin, George: 204-205
Kaiserlauthen: 123
Kamm, Henry: 210
Kampuchea: 156
    see also Cambodia
Kansas: 123
Karachi: 108
Karlsruhe, Smiley Barracks: 128
Karnow, Stanley: 207
Kazan, Elia: 44
Keflavik Air Force Base: 136
Kem Hong Hav: 155
Kennedy, Joe: 37
Kennedy, John F: 76, 106, 183, 204
Kennedy, Robert: 106, 107, 183
Kent State University: 36-37, 51-52,
    54-55, 111-112, 114, 120
Kentucky: 123
Kerkvliet, Benedict: 52-53, 172, 210
Khe Sanh: 73-74, 92-93

Khmer Krom minority in Vietnam and
   Cambodia: 160
Khmer Rouge: 152-161
Khmer Serai: 25
Khomeini, Ayatollah: 177
Khrushchev, Nikita: 32, 47
Kiernan, Ben: 200, 209-210
Killeen, Texas: 129
Killing Fields, see Cambodia after 1975
Kimura, Tetsusaburo: 209
King Sihanouk, see Sihanouk
King, Martin Luther: 59, 86, 87, 88,
   107, 108, 109, 127, 177
King, Rodney: 194-195
Kirtland Air Force Base: 124
Kissinger, Henry: 112, 138, 140, 177,
   207, 210
Kitty Hawk, USS: 142
Kleinen, John: 200
Knoxville, Tennessee: 111, 113
Knoxville College: 114-115
Kolb, Gerald: 72
Kolko, Gabriel: 33, 58, 172-174, 199,
   200, 203, 204, 205, 207, 210
Kolko, Joyce: 204
Korea: 27, 29, 30, 48-49, 55
   see also North Korea and South
   Korea
Korean War: 27, 48-51, 54, 85-86, 92,
   126
Kosovan Albanians: 35, 180-182
Kosovo War: 35, 180-183
Kovic, Ron: 117-120, 200, 207-208
Krause, Alison: 111, 112
Ku Klux Klan: 86, 107
Kurds: 177
Kuwait: 178-179
Ky, Vice-President: 53

labor unions: 30
   Russia: 14
   US: 4, 35, 36, 39-41, 42, 44-45, 47,
   61, 87, 112, 114, 130, 190-192, 195,
   196
   Vietnam: 94, 95, 172, 173
Labour Party, British: 23, 39
Lacoutre, Jean: 203

Ladies Home Journal: 69
land: 9-11, 25, 29, 30-31, 33-34, 68,
   99, 150, 163, 168, 172
   cooperatives: 147, 150-151, 163,
   170
   reform: 16-17, 26-27, 30-31, 33-34,
   57, 150, 155, 163
   village land: 7, 9-11
landlords: 2, 7, 10, 11, 16-17, 24-25,
   26, 30-31, 39, 61, 144
Laos: 7, 13, 21, 25, 27, 56, 67-69, 110,
   143
Latin America: 56-57
Latino minority in the US: 124, 193
Le Cao Dan: 210
Le Van Chan: 32-33, 34
Le Van Tiem: 25
Lebanon: 55, 177-178
left, US: 5, 41-47, 85-88, 185-191
Lembcke, Jerry: 184, 200, 211
Lemus, Miguel: 133
Lewin, Moshe: 203
Lewinsky, Monica: 36
liberals, US: 40, 45, 55, 86, 87, 89,
   107, 113, 176, 183
Lindisfarne, Nancy: 89
Lindquist, John: 134
Lipsitz, George: 204
Lodge, Henry Cabot: 52
Loewen, James: 89
Lon Nol: 110, 152, 153
Long An province: 33, 34, 96
Long Beach: 124
Long Island: 117
Los Angeles: 38
   riots 107, 112, 194-195
Louisiana: 123
Lovett, Robert: 36-37
Luici, Jeri: 81
Lumumba, Patrice: 51
Luong, Hy Van: 203

MacArthur, Douglas: 48
MacArthur, John: 210
MacCarthy, Eugene: 106, 107
MacNaughton, John: 55
Malaysia: 55, 59, 159, 168-169

Malcolm X: 122, 177
Manchester, New Hampshire: 53
mandarins: 12-13, 19, 24-25, 28
Mandela, Nelson: 177
Mangold, Tom: 199, 206
Mao Tse Dung: 28, 155
Marin, P: 206
marine corps (USMC): 56, 73-74, 76,
    84, 85, 86, 117, 120, 126, 134-135,
    139-140, 142, 178
market
    ideology of the: 167-168
    resistance to the: 171-173
Marqusee, Mike: 206
Marr, David: 199
Marshall, Phil: 210
Martin, Marie: 164-165, 210
Marx, Karl: 94
May 1968: 108
McCarthy, Joe: 40, 45, 106
McCarthy, Lieutenant Colonel R: 128
McCarthyism: 40-47
    see anti-Communism in the US
McCoy, Alfred: 205
McNair Barracks: 123
McNamara, Craig: 88
McNamara, Robert: 37-38, 62, 76, 80,
    88, 104, 183, 205
media, US: 35-36, 69, 88, 90, 93, 94,
    100, 101, 102, 108, 121, 135, 145,
    162, 176, 179, 184-185
Medina, Captain Ernest: 102
Mekong Delta: 7, 18, 33, 50, 93, 150-
    151, 172
Methodist ministers: 114
Mexico: 22
    Guadalajara, Village in the Sun: 117
    Mexico City: 108
Michigan State: 85, 89
Middle East: 35
Miles, Joe: 122
Miller, Jeffrey: 111, 112
Milosevic, Slobodan: 181-182
Mimi's Flamboyant Bar: 99
mines: 75, 131, 132, 134
'Minh' from Beautiful Waters: 11-12,
    16, 23

Minh, General: 52, 97
Mishel, Lawrence: 211
Mississippi: 86, 114
Mississippi Freedom Democratic Party:
    86
Missoffe, François: 150
Missouri: 123
Mitchell, John: 110
Mobutu, President: 51
Moise, Edwin: 203
Molina, marine serving with
    Kovic: 118-119
Monks, William: 141
Montenegro: 180
Moody, Kim: 211
Morocco: 55, 177
Moser, Richard: 200, 208
Mossadegh: 51
Munkirs, John: 204
Murray, Philip: 42
music: 126-127
Muslim, see Islam
mutiny, see fragging
My Lai massacre: 102-104, 130-132,
    200
My Thuy Phong, see Beautiful Waters

Nagasaki: 20, 39, 91
napalm: 50, 69, 176
Nation of Islam: 88
National Guard: 108, 111, 114, 129
National Liberation Front (NLF): 1, 3,
    9, 25, 50-53, 55, 65, 75, 82, 92, 93,
    94, 97, 98, 102, 104, 108, 137, 140,
    145-146, 150, 152
National Recovery Act, US: 41
National Security Council: 54
nationalism: 24, 55, 57
    see also Guomindang and Viet Minh
Native Americans: 107
Navasky, Victor: 204
Nazi Germany: 14, 24
Neale, Jonathan: 5, 110, 111
Nehru: 57
Nelligen army base: 128
Nepal: 55
    Gurkhas: 23

New Deal: 41
New Hampshire: 53, 106
New Jersey: 123, 141
New Mexico: 124
New York: 38, 86, 87, 195
New York City: 86
*New York Times*: 76
Newport: 124
newspapers, anti-war: 122-124, 126,
    129, 136, 176
*Newsweek*: 139, 197, 211
Ngo Van Diem: 28-29
Ngo Van Xuyet: 174, 203
Ngo Vinh Long: 209
Ngoc Bo Ray: 96
Nguyen Than Linh: 80
Nha Trang: 144
Nhu, Madame: 52
Nike: 197
*Nitro*, USS: 141
Nitze, Paul: 91
Nixon, Richard: 52-53, 105, 109, 110,
    111, 112, 113, 138, 140, 148-149,
    152
NLF, *see* National Liberation Front
Nong Dan: 172
Norfolk: 141
North Atlantic Treaty Organization
    (NATO): 166, 181-183
North Carolina: 122
North Korea: 48
North Vietnam
    government: 1, 27, 28, 49, 95, 108,
    147-148, 153
North Vietnamese Army (NVA): 66,
    73, 92-93, 96, 138, 199
novels: 66, 96
nuclear weapons: 20, 39-40, 47, 49, 53,
    109

O'Brien, Tim: 130-132, 133, 136, 208
Oai, Dr: 63-64
Oak Ridge, Tennessee: 113
Oakland: 125
    draft riots: 125
officers, US anti-war: 3, 136-137
Ohio: 124

oil: 39, 51, 58, 178-181
Okinawa: 124
Olney, Dennis: 124-125
Operation Ranch Hand, *see* Agent
    Orange
*Oriskany*, USS: 141
*Overseas Weekly*: 128

Pakistan: 108
Palestine: 55, 177-178, 181
Panzer Barracks: 128
Parenti, Christian: 211
Paris: 123
Paris peace talks and agreement: 107,
    108, 109, 137, 140, 143, 148, 153
Pathet Lao: 25, 67
Payton, Greg: 86
peace protesters, *see* protests
peaceful coexistence: 32, 149
peasants: 10-34, 39, 48, 50, 53, 61, 70,
    77, 78, 81, 84, 93, 94, 95, 98, 104,
    147, 148, 150, 156, 161, 163, 164,
    166, 168, 171-174
Pennycate, John: 199, 206
Pentagon: 3, 36-38, 53-54, 56, 61, 62,
    63, 88, 90, 91, 104-105, 138, 139,
    142, 143, 177
Petit, Michael: 210
Pham Van Bich: 210
Philadelphia: 121, 173
Philippines: 30, 51, 130, 173
Phoenix program: 97-98, 99
photographers, *see* media
Phu Ninh: 19
'Pinkville', *see* My Lai
*Pioneer Contender*, USS: 145
Pitts, Lieutenant Fred: 137
Plain of Jars: 67-69
plantations: 8
*Playboy*: 134
Plonka, Del: 75
poison gas: 80
Pol Pot: 155, 158, 160, 162-164
    Chinese support for: 157, 162-165
    US support for: 162
Poland: 55, 108

police
  US: 107, 93, 95, 110, 112, 114
  Vietnamese: 10, 11, 14, 19, 22, 24,
    30, 32, 33, 97, 154, 172
Porter, Gareth: 210
Portugal, government of: 55, 176
post-traumatic stress disorder: 185-189
pot, *see* drugs
Potsdam: 21
Powell, General: 129, 179, 211
Powers, Richard: 204
Prague, Russian tanks: 108
Pratt, John: 199, 205, 207
Preis, Art: 204
Priest, D: 211
prison
  Cambodia: 161
  US: 45, 47, 175, 191-194
prisoners of war, US (POWs): 65, 184
propaganda: 26, 34, 42, 141, 163
prostitution: 99-100, 117-118, 165, 171
protests
  GIs: 124-125, 128-130, 136-137,
    140-142
  Serbia: 182
  students, Saigon: 195
  students, US: 85-87, 89-90, 111-
    115, 120, 128-129
  US: 3, 5, 48, 55, 107, 109-115, 120-
    122, 107-108, 152, 183-184
  Vietnam: 52
  veterans: 79, 120-122
  1968: 3, 92, 93, 95-96, 106, 107-
    109, 129, 133, 196
  *see also* riots and GIs revolt
Pruitt, Sergeant Dan: 124
psychiatry: 185-189
pyschological problems, veterans: 183-
  189
public opinion, US: 48, 89, 92, 126,
  176, 182-183
Pursat: 160

Quang Ngai province: 102-104
Quang Tri: 134
Quynh leprosarium: 63

race relations
  Cambodia : 158-160
  US: 4, 42-43, 45, 59-60, 86-88, 89,
    107, 114-115, 127-128, 129, 132,
    142, 177, 178, 190-195
  US armed forces: 122, 128, 132,
    136, 142
Ralph: 71, 115
  his father: 71
  his mother: 115
*Rambo: First Blood*: 183
*Ramparts Magazine*: 87
RAND corporation: 104
rape: 98, 100-103, 163, 193
Reagan, Ronald: 44, 112, 148, 184, 191
Rear Echelon Mother Fuckers: 132
*see also* Pentagon
Red Army, *see* China
Red River Delta: 7, 10, 151, 1700
Rees, John: 203
refugees: 67, 148, 181
reparations, US to Vietnam: 148
Republic of South Vietnam, *see* South
    Vietnam
Republican Party: 37, 40, 48, 109
Reserve Officer Training Corps
    (ROTC): 111, 112, 136
Resor, Stanley: 91
Reuther, Walter: 44
Revere, Paul: 121
Rex Hotel: 171
Rhode Island: 124
Ribicoff, Abraham: 108
rice: 7, 8, 10, 18, 58, 67-68, 71, 83,
    146, 148, 150-152, 155-158, 163-
    164, 166-168, 170-171
Rice, Captain Al: 137
riots, US: 59, 107, 108, 112, 127, 129,
    190, 194, 196
  *see also* protests
Riverside Church, New York: 87
Robinson, Geoffrey: 205
Rockefeller, John D: 38
Rockefeller Foundation: 37
Rockefeller, Nelson: 53
Rockne, Knute: 50, 204
Romania: 40, 55

Romo, Barry: 135-136
Roosevelt, Franklin: 37, 40
Rostow, Walt: 50
ruling class: 30, 61
   Cambodia: 4, 156
   China: 149
   Russia: 148
   US: 36-40, 42-48, 59, 90, 92, 104-
   106, 108-109, 113, 144, 145, 148,
   175, 176, 183, 189, 190, 194, 196,
   204
   Vietnam: 2, 4, 24-25, 30, 165, 173
Rusk, Dean: 37, 58, 91
Rusk, Richard: 91
Russia
   government: 2, 4, 13, 18, 21, 27, 30,
   39, 45-49, 56, 61, 66, 130, 147-150
   aid to Vietnam: 148-150, 165
   army: 14
   fall of dictatorship in 1989: 55, 165,
   178
   tanks in Czechoslovakia: 108
   see also state capitalism, Stalinism,
   Russian Revolution, Sino-Soviet
   split
Russian Revolution: 13, 22, 43, 55,
   110, 122, 139, 174, 201
Rwanda: 191

Sa Thay: 96
sabotage: 142
Sahlins, Marshall: 85
Saigon: 7, 21, 92, 93, 95-96, 97, 148,
   150-151, 171
   fall of: 147, 150
   insurrection: 22-23, 173-174
San Diego: 140
San Francisco: 86, 125
Saudi Arabia: 55, 177-179
Schell, Jonathan: 206
Scheuer, Sandy: 111, 112
Scholars' Revolt: 12
Schmidt: 211
Schrecker, Ellen: 204
Schroeder, William: 112
Schwartz, Nancy: 204
Scranton, Governor: 53

Screaming Eagles: 98
Screen Actors Guild: 44
Screenwriters Guild: 45
Seattle: 195-197
Sen Osman: 158
Seng Horl: 157-158
Serbia: 35, 180-184
Serbs in Kosovo: 35, 180-181
Shah of Iran: 48, 51
Shanghai: 15
Shawcross, William: 200, 209, 210
Shea, Dick: 92, 207
Shilts, Randy: 211
Sihanouk, King Norodom: 110, 152,
   163, 165
Sim, Kevin: 103, 200, 207
Simons, Geoffrey: 211
Simpson, Varnado: 102-104
Sino-Soviet split: 148-150
Skull and Bones club: 36
Smiley Barracks: 128
Smith, Captain Frank: 137
Smith, Sharon: 211
Snepp, Frank: 99-100, 207
Socialist Workers Party (SWP) in the
   US: 122-123
soldiers, see GIs
Son-Duong: 25
songs, anti-war: 69-71
Soupanavong: 67
South Africa: 55, 176-177
South Korea: 48, 50-51
South Vietnam
   government: 1, 27, 28-34, 49, 53,
   62, 88, 95, 143, 144
   economy: 30-31, 144
   government forces: 33, 50-51, 45,
   62, 140
   air force: 99
Southern Christian Leadership
   Conference: 88
Souvannaphong: 67
soviets: 13
Soviet-American Friendship
   League: 45
Soviet Union: 40, 57, 140
Sowders, Ed: 136

Spain: 43, 45
Special Branch: 43
spitting, myth of: 184
Spofford, Tim: 207
Srey Pich Chnay: 155
Sri Lanka: 108-109
Stacewicz, Richard: 200, 208
Stalin, Joseph: 14, 15, 32, 43, 47, 149, 155-156
Stalinism: 15, 22, 148-149
    see also state capitalism
Stanford University: 88
Starbucks: 196
State Department: 110
state capitalism: 14, 15-16, 28, 30, 32, 39-40, 45-46, 147-148, 151, 156-157, 169, 190, 201
Steelworkers: 42
Steinberg, Barry: 136
Steptoe, Lamont: 132
Stevenson, Adlai: 45
strikes
    Cambodia: 155
    Iran: 177
    Karachi: 108
    students, US: 112-115
    US: 36, 40-42, 43, 44, 191-192, 195
    Vietnam: 172-173
students: 85, 86, 88, 89, 94, 107-108, 111-115
Students for a Democratic Society (SDS): 85, 107
Student Non-Violent Coordinating Committee (SNCC): 86
Stuttgart: 128, 123
style of this book: 4
Subic Bay: 123, 142
Sudan: 55, 177
Sukarno: 57-59
Sumatra: 58
Supreme Court, US: 193
SVN see South Vietnam
Sweden: 60
Syria: 177

Taft, Senator: 42, 46
Taft-Hartley Act: 42, 44

Takeo village: 158
Tam Eng: 158
Tate, Atticus: 78-80
taxes, Vietnam: 8, 147, 150
*Taxi Driver*: 183
Tay Ninh province: 31
Taylor, K: 211
Te: 25-26
Teamsters Union: 36, 195
television, *see* media
Tennessee: 123
    University of: 111, 114
Tep Ibrahim: 159
Tet Offensive: 92-99, 104, 106, 108, 150-151
Texas: 123
Thai Binh province: 172
Thailand: 55, 108, 142, 143, 162-163, 168, 173, 200
Thanh Hoa province: 172
Thayer, Carlyle: 204
therapy, *see* psychiatry
Thieu, General and President: 53, 97, 143, 144
Thomas Jr, Allen: 127
Thud Ridge: 65
Tiananmen Square: 174
*Time*: 139
Tine, Warren Van: 204
Tonkin Gulf incident: 54
Tonry, Michael: 211
torture: 98, 102, 104, 161
tours of duty: 72
Trotsky, Leon: 22, 201
Trotskyists: 22, 23, 122-123, 174
Trujillo: 208
Trullinger, James: 9, 98, 203, 204, 206
Truman, Harry: 38, 40, 45, 106
Truong: 10
Truong Nhu Tang: 65-66, 205, 207
Tu Hua: 99
Tunisia: 55, 177
tunnels: 80-82, 83, 93, 99, 136
Tuol Sleng prison: 161
Turkey: 55, 108, 179, 181-182, 193
Tuso, Joseph: 69, 205

U Tapao Air Base: 142
UAW, *see* United Auto Workers
UN, *see* United Nations
Ungpakorn, Ji: 200
unification of Vietnam: 150
Union Pacific Railroad: 36
unions, *see* labor unions
United Auto Workers (UAW): 37, 40, 42, 44, 88
United Fruit Company: 51
United Nations (UN): 48, 67, 162, 165, 180-181
United Parcel Service (UPS): 195
United States (US)
    government: 1, 5, 18, 21, 27, 28, 30, 35, 36, 39, 47, 49, 55, 59, 60, 65, 72, 73, 105, 108, 110, 119, 140, 142, 143, 148, 149, 152, 162, 163, 178, 179, 180-181, 182, 189
    embassy in Saigon: 54, 92, 93, 99
    foreign policy outside Vietnam: 35-36, 39-40, 50-51, 56-60, 149, 175-184
    decision to intervene in South Vietnam: 50-56, 60, 61
    invasion of Cambodia, 1970: 110-113, 152
    reparations: 143-4
Universities and colleges
    Berkeley, University of California at: 85, 129
    Cornell: 85-86
    Dartmouth College: 89
    Jackson State: 114
    Kent State: 111-115
    Knoxville: 114-115
    Michigan State: 85, 89
    Stanford: 88
    Tennessee: 111, 114
    Vermont: 89
    Wisconsin at Madison: 196
Unsatisfied Black Soldiers: 128
US Communist Party: 42-47, 86, 88, 194
US Declaration of Independence: 20
US House of Representatives, *see* Congress

VA, *see* Veterans Administration
Valentine, Douglas: 207
Van Tine, Warren: 204
Vermont, University of: 89
Versailles peace conference: 13
Veterans Administration (VA)
    hospitals: 119-120, 185-189, 192
veterans
    US: 83, 111, 114, 117-121, 122, 123, 127, 139, 141, 182-189, 200
    Vietnamese: 96, 200
Vichy regime: 17
Viet Cong: 1, 3, 50, 62-63, 73, 77-79, 80, 81, 82, 86, 93, 97-98, 99, 102, 109, 110, 140
    *see also* National Liberation Front
Viet Minh: 17-20, 22-27, 80, 98, 145
Vietnam
    after 1975: 200
    independence from China: 7
    independence from France: 15, 17-20, 21, 22, 27
    war with Cambodia: 159-165
    war with China: 162-163
    unification: 50
    *see also* North Vietnam and South Vietnam
*Vietnam GI*: 122
Vietnam syndrome: 176-183
Vietnam Veterans Against the War (VVAW): 120-122, 141, 184-185, 200, 206
Vietnamese Communist Party: 12-27, 61, 94, 199
Vietnamese minority in Cambodia: 159-160
Vietnamese New Year, *see* Tet
Village in the Sun, *see* Mexico, Guadalajara
Village Liberation Women's Committee: 104
Vo Hoang Le: 81
Vo Thi Mo: 82, 99, 104
Vo Van An: 29

Wall Street: 37
Washington: 4, 5, 54

*Washington Post*: 142
Washington, demonstrations: 109-110
Watkins, Susan: 207
Watts, William: 91
Wells, Tom: 90-91, 199, 205, 206, 207
Wesseling, Louis: 207
Westheider, James: 127, 206, 208
Westmoreland, General William C: 73, 79, 92-93, 104-105, 107, 125, 139
Wilcox, Fred: 211
Williams, Roger: 125
Williams, Soapy: 37
*Winston Salem-Journal*: 106
Wisconsin, University of: 196
Wise Men: 106
women's oppression: 169-171, 190-191
  *see also* birth control, prostitution, rape
Women's Army Corps School: 123
Woodward, Bob: 211
workers
  Hungarian: 113
  Karachi: 108
  Palestinian: 107
  Prague: 108
  Russian: 13-14
  Third World: 192
  US: 3, 4, 44, 47, 82, 87, 89, 113-115, 117-121, 128, 129, 130, 183, 190-192
  Vietnamese: 4, 8, 15, 16, 17, 22, 23, 30, 31, 94, 95, 147-148, 151, 167, 172-174
working class: 3
  Russian: 13, 22
  US: 71, 83, 88, 89, 90, 113-115, 125, 126, 130, 136, 176, 186, 189, 190, 191
  Vietnamese: 23, 94
  *see also* workers
World Bank: 38, 104, 148, 168
World Trade Organization (WTO): 195-197
World War One: 13, 36, 40, 43, 122
World War Two: 1, 17-18, 21, 39, 41, 45, 48, 62, 81, 83, 105, 112, 153
Wright-Patterson Air Force Base: 124

Yale University: 36
Yalta: 21
Yippies: 90, 107, 113
Young, Allan: 185-189, 200, 211
Young, Marilyn: 89, 199, 203, 204, 205, 206, 208
Yugoslavia: 55, 108, 180-183

Zhai, Quiang: 200, 204
Zhou Enlai: 28
Zippo: 131